Apostle Donald Spellman has masterfully laid out the components of the Kingdom of God—Grace! Declaring that Grace is a magnificent quality, Apostle Spellman supports his claim through Scripture which clearly show that Grace is full of splendor and the glory of God. In this respect, Grace is Divine and, therefore, free and universal in its natural tendency; it is without restraint, and thus established permanently in contrast with debt.

In *God's Magnificent Grace,* Apostle Spellman not only shows us the benefits of Grace, but also lets us know that God's unmerited favor is not a license to sin. The spiritually mature saint understands that Grace is more powerful than sin. However, in the religious mindset, many Believers continue to sin, citing Romans 5:20b, *"But where sin abounded, graced abounded much more."* But as we learn from Romans 6:1-2, Believers should not continue in sin even though grace does abound. As taught in Scripture, Believers are never to use Grace as a cloak for unrighteousness, which implies that Grace is not freedom from sin; it is the power of God freely granted to Believers to live a holy life through faith in Jesus Christ. In short, Grace is God's way of giving Believers better than they deserve.

Spellman graciously lays out the manifold components of Grace, pounding home the fact that God's Grace is truly magnificent. How magnificent? Grace is what Believers receive when their spiritual maturity does not keep pace or exceed the manifold temptations of the world; even when it should.

As you read and digest the contents of this book, you will never again hesitate to *"come boldly to the Throne of Grace, that you may obtain mercy and find grace to help in time of need"* (Hebrews 4:16). Apostle Donald Spellman shows us that we are empowered by Grace. Therefore, let us not frustrate the grace of God; but as workers together with Him, I implore you not to receive the grace of God in vain.

Living in a 21ˢᵗ Century world, *God's Magnificent Grace* has never been more appealing!

—Dr. James Brewton
Apostle, Bishop, Senior Pastor,
Community Empowerment Ministries, Inc., Allendale, SC
Community Empowerment Family Worship Ministry, Inc., Claxton, GA
President,
The Identity Institute School of Ministry
Author,
From Footmen to Horseman
Back Porch Meditations, Holy Spirit Revelations
A Slave of Circumstance

In Reverend Donald Spellman's new book "God's Magnificent Grace", he so beautifully reveals biblical analogies to teach us how grace is not earned, but is a gift that all Christians should embrace, but not abuse or use as a free pass to Heaven.

I am amazed at how clear he makes to us as believers, God's patience and love, as well as the importance of strong faith, tenacity of repentance, and the study of God's word.

Reverend Spellman is a master at connecting the Old and New Testaments regarding God's amazing grace. I applaud him in yet another blessing to Christians and non-Christians alike with this new book.

Dale A. Miles, DMD
Savannah, Georgia

Apostle Spellman lays out his case before the Jury of his peers in Christendom, and with half-hearted saints who would use God's Grace to continue in the very Sin that Jesus delivered us from and also for sinners who have yet to receive Jesus Christ as their Lord and Savior.

He brings evidence to his case by supporting it his stand, by addressing scripture from the Old and New Testament of the Holy Bible.

God has often times in scripture shown Grace to those He has favored. God is Sovereign and when he renders grace to an individual, it is not because he or she is good or deserving of it. Grace is given by God favoring an individual with his unmerited favor. Let's be clear none of us are worthy of his grace, but when it's poured out upon us in our lives, I have to echo the Apostle, "We don't have a license to sin." I'm a recipient of that unmerited favor.

Apostle Spellman brings out these points and more in this book. He also has the where with all to understand that others will need more insight on the complexities sometimes misunderstood by Grace to have a Question and Answer section at the end of the book.

Apostle Spellman has been studying and writing books for some time now. I am so very proud that God has endowed him with this gift to write books and to do so with the heart of the reader in mind.

I've known Apostle Spellman for over 34 years; he's a man of integrity, a loving husband, a great father and grandfather. I humbly endorse this book and recommend it to others, to help us all better understand that could easily be misunderstood. Let us all continue in Grace and in the Service of our Lord and Savior Jesus Christ.

With a Godly Reverence to the Author,

Pastor Steven E Butler
House of Deliverance Church of God in Christ
Grovetown, Georgia

GOD'S MAGNIFICENT GRACE

The Benefits of Grace and Why God's
Unmerited Favor Is Not a License to Sin

Questions and Answers Worksheets Included

Donald Spellman

ISBN 978-1-0980-8268-0 (paperback)
ISBN 978-1-0980-8269-7 (digital)

Christian Faith Publishing, Inc.
832 Park Avenue
Meadville, PA 16335
www.christianfaithpublishing.com

Printed in the United States of America

To the Body of Christ

But God, who is rich in mercy, because of His great love with which He loved us, even when we were dead in trespasses, made us alive together with Christ (by grace you have been saved), and raised us up together, and made us sit together in heavenly places in Christ Jesus, that in the ages to come He might show the exceeding riches of His grace in His kindness toward us in Christ Jesus.

—Ephesians 2:4–7

CONTENTS

ACKNOWLEDGEMENTS

It was Jesus who said "I can of Myself do nothing." In comparison, I knew when I first started writing I needed the Lord's guidance, enablement and blessings. He alone deserves all glory, praise and honor. For I am always humbled and grateful that "I can do all things through Christ who strengthens me."

My beautiful wife Sheila and I have been married for the last 35 years, I am extremely grateful to the Lord for her. Thanks for your patience and understanding. All authors know the time and effort it takes writing a book, that being said it helps to have a supportive spouse, and I'm grateful God has given her to me. I look forward to being with you for the next 35 years and more. There's no one greater in my life with the exception of Jesus and the Holy Spirit.

The making of a book requires a succession of hard work, steps and entities. First, I had to produce a manuscript and then attain a good publisher. I am thankful for "Christian Faith Publishing" for all their time consuming work into making the book a reality. Thanks a million!

I'm very thankful to Pastor Steven Butler, Dr. James Brewton and Dr. Dale Miles, who wrote an endorsement concerning this book. Men of God, please know that I am forever grateful that you would allow me to take of some of your precious time. "The Lord bless you and keep you; the Lord make His face shine upon you, and be gracious to you; the Lord lift up His countenance upon you, and give you peace" (Numbers 6:24-26).

And finally, I am thankful to God for these people who have been there for our ministry over the years, Prophet Adair Johnson, Michael Spellman (Spellman's Computers), Evangelist Shirley Spellman and Deacon Tony Gibson. There are more people who could have been added to this list, I pray you understand the list would have been too long. But I thank God for you all as well.

INTRODUCTION

It's mind-boggling that when it comes to God's grace, some believers are hesitant to preach or teach on the subject or simply avoid it. While sitting in my office one day, thinking what the reason could be, I came to one conclusion. Could it be many spiritual leaders believe the members of their congregations would abuse or take it in vain (see Romans 6:1–2; 2 Corinthians 6:1)? To those who struggle with this sort of rationale, there's no need to worry or fear since Jesus was "full of grace and truth" (see John 1:14).

If ever there should be a question about most opposites in the Bible, what comes to mind immediately would be the Mosaic Law and the dispensation of God's grace. They are different as night and day, rain and sunshine, hot and cold, and so on. And the most important distinction is they were given at different dispensations. John 1:17 says, "For the Law was given through Moses, but grace and truth came through Jesus Christ."

In case you're not familiar with the meaning of grace, here's a concise definition taken from *Nelson's New Illustrated Bible Dictionary.* Grace is favor or kindness shown without regard to the worth or merit of the one who receives it and in spite of what that person deserves. Grace is one of the key attributes of God. Exodus 34:6 says, "The Lord God is merciful and gracious, longsuffering, and abounding in goodness and truth." Therefore, grace is almost always associated with mercy, love, compassion, and patience.

In the Old Testament, the Hebrew term used is *chen,* which is defined as favor, grace, or charm; grace is the moral quality of kindness, displaying a favorable disposition. In the King James translation, "chen" is translated as grace thirty-eight times, favor twenty-six times, twice as gracious, once as pleasant, and once as precious.

The Greek word for grace is *charis.* It has various uses, an objective that bestows or occasions pleasure, delight, or causes favorable regard. This word *charis* also appears in another form in the word *charisma. Charisma* is the word that is used for the gifts of the Holy Spirit and for various other manifestations. Charisma means "grace made manifest or made specific." *Charis* is "grace, in general;" charisma is the specific manifestation of that grace in someone's life.

There are two important facts concerning grace. First, we cannot earn it nor do we deserve it. Anything we earn or deserve is not grace. Second, grace is normally received by faith. Ephesians 2:8–9 says, "For by grace you have been saved through faith and that not of yourselves; it is the gift of God, not of works lest anyone should boast."

Someone defined "G-R-A-C-E" as "God's riches at Christ's expense." There are only two possible ways to achieve righteousness, and if you are born again through the blood of Christ, you are going to follow one or the other. One is by the works of the law, and the other is by grace through faith (see Romans 10:3–4).

While speaking with a gentleman one day, he told me about someone who struggled to let go of many old covenant rituals. Interesting enough, even though he explained to him how Jesus is the mediator of a better covenant established on better promises, he still could not embrace those facts. Unfortunately, this is not an isolated problem with one individual. There are multitudes in the Body of Christ who operate in legalism and religious tradition who have this mentality. This among other reasons is why I was led to write this book.

We should bear in mind the flesh hates, and the devil detests grace because it eliminates self-righteousness. Having the right perspective and understanding what it means will prompt us to give God all the glory and honor that is only due to Him, for Paul said, "He that glorieth, let him glory in the Lord" (see 1 Corinthians 1:31).

Satan's primary objective is to exalt himself above God, and if allowed, he will copartner with our flesh to accomplish that mission. He has deceived multitudes into operating in the flesh apart from God's grace. He is a great deceiver, and his lies are a means to an end, for Jesus said, "He is a liar and the father of it" (see John 8:44). His methods are designed to silence or pervert the Gospel (God's grace to you and me).

The sinner is one of the most important reasons for the existence of God's grace. Why? Because before we came to Christ, we were dead in trespasses and sins, undeserving, ill-deserving, and hell-deserving. That is the sort of person for whom the grace of God is proclaimed and exists. Titus 2:11 says, "For the grace of God that brings salvation has appeared to all men." Jesus didn't come to call the righteous to repentance; neither did He come to find goodness and righteousness with the sinner. He came to bestow righteousness on those who are not right with Him. To justify the ungodly or the guilty is a miracle only reserved for the grace of God alone (see Romans 4:5).

During biblical times, the average Jew struggled to embrace this kind of teaching. To justify the ungodly for them was considered a scandal in a sense. It was inconceivable that God would acquit a guilty, godless man. There are two reasons why I believe they had this rationale. First, during biblical times, all Jews rejected Jesus as the Messiah and therefore discarded the redemptive transaction involving God and Christ. Secondly, they failed to see the significance of belief and trust on the part of one who was godless. What they needed to understand and acknowledge is that such trust shows that the man or woman is no longer without God but rather a person who has committed themselves to everything God is and has done.

Take a lawyer for instance. It's in his or her job description to justify the innocent or to plead a case in a courtroom. The lawyer is not there, per se, to protect the guilty party. In the same way, it's not man's right nor in his power to justify the guilty. The jury and judge hold the final say whether or not the person is found guilty. In comparison, justifying the ungodly or the guilty is a miracle reserved for the grace of God alone (see Romans 4:5). Christ did not die for us because we had strength to save ourselves or that we were clicking on all the right cylinders. He died for sinners who are without strength (see Romans 5:6–10).

It's important to see that God's grace is not just limited to the New Testament. We see glimpses and examples in the Old Testament as well. The most notable illustration of grace is seen in the redemption of the Israelites from Egypt and their establishment in the promised land. If grace was dependent upon any merit on their part, it would never have taken place. However, in spite of their constant complaining, murmuring, frequent rebellion and trespasses, God's mercy and grace was extremely abundant. In chapter 3, I'll go in depth and show you more instances of grace in the Old Testament.

Jesus was full of grace and truth. He was the embodiment of grace. But interesting enough, many people are surprised to know God's grace was upon His life while on earth as well. Luke 2:40 says, "And the Child grew and became strong in spirit, filled with wisdom; and the grace of God was upon Him." This gives us much assurance and appreciation for the grace of God in our personal lives, and to know our Lord and Savior was actually a benefactor Himself.

Among the New Testament writers, Paul stands head and shoulders above them as an advocate of grace. Considering his background history. It should come as no surprise that among his contemporaries, he was the one who wrote boldly on the subject and often. For instance, Paul understood what he had become and accomplished was because of the grace of God. First Corinthians 15:10 says, "But by the grace of God, I am what I am, and His grace toward me was not in vain…yet not I, but the grace of God which was with me."

We read also Ephesians 3:7–8 that says, "I became a minister according to the gift of the grace of God given to me by the effective working of His power. To me who am less than the least of all the saints, this grace was given, that I should preach among the Gentiles the unsearchable riches of Christ."

Paul and those who comprehend God's grace are not ashamed to give credit to whom credit is due. I can honestly say as I reflect back over my own life, God's grace has been abundant upon me. In my first book, *Christ Still Heals*, I shared my experience of being diagnosed with cancer among other things and how God healed and delivered me. Did I deserve His grace and mercy upon my life? Certainly not! But as Peter says, "In truth I perceive that God shows no partiality" (see Acts 10:34). And as Paul said, "His grace toward me was not in vain," and that was certainly my case.

There are many profound books written on the subject of grace. I am optimistic this book will reaffirm the richness and beauty of grace. God's grace is absolutely magnificent. No number of pages, pamphlets, books, lectures, or messages can do justice or express the wealth and depth of His unmerited favor. Besides, with many in the Body of Christ still entrenched in various forms of spiritual bondages, it's extremely important we understand and embrace the message of grace. So get ready to go on a spiritual journey as we look at the benefits of grace and its boundaries.

1

A DEMONSTRATION OF GRACE IN THE OLD TESTAMENT

> Now the Lord descended in the cloud and stood with him [Moses] there, and proclaimed the name of the Lord. And the Lord passed before him and proclaimed the Lord, the Lord God, merciful and gracious, longsuffering, and abounding in goodness and truth, keeping mercy, forgiving iniquity and transgression and sin, by no means clearing the guilty.
>
> —Exodus 34:5–7

There are examples of God's mercy and grace in the Old Testament that help us understand and appreciate His grace and mercy in the New Testament. Early in the Old Testament, God revealed Himself as "The Lord, the Lord the compassionate and gracious God, slow to anger, abounding in love and faithfulness, maintaining love to thousands, and forgiving wickedness, rebellion and sin" (Exodus 34:6 NIV). Grace and mercy were already at work in the Garden of Eden when God responded to the fall of creation with the promise of redemption and care rather than with abandonment or destruction (see Genesis 3:15).

Additionally, the call of God to Abraham was an extension of grace to him. The blessings bestowed upon his descendants would be instrumental in bringing about a universal blessing to all the families of the earth. To seal this promise, God made a covenant with Abraham. The end purpose in which this was working was to extend His grace to the whole human race. Genesis 12:2–3 says, "And I make of thee a great nation, and I will bless thee, and make thy name great; and thou shalt be a blessing; and I will bless them that bless thee, and curse him that curseth thee; and in thee shall all families of the earth be blessed."

In a sincere confirmation of the promise to Abraham, God confirmed, "As for Me, behold my covenant is with thee...and I will establish my covenant between me and thee, and thy see after thee in their generations for an everlasting covenant, to be a God unto thee, and to thy seed after thee" (Genesis 17:4–7 KJV). Because of grace, this promise was applicable to all Abraham's offspring, not only his racial descendants, the Jews, but also to his spiritual descendants, believers from all nations. Romans 4:16 (KJV) says, "Therefore it is of faith, that it might be by grace; to the end the promise might be sure to all the seed; not to that only which is of the law, but to that also which is of the faith of Abraham; who is the father of us all."

Israel's Liberation and Deliverance from Egypt

The children of Israel redemption and deliverance was a foreshadow of God's grace with the purpose of bringing salvation to all men (see Titus 2:11). While under oppression in Egypt, the Israelites were in a hopeless and dreadful condition, and because of anguish of spirit and harsh bondage, they struggled to listen to Moses (see Exodus 6:9). It was inconceivable to believe that freedom was in sight, considering their circumstances. However, the God of grace and mercy stepped in and did something for them they could not do for themselves.

This was a presage of deliverance from the bondage of sin and death on our behalf through Christ Jesus. Romans 5:6 (AMP) says,

"While we were yet in weakness, powerless to help ourselves, at the fitting time Christ died for (in behalf of) the ungodly."

On numerous occasions, Moses stood as intercessor and mediator for the transgressions of Israel. This is comparable to how Jesus mediates and intercedes for the believer today. First Timothy 2:5 (KJV) says, "For there is one God, and one mediator between God and men, the man Christ Jesus."

We read also Hebrews 9:15 that says, "And for this cause He [Jesus] is the mediator of the New Testament, that by means of death, for the redemption of the transgressions that were under the first testament, they which are called might receive the promise of eternal inheritance."

On their way through Rephidim and reaching the desert of Sinai, the Lord called Moses and commanded him to speak to house of Jacob and to the children of Israel. God wanted Moses to remind them how they were brought out on eagle's wings. Moreover, He told them that if they would obey His voice and keep His covenant, they would be a treasured possession above all people (see Exodus 19:4–5). As an act of mercy and grace, God honored their request to have Moses as a mediator for the Israelites.

Prior to Moses passing on the message to the Israelites, he had to enter a thick darkness (a place they could not go) to commune with God. In comparison, Jesus went to the cross (a picture of darkness and dread) and a place where we were not able to go. Hebrews 2:9 (KJV) says, "But we see Jesus, who was made a little lower than the angels for the suffering of death, crowned with glory and honor that He by the grace of God should taste death for every man."

Additionally, we see the grace and mercy of God as the children of Israel committed idolatry while Moses was delayed from coming out from Mount Sinai. Allow me to share a short narrative of this horrible transgression. Despite the fact that Moses was their God-appointed leader, the children of Israel decided to ask Aaron to make them gods to lead them. Unfortunately, Aaron granted their request and made them a molten calf, and with one accord, they made a declaration, saying, "These are gods that brought us out of the land of

Egypt." The following day, the people offered burnt offerings, peace offerings, and rose up to play (see Exodus 32:3–6).

This transgression immediately came with a response of anger from God, to which He told Moses how stiff-necked the people were and to leave Him alone that His wrath may wax hot and consume them (see Exodus 32:7–10). At the outset, we see God's displeasure, but as Moses intercedes, we see His mercy and grace. Moses argues his point, saying, "Why should the Egyptians speak and say He brought them out to harm them, to kill them in the mountains and to consume them from the face of the earth" (see Exodus 32:12).

Moses went on to make a case by saying remember Abraham, Isaac, and Israel, "Your servants in whom You made a covenant with (v. 13)." Without hesitation, after Moses had made an end to interceding as a priest for the people, the Lord repented of the evil which He intended to do. So with Moses interceding, we're shown a parallel in which Jesus steps in to thwart the wrath of God against His people. Ephesians 2:13 says, "But now in Christ Jesus you were once were far off have been brought near by the blood of Christ."

As it were prior to salvation, we too "once conducted ourselves in the lusts of our flesh, fulfilling the desires of the flesh and of the mind, and were by nature children of wrath, just as the others" (see Ephesians 2:3). As a result of our rebellious behavior, God's wrath was revealed from heaven against all ungodliness and unrighteousness of men (see Romans 1:18). Since this unrighteousness made God hostile toward us, Jesus has become our High Priest, offering not just prayers but also Himself as a sacrifice for our sins.

> But this man, because He continued forever, hath an unchangeable priesthood. Wherefore He is able also to save them to the uttermost that comes unto God by Him, seeing He ever liveth to make intercession for them. For such an High Priest became us, who is holy, harmless, undefiled, separate from sinners, and made higher than the heavens. Who needed not daily, as those High Priests, to offer up sacrifice, first for His

own sins, and then for the peoples for this He did
once, when He offered up Himself. (Hebrews
7:24–27 KJV)

The Negative Report of the Spies

Once more, Israel had need of God's intervention and His
grace for another transgression committed. God instructs Moses
to send a man from every tribe of Israel to spy out the promised
land (Numbers 13:1–33). So at the command of God, Moses relays
the message, saying, "See what the land is and the people that dwell
therein, whether they are strong or weak, few or many, good or bad?"
He also instructed them to be of good courage. The men did precisely as Moses instructed them to do. They brought back a cluster of
grapes, pomegranates, and figs.

After searching out the land for forty days, they returned to
Moses, Aaron, and to the congregation of the children of Israel with
their report. The report they gave was that the land was flowing with
milk and honey. However, they began to speak negative, saying the
people were too strong and the cities were fortified. Moreover, they
said there were giants in the land, but Caleb gave a different report,
as did Joshua, who said they were able to possess the land in spite of
the other's report.

Proverbs 18:21 says, "Death and life in the power of the tongue,
and those who love it will eat its fruit." The spies, with the exception
of Joshua and Caleb, prevented their tongues from coming in agreement with what the Lord had told them. Instead, they allowed physical senses, particularly their sight, to shape what came from their
mouths. What's more, they had an opportunity to build the faith of
the congregation, but instead, they fed them unbelief. In short, they
spoke death instead of life.

So the congregation of Israel lifted up their voices and wept
upon hearing the report of the spies who spoke negative. Thus, they
would have stoned Joshua and Caleb as well, except the Lord appeared
in the tabernacle of the congregation. He spoke unto Moses, saying,

"How long will these people provoke Me?" With God's wrath kindling and His intention to smite them with pestilence, Moses intercedes again as a priest on the behalf of the people.

> And Moses said to the Lord, then the Egyptians will hear it, for by Your might You brought these people up from among them… And now, I pray let the power of my Lord be great, just as You have spoken, saying the Lord is longsuffering and abundant in mercy, forgiving iniquity and transgression; but He by no means clears the guilty, visiting the iniquity of the fathers on the children to the third and fourth generation. Pardon the iniquity of this people I pray, according to the greatness of Your mercy, just as You have forgiven this people, from Egypt even until now. Then the Lord said I have pardon according to your word, but truly as I live all the earth shall be filled with the glory of the Lord. (Numbers 14:13, 17–21)

The narrative concerning the Lord's mercy and grace has not changed since the time of Moses and the Israelites. He is still "the same yesterday and today and forever" (Hebrews 13:8). God has promised through His Word that He would give men and women a chance to come to Him. He's "not willing that any should perish but that all should come to repentance" (see 2 Peter 3:9 KJV).

God's grace and mercy were very much evident in the Old Testament. Just as Moses interceded for the Israelites, to this day, Jesus still intercedes and acts as a High Priest for us. If we fall from grace and repent, we can be restored back into fellowship with God.

Proverbs 24:6 says, "For a righteous man may fall seven times, and rise again, but the wicked shall fall by calamity." Our getting back up again is related to God's grace and Jesus intercession for us, for "He [Jesus] is able also to save them to the uttermost that come unto God by Him, seeing He ever liveth to make intercession for them" (see Hebrews 7:25).

The Altar of the Earth

> An altar of the earth you shall make for Me, and you shall sacrifice on it your burnt offerings and your peace offerings, your sheep and your oxen. In every place where I record My name I will come to you, and I will bless you. (Exodus 20:24–26)

The altar of the earth in which God commanded Moses to make is another good example of grace and mercy in the Old Testament. Moses was instructed only to use the altar for burnt offerings, peace offerings, sheep offerings and oxen. In addition, the altar was to be made of stone and not out of hewn stone with no tools used upon it or else it would become polluted, and no steps were to be made also, lest their nakedness be exposed.

A closer look unfolds a revelation of grace behind the instruction God gives Moses. Let's look first at the altar of earth, which speaks of humility. This speaks of the fact that the impoverished and destitute of God's people can erect an altar with materials found anywhere. This lets us know we're without excuse as it relates to worshipping God. For every believer in Christ can erect a posture or attitude of worship. The Lord Jesus doesn't require any expensive offering. Both non-Christian and Christian alike can come at any time and from anywhere before the throne of grace. Hebrews 4:16 (KJV) says, "Let us therefore come boldly unto the throne of grace, that we may obtain mercy, and find grace to help in time of need."

Please note the instructions to make the altar out of regular stones and not hewn stones. This speaks to the fact that we cannot earn righteousness on the basis of works and that Christ is the only one who can justify us. Romans 4:4–5 (KJV) says, "Now to Him that worketh is the reward not reckoned of grace but of debt, but to him that worketh not, but believeth on him that justifieth the ungodly, his faith is counted for righteousness."

While taking in His last breath on the cross, Jesus made a firm declaration. He said, "It is finished" (see John 19:30). God instructing Moses not to use a tool on the altar of stone "less it becomes polluted" speaks a fact that we can nullify God's grace and the finished work of Christ by attempting to add our works of righteousness.

> But after that the kindness and love of God our Savior toward man appeared, not by works of righteousness which we have done, but according to His mercy he saved us, by the washing of regeneration, and renewing of the Holy Ghost, which He shed on us abundantly through Jesus Christ our Savoir, that being justified by His grace, we should be made heirs according to the hope of eternal life. (Titus 3:4–7 KJV)

The fact there were no steps leading to the altar is one of the most remarkable things about the altar of stone. This gives us the understanding it was accessible and within reach for the desperate and worthless sinner. For those of you who need a Savior, you don't have to wait until you have attained righteousness to receive Christ. He came to seek and save that which is lost. He'll meet us right where we are and whatever level of spiritual despair we're in for "whosoever wishes, let him take the free gift of the water of life freely" (see Revelation 22:17). It makes no difference what your present condition is and where you're at in life. He's ready to save you with His abundance of grace.

> But the righteousness which is of faith speaketh on this wise, say not in thine heart, who shall ascend into heaven? That is to bring Christ down from above, or who shall descend into the deep? That is to bring up Christ again from the dead, but what saith it? The word is nigh thee, even in

thy mouth, and in thy heart that is, the word of faith, which we preach; that if thou confess with thy mouth the Lord Jesus, and shalt believe in thine heart that God hath raised Him from the dead, thou shalt be saved. (Romans 10:6–9 KJV)

The Blood of the Covenant

The blood of the covenant is another example of grace and mercy in the Old Testament. After a few days of receiving instructions concerning the law at Mount Sinai, Moses is given directives about the blood of the Covenant. The covenant is firmly declared in the presence of the people and written down by the hand of Moses. They were to offer burnt and sacrifice peace offerings of oxen unto the Lord. The blood of the offerings is to be carefully placed in basins. One-half is to be sprinkled on the altar and the rest on the people. Let's see what God instructed them in detail concerning this blood of the covenant.

And Moses came and told the people all the words of the Lord, and all the judgments; and all the people answered with one voice, and said all the words which the Lord hath said will we do. And Moses wrote all the words of the Lord, and rose up early in the morning and builded an altar under the hill, and twelve pillars according to the twelve tribes of Israel, and he sent young men of the children of Israel, which offered burnt offerings and sacrificed peace offerings of oxen unto the Lord. And Moses took half of the blood, and put it in basins; and half of the blood he sprinkled on the altar, and he took the book of the covenant, and read in the audience of the people; and they said, all that the Lord hath said will we do, and be obedient. And Moses took the blood

and sprinkled it on the people and said behold
the [blood of the covenant] which the Lord
hath made with you concerning all these words.
(Exodus 24:3–8 KJV)

The blood that was poured on the altar speaks of the death of Christ for our sins. The blood spoken about in the Old Testament represents life. In comparison, the blood poured out upon the altar is the life of Christ poured out for us. Mark 10:45 (KJV) says, "For even the Son of man came not to be ministered unto, but to minister and to give His life a ransom for many."

The blood that was preserved in the basins and sprinkled upon the people speaks of the resurrection life of Christ and the continued intercession He makes for His people. Hebrews 7:25 (KJV) says, "Wherefore He is able also to save them to the uttermost that come unto God by Him, seeing He ever liveth to make intercession for them."

When Christ went to the cross, He conquered death and is now seated at the right hand of the Father. We know from those facts that He lives forever, and because He lives, He's able to save to the uttermost. Whosoever calls on the Lord can be saved. The Apostle Paul, in writing to the believers at Rome, described it this way, "Who is he that condemneth? It is Christ that died, yea rather, that is risen again, who is even at the right hand of God, who also maketh intercession for us" (Romans 8:34 KJV).

The blood in the basins also speaks of His continued indwelling to sanctify and keep us in fellowship with God. In short, the shed blood is the death on Calvary and the sprinkled blood is the resurrection life of Christ that is shed abroad in our hearts with the purpose of cleansing, sanctifying, and sustaining our spiritual life. The one is His life given for us the other is His life in us.

Galatians 2:20 says, "I have been crucified with Christ; it is no longer I who live, but Christ lives in me; and the life which I now live in the flesh I live by faith in the Son of God, who loved me and gave Himself for me."

The City of Nineveh and a Rebellious Prophet

Nineveh was rebellious in the eyes of the Lord, an ancient capital city of the Assyrian empire founded by Nimrod (see Genesis 10:8). Because the wickedness of Nineveh was so apparent, God commissioned Jonah the son of Amittai to go and preach against the city (see Jonah 1:2). But instead of the prophet walking in obedience, he fled in the opposite direction on a ship headed toward Tarshish.

In comparison, this is often the response of those who walk in disobedience. They run and hide from the presence of the Lord as was the case with Adam and Eve when they disobeyed God in the Garden (see Genesis 3:8). In order to get Jonah's attention, God sent an enormous wind while he was asleep on the ship. It appears that this is always the case with our Lord. He is longsuffering and full of mercy. He sends a warning before destruction.

It's imperative that when the Lord places us on an assignment not to rebel or turn a deaf ear from His instructions because He might send a storm to get our attention. Hebrews 12:6, 11 (KJV) says:

> For whom the Lord loveth He chasteneth and scourgeth every son whom He receiveth... Now no chastening for the present seemeth to be joyous, but grievous; nevertheless, afterward it yieldeth the peaceable fruit of righteousness unto them which are exercised thereby.

Jonah had not only placed his life in jeopardy but those he came in contact with. The story goes on to describe how the storm was raging and the crew members were terrified. All of these things happened while Jonah was sound asleep at the bottom of the ship (see Jonah 1:4–5). Note that there are times when love ones and friends are at risk because of an individual who choose to walk in rebellion and disobedience. Jonah knew that the only solution was for his fellow crew members to throw him overboard into the sea (v. 12). The men disregarded what he suggested and continued to try to bring the ship to land, but the wind was contrary against them (v. 12).

It's important to we see that no matter how we try to make things better, if anyone willfully walks in disobedience, it will definitely cause great pain. Consider Esau who devalued and sold his birthright for a stew of lentils or a morsel of food. Hebrews 12:17 says, "He was rejected for he found no place for repentance, though he sought it diligently with tears." During biblical times, a birthright was a right, privilege, or possession to which a person, especially the firstborn son, was entitled by birth.

Circumstances worsened for Joseph as God allowed him to be swallowed up by a great fish (sort of a furnace of affliction) to get His attention (see Jonah 1:17). In comparison, because of God's grace and mercy every now and then, if we chose to disobey, He'll do the same for us. At various times, God will use different methods to warn those who walk in disobedience. Having no place to run, Jonah eagerly seeks God's face. Jonah 2:1–2 (KJV) says, "Then Jonah prayed unto the Lord His God out of the fish's belly, and said I cried by reason of mine affliction unto the Lord, and He heard me; out of the belly of hell cried I and thou heardest my voice."

Jonah didn't deserve another chance, but God is merciful, slow to anger, and full of compassion. He spoke to the fish, and it vomited him out on dry land. The Bible says the "word of the Lord came to Jonah the second time" (see Jonah 3:1). The phase indicating "the second time" shows us that when we blow it, God is a God of second times or chances. He gives us what we don't deserve and blesses us when we should have been judged.

The devil knew if Jonah had obeyed God the first time, Nineveh would have repented earlier. But as it were, Jonah, upon his second commission, preached to the people of Nineveh, and they repented. Jonah 3:5, 10 says:

> So the people of Nineveh believed God, and proclaimed a fast and put on sackcloth from the greatest of them even to the least of them…

> And God saw their works that they turned
> from their evil way; and God repented of the evil
> that had said that he would do unto them; and
> He did it not.

This was a moment of celebration. The people of Nineveh had repented, and God had ceased from judging the land with destruction. But no, this wasn't enough for Jonah. He was disappointed and angry. Jonah 4:2–3 (KJV) says:

> And he prayed unto the Lord and said, "I
> pray thee, O Lord was not this my saying when
> I was yet in my country? Therefore, I fled before
> unto Tarshish; for I knew that thou art a gracious
> God, and merciful slow to anger and of great
> kindness and repentant thee of the evil, therefore
> now O Lord take I beseech thee my life from me;
> for it is better for me to die than to lie."

Instead of God giving into the demands of Jonah's request, He had yet another lesson to teach him. The Lord prepared a gourd to cover him from the heat, but shortly thereafter, he ordered a worm to destroy the gourd, leaving Jonah fainting and wanting to die. God understood that Jonah's priorities and heart was not in the right place. He had more compassion on a gourd than the people of Nineveh. Jonah 4:11 (KJV) says, "And should not I spare Nineveh that great city, wherein are more than six score thousand persons that cannot discern between their right hand and their left hand; and also much cattle?"

We can learn a lot from the story of Jonah and Nineveh, a rebellious prophet, a rebellious people, and a gracious God. It's remarkable to see that the Lord was patient with the prophet and longsuffering toward Nineveh. Second Peter 3:9 says, "The Lord is not slack concerning His promise, as some count slackness, but is longsuffering toward us, not willing that any should perish but that all should come to repentance." This shows us the extent of God's mercy and grace as He forgave both parties to accomplish His goal. What a wonderful and gracious God we serve!

God's gracious interventions under the Old Covenant (before Jesus) were intended to reveal the role of the church in His plan for redeeming the world. The institutions of the Old Covenant held only a temporary form of God's grace. The ultimate expression of that grace came in the New Covenant when Jesus completed His work. Hebrews 8:6–7 (KJV) says, "But now hath He obtained a more excellent ministry, by how much also He is the mediator of a better covenant, which was established upon better promises. For if that first covenant had been faultless, then should no place have been sought for the second."

Short Review of God's Grace Manifest in the Old Testament

- The call of God to Abraham was an extension of grace to him. The blessings God offered to Abraham's descendants would be instrumental in bringing about a universal blessing to "all the families of the earth." To seal this promise, God made a covenant with Abraham, the end purpose in which He was working was to extend His grace to the whole human race (see Genesis 12:2–3).

- The children of Israel's redemption and deliverance was a foreshadowing of God's grace with the purpose of bringing salvation to all men (see Titus 2:11). This was a presage of deliverance from the bondage of sin and death on our behalf through Christ Jesus. Romans 5:6 (AMP) says, "While we were yet in weakness, powerless to help ourselves, at the fitting time Christ died for (on behalf of) the ungodly."

- The Lord's mercy and grace have not changed since the time of Moses and the Israelites. He is still "the same yesterday and today and forever" (see Hebrews 13:8). God has promised through His Word that He would give men and women a chance to come to Him. He is not willing to destroy people but to save them (see 2 Peter 3:9).

- The altar of earth, which represents humility, speaks of the fact that the impoverished and destitute of God's people could erect an altar and the materials could be found anywhere. This lets us know that we are without excuse when it comes to worshipping God. For every believer in Christ can erect a posture or attitude of worship. The Lord Jesus doesn't require any expensive offering, both non-Christian and Christian alike can come at any time and from anywhere before the throne of grace (see Hebrews 4:16).

- The blood that was poured on the altar speaks of the death of Christ for our sins. The blood spoken about in the Old Testament represents life. In comparison, the blood poured out upon the altar is the life of Christ poured out for us. Mark 10:45 (KJV) says, "For even the Son of man came not to be ministered unto, but to minister and to give His life a ransom for many."

- It's imperative that when the Lord places us on an assignment not to rebel or turn a deaf ear from His instructions because He might send a storm to get our attention. Hebrews 12:6, 11 (KJV) says, "For whom the Lord loveth He chasteneth and scourgeth every son whom He receiveth… Now no chastening for the present seemeth to be joyous, but grievous; nevertheless, afterward it yieldeth the peaceable fruit of righteousness unto them which are exercised thereby."

- Jonah didn't deserve another chance, but because God is merciful, slow to anger, and full of compassion, He spoke to the fish, and it vomited him out on dry land. The Bible says the "word of the Lord came to Jonah the second time" (see Jonah 3:1). The phase indicating "the second time" shows us that when we blow it, God is a God of second times or chances. He gives us what we don't deserve and blesses us when we should have been judged.

Life's Application

God's gracious interventions under the Old Covenant (before Jesus) were intended to reveal the role of the church in His plan for redeeming the world. The institutions of the Old Covenant held only a temporary form of God's grace. The ultimate expression of that grace came in the New Covenant when Jesus completed His work. In order for us to benefit from what Jesus has done, we must receive Him. This is essential because He is the mediator of a better covenant, which was established upon better promises.

Scripture Reference

Now the Lord descended in the cloud and stood with him [Moses] there, and proclaimed the name of the Lord. And the Lord passed before him and proclaimed, the Lord, the Lord God, merciful and gracious, longsuffering, and abounding in goodness and truth, keeping mercy, forgiving iniquity and transgression and sin, by no means clearing the guilty. (Exodus 34:5–7)

2

THE ESSENTIAL FACTS ABOUT GRACE

> Blessed be the God and Father of our Lord Jesus Christ, who has blessed us with every spiritual blessing in the heavenly places in Christ, just as He chose us in Him…according to the good pleasure of His will, in the praise of the glory of His grace, by which He made us accepted in the beloved. In Him we have redemption through His blood, the forgiveness of sins, according to the riches of His grace.
>
> —Ephesians 1:3–7

God's grace covers every area of our lives from salvation, physical healing, financial sufficiency, and provision to carrying out ministry and so on. If it's in God's plan and purpose for our lives, He will give us enough grace in order for us to operate in it. Without it, we're incapable of carrying out His purposes on earth. Philippians 2:13 says, "For it is God who works in you both to will and to do for His good pleasure."

The Old Covenant was superseded by the New Covenant that presented the full manifestation of God's grace. The law was a temporary measure that prepared for the grace that was to come by faith in Jesus Christ. In relation to this, here's what Paul said to the church at Galatia.

> But before faith came, we were kept under the law, shut up unto the faith which should afterwards be revealed. Wherefore the law was our schoolmaster to bring us unto Christ, that we might be justified by faith. But after that faith is come, we are no longer under a schoolmaster, for ye are all the children of God by faith in Christ Jesus. For as many of you as have baptized into Christ have put on Christ. There is neither Jew nor Greek, there is neither bond nor free, there is neither male nor female; for ye are all one in Christ Jesus. And if ye be Christ's, then are ye Abraham's seed, and heirs according to the promise. (Galatians 3:23–29, KJV)

Our grace account with God is full enough to withdraw on every need, and according to Paul our, "God shall supply all your need [spiritually, emotionally, physically] according to His riches in glory by Christ Jesus" (see Philippians 4:19). We can never overdraft our grace account with God because He has more than enough to cover us. We have a spiritual overdraft protection plan, and Jesus has covered and, should I say, paid the expenses. Psalm 23:1, 5 says, "The Lord is my shepherd; I shall not want... Thou anointest my head with oil; my cup runneth over."

What does that mean to you and me? It means we're spiritual millionaires! The problem with what I just stated is that many Christians do not understand they can be rich in God's grace. Paul told the believers at Ephesus they were blessed in heavenly places:

> Blessed be the God and Father of our Lord Jesus Christ, who has blessed us with every spiritual blessing in the heavenly places in Christ, just as He chose us in Him before the foundation of the world, that we should be holy and without blame before Him in love, having predestined us to adoption as sons by Jesus Christ to Himself,

according to the good pleasure of His will, in
the praise of the glory of His grace, by which
He made us accepted in the beloved. In Him we
have redemption through His blood, the forgiveness of sins, according to the riches of His grace.
(Ephesians 1:3–7)

Please observe how in the present tense, Paul is giving thanks
for blessings we already have. These blessings are for every area of our
lives. This gives the understanding why spiritual blessings are located
in heavenly places. Unfortunately, many Christians have placed their
affections on earthly things instead of spiritual things. Colossians
3:1–2 (KJV) says, "If ye then be risen with Christ, seek those things
which are above, where Christ sitteth on the right of God, set your
affection on things above, not on things on the earth."

The scripture above references just a few of the spiritual blessings God in His rich grace has already giving us because of the atonement of Christ. Please bear in mind this list does not fully exhaust
everything we have as a result of God's grace. So how do we receive
these spiritual blessings? As a born-again believer in Christ, all we
simply have to do is to withdraw from God's spiritual bank of grace.

As I stated earlier, faith is the withdrawal slip, grace is our
account number, figuratively speaking. Faith is the channel through
which all our spiritual blessings flows, while grace is the fountain or
stream that flows through that channel. In other words, faith is the
aqueduct along which the flood of mercy flows down upon us. The
aqueduct was a water system in Rome that carried water into the
city. An aqueduct had to be kept together in order to carry the flow
of water.

Likewise, our faith must be true and sound that it may become
a solid channel of mercy to our souls. We must bear in mind that
faith is only the channel or aqueduct and not the fountainhead. The
blessings of the Lord can come to us, even though our faith is that of
a mustard seed because the blessing lies in the grace of God and not
in our faith. Before we go any further, I think it's worth showing you

what we have in our grace account. Please observe a few listed below; however, this doesn't fully exhaust all of what we have through grace.

- We are the righteousness of God. Second Corinthians 5:21 (KJV) says, "For He hath made Him to be sin for us, who knew no sin; that we might be made the righteousness of God in Him." When Jesus becomes Lord and Savior of our lives, we make an exchange—our sin for His righteousness. Our sin is poured into Christ at His crucifixion; His righteousness is poured into our conversion.

- We are sons and heirs. Galatians 4:7 (KJV) says, "Wherefore thou art no more a servant, but a son; and if a son, then an heir of God through Christ." As children of God, we share with Christ Jesus all the privileges of God's resources; we are given the right to claim what Jesus has provided for us. Second Corinthians 1:20 says, "For all the promises of God in Him are Yes and in Him Amen, to the glory of God through us."

- We have been adopted. Ephesians 1:5 (KJV) says, "Having predestinated us unto the adoption of children by Jesus Christ to himself, according to the good pleasure of His will." The Greek word for predestinate is *proorizo*. It has a special reference to that which the subjects of God's foreknowledge are predestinated. The word *predestined* also means predetermined. In Roman law, adopted children had the same rights and privileges as biological children. In addition, the adopted child was guaranteed all legal rights to his father's property.

- We have all our needs supplied. Philippians 4:19 (KJV) says, "But my God shall supply all your need according to His riches in glory by Christ Jesus." We also read, "The Lord is my shepherd; I shall not want" and "The earth is the Lord's and all its fullness, the world and those who dwell therein" (see Psalm 23:1, 24:1). Embracing these biblical facts can assure us that God will meet all of our needs—spiritual, emotional, financial, and physical!

- We have been justified and have access to God. Romans 5:1–2 (KJV) says, "Therefore being justified by faith, we have peace with God through our Lord Jesus Christ; by whom we also have access by faith into this grace wherein we stand, and rejoice in hope of the glory of God." There is no more enmity between us and God and no more sin blocking our relationship with Him. We owe thanks to Jesus who paved the way for this peaceful relationship to take place.
- We have been reconciled. Second Corinthians 5:18 (KJV) says, "And all things are of God, who hath reconciled us to himself by Jesus Christ, and hath given to us the ministry of reconciliation." We are no longer God's enemies and strangers to Him. According to *Merriam-Webster's Dictionary*, the word *reconcile* means "re-establish friendship between; to settle or resolve, as a dispute; to bring (oneself) to accept."
- We are reconciled or reunited to God by the death of Christ on the cross. Ephesians 2:14, 16 says, "For He [Christ] Himself is our peace, who has made both one, and has broken down the middle wall of separation…and that He might reconcile them both to God in one body through the cross, thereby putting to death the enmity."
- We are sealed with the Holy Spirit. Ephesians 1:13 (KJV) says, "In whom ye also trusted, after that ye heard the word of truth, the gospel of your salvation; in whom also after that ye believed, ye were sealed with that Holy Spirit of promise." The Holy Spirit is God's seal and assurance that we belong to Him. The promise is we are filled by the Holy Spirit; it shows we are truly his; it reveals the authenticity of our faith. It establishes the fact we are God's children and guarantees eternal life for us.
- We are God's workmanship created to do good works. Ephesians 2:10 (KJV) says, "For we are his workmanship, created in Christ Jesus unto good works, which God hath before ordained that we should walk in them." We were

saved with the intent to carry out good works. We are God's work of art, His masterpiece. Only God through Christ's death on the cross can save us, and then he can use us for His service and glory.

- We have spiritual fullness. John 6:35 (KJV) says, "And Jesus said unto them, I am the bread of life; he that cometh to me shall never hunger; and he that believeth on me shall never thirst." Natural food sustains human life. Because Jesus says He has life in himself, we will never thirst or hunger spiritually when we receive Jesus as our personal Lord and Savior.

- We have obtained an inheritance. Ephesians 1:11 (KJV) says, "In whom also we have obtained an inheritance, being predestinated according to the purpose of Him who worketh all things after the council of His own will."[1]

Growing in Grace

There is one important thing we must bear in mind concerning grace, and that is it has boundaries. What that mean is the things it will allow and the things it will not permit. I will cover those in chapter 3, but for now, I would like to ask you this important question: do you know we must grow in grace? It was Peter who said, "But grow in the grace, and knowledge of our Lord and Savior Jesus Christ" (see 2 Peter 3:18).

I strongly believe it should be the desire and goal of every born-again Christian to want an increase of grace upon their walk in Christ. What I mean is what we have already received should encourage us to petition for more. That does not mean we are ungrateful, selfish, nor discontented. It simply indicates we are hungry and thirsty for more of Christ who, as we know, was full of grace and truth (see Matthew

---

[1] Quotations taken from Donald Spellman, *Freedom from Spiritual Bondage*, copyright © 2019, by Kingdom House Publishing, Lakebay, Washington, pp. 90–91.

5:6). It also suggests we're not merely satisfied with where we are presently but are willing to meet the challenges to grow in grace.

God is always in the business of increasing and multiplying. God told Abraham to walk before Him and be perfect. In other words, walk in total obedience, and I will multiply thee exceedingly (see Genesis 17:1–2). In addition to that promise, God told him that if he would follow Him, He would make him exceedingly fruitful (see Genesis 17:6). Observe the promise that Jesus makes which is comparable to what God told Abraham:

> I am the vine; you are the branches. He who abides in Me and I in him, bears much fruit; for without Me you can do nothing. If anyone does not abide in Me, he is cast out as a branch and is withered; and they gather them, and throw them into the fire, and they are burned. If you abide in Me, and My words abide in you, you will ask what you desire, and it shall be done for you. By this My Father is glorified, that you bear much fruit, so you will be My disciples. (John 15:5–8)

In Paul's letter to the believers at Rome, it shows us how we have access by faith; because of grace and the current graces, we have produced more. They are multiplied over and over again. Romans 5:2–4 (NIV) says, "Through whom we have gained access by faith into this grace in which we now stand. And we rejoice in the hope of the glory of God. Not only so, but we also rejoice in our sufferings because we know that suffering produces perseverance, perseverance, character; and character hope."

Notice there is a two-sided reality of grace in Christ as a believer. First, we are complete in Christ, and our acceptance with Him is secure. Secondly, we are growing in Christ and we're becoming more and more like Him. Philippians 1:6 (KJV) says, "Being confident of this very thing, that He which hath begun a good work in you will perform it until the day of Jesus Christ." The tribulations we endure are means by which our growth is obtained. James 1:3 says, "Knowing that the testing of your faith produces patience."

When young children begin to grow into adulthood, we say they're experiencing growth pains. In comparison, the believer in Christ also undergoes spiritual growth pains. This assures them of the fact they're growing in grace. God has given us the grace to endure trials without sustaining loss or deterioration. Jude 24 says, "Now unto Him [Jesus] who is able to keep you from stumbling, and to present you faultless before the presence of His [God] glory with exceedingly joy."

To understand how a believer in Christ grows in grace, let's look at the process and development of a natural fruit tree. First, the seed must be planted in the ground. Afterward, a root starts growing deep down into the soil, and a sprout begins to rise upward. Over a period of years, the sprout grows into a fruit tree. In the course of time, a blossom appears on the tree. These eventually fall off, and fruit begins to develop. In the first years of growth as the tree becomes strong, the blossoms and young fruit must be plucked off with the purpose of the tree's root system being developed to support the weight of the tree.

Simultaneously, while the tree is vulnerable, fragile, and growing through its various stages, it must withstand the storms and winds that blow against it. Moreover, the winter frost may even destroy its blossoms. Finally, the tree is fully developed to withstand the adversities of storms and winter frost. It now has the capacity to yield fruit.

In comparison, believers in Christ go through a process. First, the Word is planted in us with the purpose developing a root system. We are then pruned back in order to develop stronger fruit. John 15:2 (AMP) says, "He [Jesus] cleanses and repeatedly prunes every branch that continues to bear fruit, to make it bear more and richer and more excellent fruit." Simultaneously, while this is taking place, the tests of life come to develop character in us(see James 1:2–4).

Finally, we are compared to a palm tree which in the winter months does not change its appearance; the more it is pressed down, the more it grows. Let's now take a close look at Peter's second letter to the church. In the first few verses, he starts off by explaining the necessity of cultivating Christian graces by adding on to our faith. Here's how he explains it to the believers:

> Grace and peace be multiplied unto you through the knowledge of God, and of Jesus our Lord, according as His divine power hath given unto us all things that pertain unto life and godliness, through the knowledge of Him that hath called us to glory and virtue; whereby are given unto us exceeding great and precious promises; that by these ye might be partakers of the divine nature, having escaped the corruption that is in the world through lust. And beside this, giving all diligence, add to your faith virtue; and to virtue knowledge; and to knowledge temperance; and to temperance patience; and to patience godliness brotherly kindness; and to brotherly kindness charity, for if these things be in you, and abound, they make you that ye shall neither be barren nor unfruitful in the knowledge of our Lord Jesus Christ. (2 Peter 1:2–8 KJV)

There are multitudes of well-meaning Christians who are unwilling to search the scriptures and find out what belongs to them. The discipline of a personal prayer life and Bible study is not on their list of things to do. The Bible tells us that God's people perish because of a lack of spiritual knowledge and rejection of knowledge (see Hosea 4:6). Although we must rely on God's enabling grace for everything we encounter in life, and because grace has made it possible for us to be heirs of eternal life, we must still maintain good works.

Titus 3:7–8 (KJV) says, "That being justified by His grace, we should be made heirs according to the hope of eternal life, this a faithful saying, and these things I will that thou affirm constantly, that they which have believed in God might be careful to maintain good works, these things are good and profitable unto men." Let's now go briefly go over these successive stages of spiritual qualities that should increase in the life of the believer (see 2 Peter 1:2–8).

The first successive stage is to "add to our faith virtue" (v. 5). Virtue is goodness, honesty, integrity, moral excellence and strength. It is also a quality that is applied to every area of our lives. Whatever we do in life should be birthed out of excellence. Colossians 3:23 says, "And whatever you do, do it heartily [whole heart], as to the Lord and not to men." Virtue is essential in our walk to maintain good works and to excel in the grace God has given us. Virtue gives us the courage and strength to push forward, for Proverbs 28:1 says, "the righteous are bold as a lion."

What's more, regarding the word *virtue*, Matthew Henry's commentary is quoted by saying:

> Let not your hearts fail you in the evil day,
> but show yourselves valiant in standing against
> all opposition, and resisting every enemy, world,
> flesh, devil, yea and death too. We have need of
> virtue while we live, and it will be of excellent use
> when we come to die.[2]

The second successive stage is to "add to our faith knowledge" (v.5). This is not theological or abstract knowledge but practical knowledge of understanding the scriptures and His revealed will through the Word. This is why we must be persistent and consistent in studying God's Word (see 2 Timothy 2:15). We must receive the spiritual knowledge the Bible has to offer. Hosea 4:6 says, "My people are destroyed for lack of knowledge; because you have rejected knowledge."

We can miss out on many promises and blessings in the Bible by refusing to accept it. The Bible has everything we need for instruction and godly living. Second Timothy 3:16 (KJV) says, "All scrip-

---

[2] Quotations taken from Matthew Henry, *Commentary on the Whole Bible New Modern Edition*, copyright © 1991, Volume 5, Hendrickson Publishers, Inc., Peabody, Massachusetts, p. 837.

ture is given by inspiration of God, and is profitable for doctrine, for reproof, for correction and for instruction in righteousness."

The third successive stage is to "add temperance" (v. 6). Temperance speaks of self-control and restraint. As believers in Christ, we must always exercise self-restraint. Discipline should be applied to every area of our lives (personalities, emotions, attitudes, appetites and thoughts). Paul's first letter to the church at Corinth gives us a beautiful illustration of how an athlete disciplines himself to compete for a prize. The picture he paints gives us a parallel concerning a believer walk in Christ.

In 1 Corinthians 9:25 (AMP), he explains it this way: "Now every athlete who goes into training conducts himself temperately and restricts himself in all things. They do it to win a wreath that will soon wither, but we do it to receive a crown of eternal blessedness that cannot wither."

Christians who have added temperance (self-control) understand the importance of living godly in this present life. Titus 2:11–12 (KJV) says, "For the grace of God that bringeth salvation hath appeared to all men, teaching us that denying ungodliness and worldly lusts, we should live soberly, righteously, and godly in this present world."

The fourth successive stage is to "add patience" (v. 6). Patience also means perseverance or endurance; all three words have the same meaning. The apostles in the early church exhorted the disciples to continue in the faith. Paul warned them that through much tribulation, we would enter the kingdom of God. This encourages those who are on the verge of giving up to keep the faith and to have patience (endurance or perseverance). Patience is the ability to overcome innumerable tests and trials. It also is the ability to last, continue or remain, to withstand hardships or adversity despite suffering.

Hebrews 6:11–12 says, "And we desire that each one of you show the diligence to the full assurance of hope until the end, that you do not become sluggish, but imitate those who through faith and patience [endurance, perseverance] inherit the promises."

Impatience is quite the opposite and will expose any weak or undisciplined areas of our personality. In a marathon, it's not speed or strength but endurance that counts. We must remember the Christian race is not a sprint but a race that requires longevity, patience (endurance, perseverance). If we have not yet attained something that God promises, we need patience (endurance, perseverance) to wait on it. This will expose many things in our character and will show if an individual will either give up waiting or trust Him to wait.

Hebrews 10:35–36 says, "Therefore do not cast away your confidence, which has great reward. For you have need of patience [endurance, perseverance], so that after you have done the will of God, you may receive the promise." The testing of our faith will produce patience, which will eventually lead to us being complete and lacking nothing.

The fifth successive stage is to "add godliness" (v. 6). This is an important stage of spiritual development. This is when a person's life is centered in God. In other words, their lives are surrendered to the Holy Spirit and are God-centered. The atmosphere changes when they enter a room and the people in that room come under strong conviction (see John 16:8).

For instance, there was a man of God who, after moments of intense prayer, entered a railway car, sat down and, without speaking a word, affected the man in the opposite seat. The gentleman was brought under strong conviction. The man blurted out, "Your presence convicts me of sin." When we allow the Holy Spirit to add this important character trait in our lives, positive things will occur. It might not necessarily happen the same way as the story I've just related, but nonetheless, lives will change, and most important, God will be glorified.

The sixth successive stage is to "add brotherly kindness" (v. 7). It is serviceable, good, and gracious. This describes how a believer should interact with their fellow brothers and sisters in Christ. In Acts 28:2, we see a pattern of how brotherly love should be displayed. For example, on an island where Paul and his fellowmen had survived a shipwreck, the barbarous people showed them great kindness. Because of the rain and cold weather, Paul and his companions were received with kindness. My friend, if barbarous people showed kindness to complete strangers, there should be no problem for us to show kindness to our fellow brothers and sisters in Christ.

In Paul's first epistle to the church at Thessalonica, he said there wasn't any need for him to write about how they should love each other, seeing God had already instructed them on the matter (see 1 Thessalonians 4:9–10). Selfishness is the enemy of brotherly kindness. When believers are only interested in their own affairs and their own well-being, it becomes extremely difficult for them to show kindness.

We must always be willing to look out for the needs of others. Romans 12:10 (KJV) says, "Be kindly affectionate one to another with brotherly love; in honor preferring one another." There's a kindness that proceeds out from the believer to all men but has special reference to those who are fellow believers in Christ. Galatians 6:10 says, "Therefore as we have opportunity, let us do good to all especially to those who are of the household of faith."

The seventh successive and final stage is to "add charity" (v. 7). Charity is the same as love or compassion. It is equivalent to the love Christ demonstrated on the cross when He prayed for those who crucified Him. It is the same identical love that Stephen demonstrated while he was being stoned to death, asking the Lord to lay it not to their charge. Love is a by-product of our new life in Christ.

When Christians truly love each other, it will have an impact that goes far beyond their neighborhoods and communities. Jesus said that when believers love each other, it will validate their claim as His disciples. John 13:34–35 (KJV) says, "A new commandment I give unto you, that ye love one another; as I have loved you, that ye also love one another, by this shall men know that ye are my disciples, if ye have love one to another."

The love of God is always directed outward toward others, not inward toward ourselves. One of the most beautiful explanations of charity (love) is found in Paul's first letter to the believers at Corinth where he says:

> Love is patient, love is kind. It does not
> envy, it does not boast, it is not proud. It is not

> rude, it is not self-seeking, it is not easily angered, and it keeps no record of wrongs. Love does not delight in evil but rejoices with the truth. It always protects, always trusts, always hopes, always persevere, love never fails. (1 Corinthians 13:4–8 NIV)

Love can always be known by the actions it prompts. It is not in mere words but in deeds and truth.

Up to this point, I have explained the benefits of grace and the indispensable blessings it brings to believers and the indirect impact it has on nonbelievers. The question we must ask is, can an individual receive the grace of God in vain? The answer is yes. God's grace can be received in vain. Second Corinthians 6:1 (KJV) says, "We then, as workers together with Him, beseech you also that ye receive not the grace of God in vain."

One thing we must bear in mind is Paul had always sought evidence of a lifestyle of the Gospel in the converts abroad. The same should hold true with those of us who are saved. It cost God His Son Jesus, and the outpouring of His grace should not be taken lightly. The Gospel itself is a message of grace. It would be in vain for anyone to hear unless we believe it and act on it. I've come to understand it is our responsibility to compel people to accept God's mercy and grace. Once we have become benefactors of that grace, we should never take it for granted.

Can we frustrate the grace of God? The answer is emphatically yes. Anytime we try to gain a right standing with God other than through the atonement of Christ, we frustrate God's grace. Paul in his epistle to the Galatians warned them about the folly of believing righteousness comes through the keeping of the law. Galatians 2:21 (KJV) says, "I do not frustrate the grace of God; for if righteousness come by the law, then Christ dead in vain."

The word *frustrate* means to discourage, prevent, hinder, and obstruct. So in short, Paul said we *discourage, prevent, hinder,* and *obstruct* the grace of God when we try to obtain righteousness through the Mosaic Law. In other words, the doctrine of justification of the law required works to obtain righteousness. In favor of grace, Paul showed the believers at Rome how works nullifies grace. Romans 11:6 (KJV) says, "And if it by grace, then is it no more of works; otherwise grace is no more grace. But if it be of works, then is it no more grace; otherwise work is no more work."

In the book of Jude, there is a strong warning for those who would turn the grace of God into a license for immorality. The same warning applies to us today. Jude 4 (NIV) says, "For certain men whose condemnation was written about long ago have secretly slipped in among you. They are godless men, who change the grace of our God into a license for immorality and deny Jesus Christ for our only sovereign and Lord." These were false teachers who taught that Christians could do whatever they liked without fear of God's punishment.

In this dispensation, some Christians minimize the issue of sin, believing how they live has little to do with their faith. What a person truly believes will show up in how they live. Those who truly have faith will show it by their love, deep respect, and reverential fear for God. There is a temptation for people to say it's okay to sin and to say, "After all, you will be forgiven."

However, Paul said to the believers in Rome, "Shall I continue in sin that grace may abound? Certainly not!" (see Romans 6:1-2). In chapter 4, in an effort to balance out this teaching about grace, I will show you the things grace will not permit.

Short Review of The Essential Facts About Grace

- Our grace account with God is full enough to withdraw on every need we have. Philippians 4:19 (KJV) says, "But my God shall supply all your need [spiritually, emotionally, physically] according to His riches in glory by Christ Jesus."
- Spiritual blessing is located in heavenly places, and most Christians have their affections on earthly things instead of spiritual things. Colossians 3:1–2 (KJV) says, "If ye then be risen with Christ, seek those things which are above, where Christ sitteth on the right of God, set your affections on things above, not on things on the earth."
- Here are just a few blessings we're able to withdraw out of our grace account: we are the righteousness of God; we are sons and heirs; we have been adopted; we have all our needs supplied; we have been justified and have access with God; we have been reconciled; we are sealed with the Holy Spirit; we are God's workmanship created to do good works; we have spiritual fullness, and we have obtained an inheritance.
- God is always in the business of multiplying. Jesus said that if we depend on Him, we would bring forth much fruit and that His Father is glorified (see John 15:1–10).
- There is a two-sided reality of grace in Christ. As a believer, on one hand, we are complete in Christ, and our acceptance with Him is secure. Then on the other hand, we are growing in Christ. We are becoming more and more like Him. Philippians 1:6 (KJV) says, "Being confident of this very thing, that He who hath begun a good work in you will perform it until the day of Jesus Christ."
- Can an individual receive the grace of God in vain? The answer is emphatically yes; God's grace can be received in vain. Second Corinthians 6:1 (KJV) says, "We then, as workers together with Him, beseech you also that ye receive not the grace of God in vain." The next question you might ask is, can I frustrate the grace of God? The

answer is yes. Anytime we try to gain a right standing with God as opposed to the atonement of Christ, we frustrate God's grace (see Galatians 2:21).

- The things grace will not permit: grace will not cancel the responsibility of saved men when sin is present in their lives. Grace will not keep men saved who willfully keep sinning. Grace will not set aside all sentences for future sins. Grace will not set aside the requirements that men must meet for salvation. Grace will not allow eternal life to men who serve sin and Satan. Grace will not allow God to forgive unconfessed sins. Grace will not cancel the law of sowing and reaping as it pertains to sin.

Life's Application

God has opened a grace account for those of us who have accepted His Son. The atonement of Christ has secured this spiritual account for us. It's up to us as believers to withdraw on our spiritual inheritance because of what Christ has done and our positional standing in Him. Colossians 1:13 (KJV) says, "Who hath delivered us from the power of darkness, and hath translated us into the Kingdom of His dear son." Instead of receiving God's grace in vain or frustrating it, we should readily receive what God has given.

Scripture Reference

And God is able to make all grace (every favor and earthly blessing) come to you in abundance, so that you may always and under all circumstances and whatever the need be self-sufficient (possessing enough to require no aid or support and furnished in abundance for every good work and charitable donation). (2 Corinthians 9:8 AMP)

3

UNIVERSAL GRACE AND MERCIES

Is there any number to His [God] armies?
Upon whom does His light not rise?

That you may be sons of your Father in
heaven, for He makes His sun rise on the evil
and on the good, and sends rain on the just and
on the unjust.

—Job 25:3; Matthew 5:45

When we look at the world at large, many would ask how God can bestow grace on those who are His children and those who are not. Or how can a righteous God have mercy on both the believer and the unbeliever? One question leads to another, so in this chapter, I will do my best to answer these questions and more. In addition, I want to show you how universal grace and mercies play an important role in the life of the believer and unbeliever in the world today.

But first, here's a simple definition of universal grace and mercies. They are undeserved blessings that God gives to all people, both believers and nonbelievers. They can also be defined as the grace of God by which He gives people countless blessings that are not part of salvation. The source of universal grace does not directly flow from Christ's atoning work but from God's longsuffering patience which awaits the sinner repentance. Second Peter 3:9 (KJV) says, "The Lord is not slack concerning His promise, as some men count slackness; but is longsuffering to us-ward, not willing that any should perish, but that all should come to repentance."

Salvation cannot be claimed to the recipients of universal grace unless they repent and receive Christ. Moreover, it may at times alert people to God's goodness and mercy but will not save them. Romans 2:4 (NLT) says, "Don't you realize how kind, tolerant and patient God is with you? Or don't you care? Can't you see how kind He has been giving you time to turn from your sin?"

It is evident that God's love is complete, and He overlooks no one as it's seen in His universal provision. His universal mercy Is abundant toward all. Matthew 5:45 says, "That you may be sons of your Father in heaven; for He makes His sun rise on the evil and on the good and sends rain on the just and on the unjust."

Sunshine and rain are a necessity for the growth and development of produce. These alone are instances and proof of the goodness and mercy of God. Every person in society would be miserable without the grace and mercy of God. Sinners partake of the comforts of life with those who trust Christ as their Savior. We must bear in mind that if God wanted to, He could prohibit the sun to shine on sinners and cause it to only benefit the believer. This was the case when He prohibited the sun to illuminate upon the Egyptians and shine only on the Israelites.

Exodus 10:22–23 (KJV) says, "And Moses stretched forth his hand toward heaven; and there was a thick darkness in all the land of Egypt three days; They saw not one another; neither rose any from His place for three days; but all the children of Israel had light in their dwellings."

Let's read what Jesus said again, Matthew 5:45 says, "That you may be sons of your Father in heaven; for He makes His sun rise on the evil and on the good, and sends rain on the just and on the unjust." In this scripture, immediately what comes to mind is God's universal mercies toward mankind. The earth does not only produce thorns and thistles or remain a parched land (see Genesis 3:18). God's universal grace produces food and material for clothing, shelter, and so on. Acts 14:16–17 (KJV) says, "Who in times past suffered all nations to walk in their own ways? Nevertheless, He left not Himself without witness, in that He did good, and gave us rain from heaven, and fruitful seasons, filling our hearts with food and gladness."

Instances of Universal Grace

An extraordinary instance of God's universal grace is seen in the book of Genesis. It was about the household of Potiphar, an Egyptian who did not worship the true God of Israel. In addition, Potiphar was a captain of the guard and one who was possibly involved in international slave trading. This is further evidenced when he purchased Joseph from his jealous brothers. After Potiphar acquires Joseph from the Midianite slave traders, the story unfolds as Potiphar quickly promotes Joseph to manage his affairs in his household. Unbeknownst to Potiphar, this would prove to be an important move because the Lord blessed his house for Joseph's sake.

> And the Lord was Joseph, and he was a prosperous man; and he was in the house of his master the Egyptian. And his master [Potiphar's] saw that the Lord was with him, and that the Lord made all that he did to prosper in his hand. And Joseph found grace in his [Potiphar's] sight, and he served him; and he made him overseer over his house, and all that he had he put into his hand. And it came to pass from that time that he hath made him overseer in his house, and over all that he had, that the Lord blessed the Egyptian's house for Joseph's sake; and the blessing of the Lord was upon all that he [Potiphar's] had in the house, and in the field. (Genesis 39:2–5 KJV)

Another example of universal grace is found in Genesis 31 regarding Jacob's father-in law, Laban. It appeared that Laban had shrewd dealings in everything from marriage, deceitful labor transactions, and management negotiations. Similar to Potiphar, Laban did not serve the true God of Israel. This is also evidenced in his worship of other gods. Jacob, after many years of working for his shrewd father-in-law, decided to leave and take his wives Rachel and Leah. While he was leaving, Rachel decided to take her father's gods.

This further adds validity to the fact Laban was not a follower and worshipper of the true God of Israel, Genesis 31:30 (KJV) says, "And now, though thou wouldest needs be gone because thou sore longest after thy father's house, yet wherefore hast thou stolen my gods?" Prior to Jacob leaving his father-in-law, Laban found himself reaping the blessings of universal mercies. Not because he worshipped the God of Israel, but he was blessed for Jacob's sake. Genesis 3:27 (KJV) says, "And Laban said unto him, I pray thee, if I found favor in thine eyes, tarry; for I have learned by experience that the Lord hath blessed me for thy sake."

These examples clearly show that men and women who are not serving or worshipping God receive countless universal grace blessings at the expense of someone who lives a righteous life. Another example of God's universal grace and mercies is seen in the institution and the placement of civil government. Government is a gift of universal grace to restrain immorality in the world.

> Let every soul be subject unto the higher powers. For there is no power but of God; the powers that be are ordained of God. Whosoever therefore resistant the power, resistant the ordinance of God; and they that resist shall receive to themselves damnation. For rulers is not a terror to good works, but to the evil. Wilt thou then not be afraid of the power? Do that which is good, and thou shalt have praise of the same. For he is minister of God to thee for good, but if thou do that which is evil, be afraid; for he beareth not the sword in vain; for he is the minister of God, a revenger to execute wrath upon him that doeth evil. (Romans 13:1–4 KJV)

Human government, law enforcement, police departments, and judicial systems all provide restraints to evil and are products of universal grace. For example, the police department is "God's servants for your good." They are servants to execute wrath on lawlessness and criminals. On the other hand, judicial systems can be corrupt and actually promote evil rather than good. Even now as we speak, police brutality is on the rise with people of color being the targets of this evil. Like any other product of universal grace, those blessings can either be used for good or evil.

There are scores of unbelievers who are gifted with talents and skills. Some are carpenters by trade, machinists, welders, musical instrument makers, bookmakers and so on. Case in point: those who have the occupation of a carpenter are able to construct a sanctuary, seminary building, ministry headquarters, and a Christian school while a musical instrument maker can make pianos, drums, keyboards, and similar instruments that will be used in church settings, workshops or conferences.

Likewise, a bookmaker can create Bible binders and Sunday schoolbooks that will be used in many churches. God has given universal grace for the good of mankind, and without it, many would suffer in the world.

Universal Grace Does Not Save People

Because of God's universal grace, unbelievers bring many things to society. However, universal grace and mercy does not save people in spite of all the good they bring to the world. The thing we should bear in mind is doing good deeds never saves people, only genuine repentance and faith. Romans 3:10–12 (KJV) says, "As it is written, there is none righteous, no not one; there is none that understandeth, there is none that seeketh after God. They are all gone out of the way they are together become unprofitable; there is none that doeth good, no not one."

It was David who wrote, "You [God] created my inmost being; you knit me together in my mother's womb... I am fearfully and wonderfully made" (see Psalm 139:13–14). Although we were "fearfully and wonderfully made" prior to salvation, we all had become "unprofitable" and incapable of doing good without Christ. Our actions might have been morally good, but it did not stem from an origination of faith, "for whatsoever is not of faith is sin" (see Romans 14:23).

A misunderstanding and misinterpretation of the grace of God can easily develop in the mind of unbelievers. God's universal grace upon them is no indication he has given them favor. Acts 14:16–17 (KJV) says, "Who in times past suffered all nations to walk in their own ways. Nevertheless, he left not himself without witness, in that he did good and gave us rain from heaven, and fruitful seasons, filling our hearts with food and gladness."

God has never left His people without a "witness or testimony" the things I had mention before, like "rain and crops" are evidences of God's goodness. Romans 2:4 (KJV) says, "Or despiseth thou the riches of His goodness and forbearance and longsuffering; not knowing that the goodness of God leadeth thee to repentance?" In an earlier letter to the believers at Rome, Paul wrote about the facts of nature which leave people without an excuse for walking in unbelief. Romans 1:19 (NIV) says, "For since the creation of the world God's invisible qualities—His eternal power and divine nature—have been clearly seen, being understood from what has been made, so that men are without excuse."

There are some unbelievers who experience God's goodness and forbearance and often have a hatred for the mercies of God. As a matter of fact, most unbelievers are more prone to sin more. Ecclesiastes 8:11 (KJV) says, "Because sentence against an evil work is not executed speedily, therefore the heart of the sons of men is fully set in them to do evil." The devil has deceived their minds with the notion that because God hasn't judged their ungodly actions, they're free to continue a life of sin. Unfortunately, what they fail to understand is judgment delayed is not judgment denied.

God Is Longsuffering

God is in the business of saving people. That's why He sent Jesus who came "to seek and save that which is lost" (see Luke 19:10).

The Lord has no pleasure in men losing their souls He "is longsuffering to us-ward, not willing that any should perish, but that all should come to repentance" (see 2 Peter 3:9). If they're honest, many become impatient when it comes to the salvation of an unsaved family member or friend. There's a temptation to drive them instead of lead to repentance. However, the Lord shows us that He leads, not drives. Hosea 2:14 says, "Therefore, behold I will allure her, and bring her into the wilderness, and speak comfortably unto her." When God releases grace in the affairs of a worthless, hell-deserving man or woman life, He's drawing them with "bands of love" (see Hosea 11:4).

I stated this earlier in the chapter that unlike saving grace, universal grace cannot save men, but it can convince them of the goodness of God and perchance lead them to repentance (see Romans 2:4). God may delay the punishment upon sin and give universal grace or temporary blessings to the sinner. But we must keep in mind that just because the punishment is delayed, it's not forgotten. Again, Ecclesiastes 8:11–13 says:

> Because the sentence against an evil work is not executed speedily, therefore the heart of the sons of men is fully set in them to do evil. But it will not be well with the wicked; nor will he prolong his days, which are as a shadow because he does not fear before God.

However, God takes no pleasure in the punishment of sinners, but He delights in the salvation of their souls. Ezekiel 33:11 says, "As I live, saith the Lord God, I have no pleasure in the death of the wicked; but that the wicked turn from His way and live." Clearly from the scriptures we read, we see how God's amazing grace compels even the worst sinner to know that in spite of Himself, God's mercy, and grace "will have all men to be saved, and to come unto the knowledge of the truth" (1 Timothy 2:4 KJV).

Short Review of Universal Grace and Mercies

- Universal grace is undeserved blessings that God gives to all people, both believers and unbelievers alike. It can also be defined as the grace of God by which He gives people countless blessings that are not part of salvation. Matthew 5:45 says, "That you may be sons of your Father in heaven; for He makes His sun rise on the evil and on the good, and sends rain on the just and on the unjust."

- The differences between universal grace and saving grace is that, universal grace, and mercies don't bring about salvation in its recipients. The source of it does not directly come from Christ's atoning work but from God's longsuffering patience that awaits the unbeliever to repent. Second Peter 3:9 (KJV) says, "The Lord is not slack concerning His promise, as some men count slackness; but is longsuffering to us-ward, not willing that any should perish, but that all should come to repentance."

- An example in the Old Testament of God's universal grace bestowed upon unbelievers is a story about a man name Potiphar, an Egyptian captain of the guard who purchased Joseph as a slave. As a result of Joseph living in his house, his household was completely blessed. Genesis 39:5 (KJV) says, "And it came to pass from the time that he had made him overseer in his house, and over all that he had, that the Lord blessed the Egyptian's house for Joseph's sake; and the blessing of the Lord was upon all that he had in the house, and in the field."

- Another example of God's universal grace and mercies is that God has put in place civil government for the restraining of evil in the world (see Romans 13:1–4).

- The goodness of God has granted universal grace to mankind. However, universal grace in itself does not save people but alerts them to the goodness of God; perchance, it might even lead them to repentance. Romans 2:4 (KJV) says, "Or despiseth thou the riches of his goodness and forbearance and longsuffering; not knowing that the goodness of God leadeth thee to repentance?"

- God may delay the punishment upon sin and give universal grace or temporary blessings to the sinner. But we must keep in mind that just because the punishment is delayed, it's not forgotten. Ecclesiastes 8:11–13 says, "Because the sentence against an evil work is not executed speedily, therefore the heart of the sons of men is fully set in them to do evil… But it will not be well with the wicked; nor will he prolong his days, which are as a shadow because he does not fear before God."

- God takes no pleasure in the punishment of sinners but rather delights in the salvation of their souls. Ezekiel 33:11 says, "Say unto them, as I live, saith the Lord God, I have no pleasure in the death of the wicked; but that the wicked turn from his way and live."

Life Application

God's abundant grace or universal grace is given to all. His goodness is seen in creation, talents, and the resources He bestows on sinful men. If for a moment the unbeliever would acknowledge universal grace upon his or her life, this would perchance lead them to repentance. It is God's will that no one perish but that all should come to repentance.

Key Scripture

That you may be sons of your father in heaven for He makes His sun rise on the evil and on the good, and sends rain on the just and on the unjust. (Matthew 5:45)

4

GRACE IS NOT LICENSE TO SIN

What shall we say then? Shall we continue in sin that grace may abound? Certainly not! How shall we who died to sin live any longer in it?

For sin shall not have dominion over you, for you are not under law but under grace. What then? Shall we sin because we are not under law but under grace? Certainly not!

—Ephesians 2:4–9, 14–15

Before I share more of what grace will do for us, we must know what it cannot do or allow. Unfortunately, there are multitudes of Christians who think it's okay to habitually sin because God's grace is accessible to us in the person of Christ Jesus. What's more, these same Christians find it to be a struggle accepting facts that grace will not rescind or cancel out the responsibility of sin when it's present in their lives. Paul writes that what a believer in Christ sows they will invariably reap. Galatians 6:7–8 (KJV) says, "Be not deceived; God is not mocked; for whatsoever a man soweth, that shall he also reap, for he that soweth to his flesh reap corruption; but he that soweth to the Spirit shall of the Spirit reap life everlasting."

Those who live a carnal life must understand the fruit that comes from their behavior will reap the harvest of spiritual death.

Romans 8:6 (KJV) says, "For to be carnally minded is death; but to be spiritually minded is life and peace." Here are two categories of people: those whose minds are controlled by their sinful nature, and those whose mind is controlled by the Holy Spirit. When we have the latter, it will yield life and peace.

Another misunderstanding some believers have is that grace will keep men and women saved who willfully keep sinning. Let's examine this for a moment.

> For it is impossible for those who were once enlightened, and tasted of the heavenly gift, and were made partakers of the Holy Ghost, and have tasted the good word of God, and the powers of the world to come, if they shall fall away, to renew them again unto repentance; seeing they crucify to themselves the Son of God afresh, and put Him to an open shame. (Hebrews 6:4–6 KJV)

The phrase "to renew them again" suggests that grace was not going to keep them. However, when we surrender to Jesus, He alone can keep us (Jude 24). Those who fall from grace must repent and return unto the Lord. Moreover, if believers have to be renewed again to repentance, then grace wasn't responsible for keeping them once they sinned and fell away.

Grace will not set aside all sentences for future sins unless one repents. Jesus made this very clear to an impotent man who he had recently healed. He gave the man enough grace for his present condition but told him that if he continued to sin, he would face future judgment. John 5:14 (KJV) says, "Afterward, Jesus findeth him in the temple, and said unto him, 'Behold, thou art made whole; sin no more, lest a worse thing come unto thee.'"

The man was obviously a believer. This suggests to us that he was grateful, similar to the leper who returned to Jesus and gave thanks after he had been healed. For Jesus to have told the impotent man not to sin anymore exposes the fact that this might have been a long-term illness and could have been the result of habitual sin in his life. The warning to him not to commit future sins also suggests he might have sinned prior to his healing. In other words, grace wasn't going to cover future sins, only repentance.

Romans 6:1–2 (KJV) says, "What shall we say then? Shall we continue in sin, that grace may abound? God forbid. How shall we, that are dead to sin, live any longer therein?" A couple of chapters later, Paul admonished the believers not to live according to the flesh but to live through the Spirit. Romans 8:12–13 (KJV) says, "Therefore, brethren we are debtors, not to the flesh, to live after the flesh, for if ye live after the flesh, ye shall die; but if ye through the Spirit do mortify the deeds of the body, ye shall live."

Grace will not lay aside the requirements that men must meet for salvation. Please do not misunderstand what I am saying at this point. I am not suggesting that works is a prerequisite for salvation. However, every one of us had to repent, confess, and have faith in the Lord Jesus for salvation (see Acts 2:38; Romans 10:9–13). Faith is the channel, and grace is the water flow in which salvation comes. To be clear here, we must understand that we're not saved on the account of our faith. Faith is the channel through which salvation flows while grace is the fountain or stream that flows through that channel.

My friends, God is not asking us to work for our salvation, but He is asking that we meet the conditions Jesus has paid for our salvation. John 1:12 (KJV) says, "But as many as received Him, to them gave He power to become the sons of God, even to them that believe on His name." Peter, being full of the Holy Spirit, on the day of Pentecost exhorted the people to repent and to be baptized for the remission of sins. As a result, three thousand souls were added to the kingdom of God.

Acts 2:37–39 (KJV) says:

> Now when they heard this, they were pricked in their heart, and said unto Peter and to the rest of the apostles, "Men and brethren, what shall we do?" Then Peter said unto them, "Repent, and be baptized every one of you in the name of Jesus Christ for the remission of sins,

and ye shall receive the gift of the Holy Ghost. For the promise is unto you, and to your children, and to all that are far off, even as many as the Lord our God shall call."

Grace was the outpouring made available to the three thousand. But when the people asked the question, "What must we do?" Peter gave them the condition or requirement.

Grace will not allow eternal life to men who serve sin and Satan. Galatians 5:19–21 (KJV) says:

> Now the works of the flesh are manifest, which are these: adultery, fornication, uncleanness, lasciviousness [lust, sexual desires], idolatry, witchcraft, hatred, variance [conflict, deviating from a standard], emulations [ambition, imitation, jealous rivalry], wrath, strife, seditions [troublemaking, agitation, treason, incitement to rebellion], heresies, envying, murders, drunkenness, reveling [to make noise or rebel] and such like; of the which I tell you before, as I have also told you in time past, that they which do such things shall not inherit the kingdom of God.

This Scripture gives us an indication that those who habitually indulge in sins of the flesh or refuse to deal with them reveal they have not received the gift of the Holy Spirit. In the following verses, we see the fruit as a result of being filled with the Spirit (vv. 22–23). The other thing we must bear in mind is the habitual practice of sin points to an unrepentant heart. This will undoubtedly keep people out of heaven.

Grace will not allow God to forgive unconfessed sins. Second Chronicles 7:14 (KJV) says, "If my people which are called by name, shall humble themselves, and pray and seek my face, and turn from their wicked ways; then will I hear from heaven, and will forgive their sin, and will heal their land." According to this Old Testament

Scripture, it was expected that God's children would receive punishment for their sins if they did not repent and turn from iniquity. The Father had set forth conditions as a means to pardon sin, and forgiveness of sins was only available if they heeded his counsel and instructions.

In the New Testament, we have a similar admonishment to repent and confess our sins, for the Apostle John says: "If we say that we have no sin, we deceive ourselves, and the truth is not in us. If we confess our sins, He is faithful and just to forgive us our sins, and to cleanse us from all unrighteousness. If we say that we have not sinned, we make Him a liar, and His word is not in us" (see 1 John 1:8–9).

In the Bible, we find that God has established a principle of seedtime and harvest, sowing and reaping. His grace will not cancel the law of sowing and reaping as it pertains to sin. Galatians 6:7–8 (KJV) says, "Be not deceived; God is not mocked; for whatsoever a man soweth, that shall he also reap, for he that soweth to his flesh shall reap corruption; but he that soweth to the Spirit shall of the Spirit reap life everlasting."

God has established a principle of seedtime and harvest that whatever spiritual seed we sow will undoubtedly bring up a spiritual crop. Grace is available for the right choices we make, but it will not cancel the repercussions and consequences of such wrong choices made. Now let's look at universal mercies and universal grace.[3]

---

[3] Quotations taken from Donald Spellman, *Freedom from Spiritual Bondage*, copyright © 2019, by Kingdom House Publishing, Lakebay, Washington, pp. 100–104.

Short Review of Grace Not a License to Sin

- Can an individual receive the grace of God in vain? The answer is emphatically yes; God's grace can be received in vain. Second Corinthians 6:1 (KJV) says, "We then, as workers together with Him, beseech you also that ye receive not the grace of God in vain." The next question you might ask is, can I frustrate the grace of God? The answer is yes. Anytime we try to gain a right standing with God other as opposed to the atonement of Christ, we frustrate God's grace (see Galatians 2:21).

- God is not asking us to work for our salvation, but He is asking that we meet the conditions Jesus has paid for our salvation. John 1:12 (KJV) says, "But as many as received Him, to them gave He power to become the sons of God, even to them that believe on His name."

- Those who habitually indulge in sins of the flesh or refuse to deal with them reveal that they have not received the gift of the Holy Spirit. In the following verses, we see the fruit as a result of being filled with the Spirit (vs. 22–23). The other thing we must bear in mind is the habitual practice of sin points to an unrepentant heart.

- God has established a principle of seedtime and harvest, sowing and reaping. His grace will not cancel the law of sowing and reaping as it pertains to sin. Galatians 6:7–8 (KJV) says, "Be not deceived; God is not mocked; for whatsoever a man soweth, that shall he also reap, for he that soweth to his flesh shall reap corruption; but he that soweth to the Spirit shall of the Spirit reap life everlasting."

5

GRACE THAT RESTORES

And when he came to himself, he said how many hired servants of my fathers have bread enough and to spare, and I perish with hunger! I will arise and go to my father, and will say unto him, father I have sinned against heaven and before thee and am no more worthy to be called thy son; make me as one of thy hired servants. And he arose and came to his father, but when he was still a great way off, his father saw him and had compassion, and fell on his neck and kissed him.

—Luke 15:17–20 KJV

The story of the wayward son is one of restoration, compassion, and grace on the undeserving. It has always been God's objective and good pleasure to restore people back to their rightful place in Him. In spite of the fall of man in the garden, God had a plan of redemption in place in the person of Christ Jesus. The story begins with the prodigal son asking his father to "give me the portion of goods that falls to me" (see Luke 15:12). This is precisely the mindset of unregenerate men and women who want things their way instead of God's way. Proverbs 14:12 says, "There is a way that seems right to a man, but its end is the way of death."

Unfortunately, some individuals rather grab instead of receive what the Father has for them. God knows when He's ready to release what He has for us, for He "will not with hold any good thing from them that walk upright" (see Psalm 84:11). He never releases something to us out of His timing or something that would harm us. The prodigal son wasn't willing to wait so he "gathered all together, journey to a far country" (see Luke 15:13).

This behavior is quite common in many homes across America, a thought of leaving at an early age but perhaps just a thought. But with this wayward son, it was more than a thought; he carried it out. Another widespread problem that both sinners and believers fall victim to is they want God to bless them with things but have nothing to do with the one who blesses them. Jesus said people sought Him out "because they ate of the loaves and were filled" (see John 6:26). They simply sought Him not because of Him but because of their bellies.

As the prodigal son began his voyage, He "journeyed to a far country" (see Luke 15:13). Satan's plan for him was put in full motion to separate and isolate him as far as he could from those who loved and cared about him. This is an old strategy from the enemy to get people as far away from God as possible. He loves to isolate them so he can move in and ultimately destroy them. John 10:10 says, "The thief [Satan] does not come except to steal, and to destroy; I [Jesus] have come that they may have life, and that they may have it more abundantly."

Have you ever watched the television channel, *National Geographic*? They would showcase various kinds of wildlife and sometimes predators. Sometimes we would witness a herd of antelope crossing a plain and moving at an extreme fast pace. When the dust finally dissipates, then along comes a slow-moving injured antelope, and suddenly, a lion that was in a crouch position jumps up and overtakes the animal. In comparison, this is the state and unfortunately the fate of many believers in Christ who are not alert.

The Apostle Peter admonished believers to, "Be sober, be vigilant; because your adversary the devil, as a roaring lion, walketh about, seeking whom he may devour" (1 Peter 5:8). We can learn a lot from the story of the prodigal son. One deceptive scheme of the devil is to deceive people into thinking the Father doesn't love them and care about them. He whispers in their ears, saying things like, "God doesn't love you. He has forgotten you," and so on. My friends, please understand if Satan can isolate you as far he can from your loved ones, that leaves no one to remind you of the Father's love for you.

Once the prodigal arrived at his destination, he "wasted his possessions with prodigal living" (see Luke 15:13). The word *prodigal* means wasteful, reckless and uncontrolled. We're told in the Bible to be good stewards over what God has entrusted in our care. Clearly the prodigal son wasn't a good steward(see 1 Corinthians 4:2). The thing we must bear in mind is that whatever God places in our hands we should allow to bless us, not curse us.

For example, take two neighbors both receive a knife as a gift for their birthdays. Each one has a different purpose for the use of their knife. One neighbor uses his knife to provide for his family by cutting meats and poultry to sell at the local meat market, while his neighbor uses his knife by killing people and committing horrible crimes. Both were given the same gift, a knife, but one chose to do right by what he received. What we all need is wisdom. Wisdom is the ability to apply or use what we have. If we don't have wisdom, we can get it (see James 1:5).

Returning back to the story of the prodigal son, we read that he went on a spending binge, and when he emptied his bag and pockets, "he had spent all" (see Luke 15:14). According to Deuteronomy 21:17, the prodigal son could have possibly received one-third of his father's estate. We can only speculate as to what he inherited with one-third of his father's assets. But nonetheless, he spent all. Consequently, when we don't trust Jesus as our Lord and Savior or leave out from His covering as Shepherd, we will find ourselves in want, spiritually, physically and emotionally.

The psalmist says, "the Lord is my shepherd, I shall not want." Yet this young man placed himself in a position of want. Proverbs 20:21 says, "An inheritance gained hastily at the beginning will not be blessed at the end." I believe it would be safe to say the prodigal son had no value nor respect for his inheritance. The fact that he initiated the acquisition of his father's estate represents arrogance and contempt. Please note that as soon as he realizes he had spent all, "he went and joined himself to a citizen of that country, and he sent him into his fields to feed swine" (see Luke 15:15).

When an individual has fallen from grace (a backslidden condition) or one who has not accepted Jesus as Savior, the end result will invariably be similar to a pigpen situation. To better understand the prodigal son circumstance (pigpen), we need to get an understanding of a pig or swine's environment. There's nothing beautiful or pleasant about being in the company of swine. For starters, there's plenty of mud and feces in which they roll around and cover themselves to keep cool.

It must have been difficult for the prodigal son to have fed them because swine are greedy and would have made it difficult for him to spread the food on the ground. What's more is that swine carry an extremely foul odor. The odor is the result of frequent bowel movements, so the ground where he was walking more than likely was covered with manure.

The prodigal son's condition declined even further. "And he would gladly have filled his stomach with the pods that the swine ate, and no one gave him anything" (see Luke 15:16). At this point, he sees himself not as his earthy father or heavenly Father sees him but as an animal desiring the same food as the swine ate. What got him to this point? In my understanding, rebellion and pride governed his behavior. There's never a time in which our heavenly Father won't provide for his children, unless we intentionally get outside His covering. David reminds us that he has never "seen the righteous forsaken, nor his descendants begging bread" (see Psalm 37:25).

Finally, the prodigal son comes to the end of himself and says, "I will arise and go to my father, and will say to him, father, I have sinned against heaven and before you" (see Luke 15:18). He realizes that everything he experienced was brought on by his own pride and rebellion. He had what we call a defining moment or a moment of truth. Thank God he came to the end of himself and allowed grace to step in and rescue him in his condition.

Unfortunately, there are people who go through things that are brought on by their own rebellious behavior. The outworking of their transgression produces self-inflicted wounds. We must never confuse the chastisement of God, the penalty brought on by sin or rebellion, with normal trials we face in everyday life. For Jesus warn us that "in the world you will have tribulation" (see John 16:33). And we're also told that "through many tribulations we must enter the kingdom of God" (see Acts 14:22). Trials and persecutions are normal as a result for living for Christ.

However, none of the above applies to the prodigal son or anyone who rebels against God. The good news is we serve a God who is full of compassion and forgives those who repent and confess. First John 1:9 (KJV) says, "If we confess our sins, he is faithful and just to forgive us our sins and to cleanse us from all unrighteousness." We read also Hebrews 8:12 (KJV) says, "For I will be merciful to their unrighteousness, and their sins and their iniquities will I remember no more."

This story ends with a loving father forgiving, embracing, and restoring his lost son. Perhaps you're reading this book and find yourself in a similar situation. I have good news for you. God is not a respecter of persons, and He'll do the same for those who come to the end of themselves.

> And he arose, and came to his father. But when he was yet a great way off, his father saw him, and had compassion, and ran, and fell on his neck, and kissed him. And the son said unto him, father, I have sinned against heaven, and in thy sight, and am no more worthy to be called thy son. But the father said to his servants, bring out the best robe and put it on him, and put a ring on his hand and sandals on his feet. And bring the fatted calf here and kill it, and let us eat and be merry. For this my son was dead and is alive again; he was lost and is found, and they began to be merry. (Luke 15:20–24 KJV)

Maybe you're saying something to the effect like, "The sins I've committed are just too great and there is no forgiveness for me at this point." Let me encourage you by saying it makes no difference as to the amount of sin(s) you've committed. Jesus assures us that "every sin and blasphemy will be forgiven men." The only sin He said that will not be forgiven is "blasphemy against the Spirit" (see Matthew 12:31). We also read in 1 John 1:9, it says, "If we confess our sins, He [God] is faithful and just to forgive us our sins and to cleanse us from all unrighteousness."

Perchance you have been out of fellowship with the Lord or you have tried to hide from His presence. If you could ask David the implications of this state, he would tell you, "Where can I go from your spirit? Or where can I flee from your presence? If I ascend into heaven, you are there: If I make my bed in hell, behold, you are there" (Psalm 139:7–8). The Bible shows us many instances of God restoring even the worst of those who have rebelled and disobeyed His Word, but grace always seems to show up at their door.

Restoration of King David

If there was ever a king who experienced the grace and mercy of God, that man was David. His difficult valley experiences would cause many to stumble, yet he kept his eyes on the Lord who was able to deliver him. At a low point in his life, he poured his heart out before God. Psalm 51:1–3 says:

> Have mercy upon me, O God, according to your loving-kindness; according to the multitude of your tender mercies, blot out my transgressions. Wash me thoroughly from my iniquity, and cleanse me from my sin, for I acknowledge my transgressions, and my sin is always before me.

Prior to David's confession of repentance, God sent the Prophet Nathan to convince him of his sin by sharing a story. Observe the magnificent wisdom of God at work, which gives us a blueprint of how to confront those who have fallen from grace. When met with this type of situation, the Bible gives us clear instructions. They must be approached and dealt with a spirit of gentleness. Galatians 6:1 says, "Brethren, if a man is overtaken in any trespass, you who are spiritual restore such a one in spirit of gentleness, considering yourself lest you also be tempted."

The means by which Prophet Nathan approached David and rebuked him was very strategic one. For one, David was a king, and to approach someone of such great authority, you had to be very careful. Fortunately, he was David's friend and one of his close counselors. Perhaps if the Lord had sent someone else, it might not have been received as well. If someone should fall from grace (a friend, close companion, or a brother or sister in Christ), reproof would be received quicker from a fellow believer than someone who is not saved. Psalm 141:5 says, "Let the righteous strike me; It shall be kindness, and let him rebuke me; It shall be as an excellent oil; let my head not refuse it, for still my prayer is against the deeds of the wicked."

David had committed some horrific transgressions. In short, he had committed adultery with Bathsheba, his neighbor's wife. And to make matters worse, in an attempt to cover his sin, he procured the death of her husband, Uriah. With this, he's not only guilty of adultery but also murder as well. The sins in which David committed are not to be taken lightly nor thought of without detestation. When he opened a door to commit adultery with Bathsheba, it was an entrance into which all other sins followed thereafter. In short, it was a canal that opened which allowed the water to gush out.

David's sins serve as a warning and stern rebuke to all believers "that he who thinks he stands take heed lest he fall" (see 1 Corinthians 10:12). The folly of those who sin is once they commit it, they feel they're invincible and continue on as if nothing ever happened. Ecclesiastes 8:11 says, "Because the sentence against an evil work is not executed speedily, therefore the heart of the sons of men is fully set in them to do evil." David fell into this category. He was carrying out his daily business as if nothing had happened, but when Prophet

Nathan showed up, his life was altered. Perhaps it never occurred to him that "his sin would find him out" (see Numbers 32:23).

After this time of reproof, David came to realize that God was merciful, so in response, he told the Lord "to have mercy on him according to thy loving-kindness, according unto the multitude of thy tender mercies" (Psalm 51:1). David neither pleads innocence nor shifts the blame to someone else. He knew he did not deserve forgiveness, but he pleaded for mercy based on God's loving-kindness. God's grace opened the door for him to be released from his burden of sin. It was, in fact, a burden because he admits it was so: "For I acknowledge my transgressions; and my sin is ever before me" (see Psalm 51:3).

David was reminded continuously of his transgression because it brought further abasement. Perhaps from that point on, he never walked on his roof without a bad memory of the time he saw Bathsheba and the spirit of lust overtook him. More than likely, he never went to sleep at night without the thought of uncleanness. What's more, every time he took a pen to write, he must have remembered how he deceitfully tried to make Uriah intoxicated by tricking him into thinking he was the father of the baby in Bathsheba's womb. The letter he wrote and placing it in his servant's hand to procure the death of Uriah must have brought back negative memories as well. With strong conviction of his conscience, it caused David to say that his "sin is ever before him" (v. 3).

When our past mistakes are brought to remembrance, it should bring about humility. It may also help us to be on guard against present temptations which may come our way. The good news is only a gracious God can remember no more the guilt of sin and the stain of sin when we repent of it. Psalm 103:11–12 says, "For as the heavens are high above the earth, so great is His mercy toward those who fear Him. As far the east is from the west, so far hath He removed our transgressions from us." We read also in Hebrews 8:12, it says, "For I will be merciful to their unrighteousness, and their sins and their iniquities will I remember no more."

It it's important to see that David was constantly aware of his sin because he had acknowledged that his sin was more than sin against man, for he had sinned in the sight of God. Not only did he commit a transgression against Uriah and Bathsheba, he had sinned against his own body and his family; but most importantly, he had disappointed God.

Proverbs 14:34 (NIV) says, "Righteousness exalts a nation, but sin is a disgrace to any people." David's confession is apparent in his desire to open up the inward and hidden parts of his being, for he asked God to, "Purge me with hyssop, and I shall be clean; wash me, and I shall be whiter than snow...create in me a clean heart, O God; and renew a right spirit within me" (see Psalm 51:7–10).

Observe how David begins by asking for external cleansing. That is what's meant by purging with hyssop. It is a ritual act of cleansing. In the natural, hyssop branches were used by the Israelites in Egypt to place the blood of a lamb on the door frames of their homes. This would keep them safe from death (see Exodus 12). It also speaks of a plea for a newly created heart and renewed right spirit. David's emphasis now shifts from the outward to inward cleansing. The expression here is a distinction that of cleansing the leper or those that were unclean by the touch of a body by sprinkling water or blood or both upon, which is applied by a bunch of hyssop.

When we need cleansing from sin, we are purged with spiritual hyssop, which is the blood of Christ that purges the conscience from dead works. It releases us from the guilt of sin and the dread of God, which shut us out of communion with him as that of a touch of a dead body, under the law which shut a man out from the courts of God's house.

The successive stages of God cleansing us from sin are a process in which external awareness happens. First we are brought to the light of our transgression, and then God is able to purge us. Secondly, we are convicted within; our conscience is alerted, which produces godly sorrow. Second Corinthians 7:10 says, "For godly sorrow produces repentance." At this point, God can cleanse us from an evil heart and renew a right spirit within us. David knew that had he not owned up to his transgressions, he would have deceived himself and forfeited the forgiveness and pardon of sin.

How many times have people sinned against God only to cover up their sin and deceive themselves? When we own up to our sins, God is ready to forgive us. First John 1:8–10 says, "If we say that we have no sin, we deceive ourselves and the truth is not in us, if we confess our sins, He is faithful and just to forgive us our sins, and cleanse us from all unrighteousness. If we say that we have not sinned, we make Him a liar, and His word is not in us."

Allow me to inject this here. There are two things that act on each other—the man who realizes he's forgiven, therefore repents, and the man who repents and is forgiven. The Holy Spirit has come with the purpose that He may overshadow men and women spirits and breathe repentance within them. There's no need for us to struggle alone if we're filled with God's precious Spirit. Through the Spirit, we have the power within to overcome every obstacle and temptation that comes our way.

David could have pushed the envelope, saying because he was a king, he deserved preferential treatment and God's blessings. However, he chose not to. Instead, he owned up to what he had done. He did not have an entitlement mentality. By owning up and confessing his sins, he positioned himself to receive God's mercy and grace. Remember, God's grace is available to us, not because of who we are but because of who He is. For it was Peter who said, "In truth I perceive that God shows no partiality" (see Acts 10:34).

The Restoration of Peter

In kingdom service, Peter was powerfully used of the Holy Spirit; however, at times, he made a few monumental mistakes that disappointed the Lord. In spite of his temporary setbacks, God's grace was present to restore him. God gave him the grace to get back up again, for Proverbs 24:16 says, "For a righteous man may fall seven times and rise again." The Bible records several instances in which Peter failed leading up to his ultimate failure in denying the Lord Jesus. Let's look at these for a moment.

Peter's first failure is trying to walk on water as Jesus bids him to come to Him. Matthew 14:29–30 says, "So He [Jesus] said come and when Peter had come down out of the boat, he walked on the water to go to Jesus. But when he [Peter] saw that the wind was boisterous, he was afraid and beginning to sink he cried out saying, 'Lord save me.'" What we learn from Peter's first failure is to never take our eyes off Jesus and entertain the problem around us. This is precisely what got Peter in trouble.

Peter's second failure is he could not discern the prophetic word concerning the Lord Jesus. Matthew 16:21 says, "From that time Jesus began to show to his disciples, that He must go to Jerusalem, and suffer many things from the elders and chief priests and scribes, and be killed, and be raised again the third day." By trying to convince Jesus of canceling His divine purpose and plan, it exposed the fact that he had a preconceived notion about what Jesus was sent on earth to do.

In comparison, we at times place the Lord's dealings on a human plane of reasoning instead of spirit discernment. We must keep in mind that God doesn't want us to be failures nor does He delight in failing us. But when we fail, and it happens to the best of us, He's right there to restore us back. First John 1:9 says, "If we confess our sins, he is faithful and just to forgive us our sins and cleanse us from all unrighteousness."

Peter's third failure transpired when Jesus was praying in the garden and approached by a band of men with weapons and torches. Peter attempted to rescue Jesus. This time it got physical instead of verbal. John 18:10–11 says, "Then Simon Peter having a sword drew it and struck the high priest's servant, and cut off his right ear. The servant's name was Malchus. So Jesus said to Peter, put your sword into the sheath. Shall I not drink the cup which My Father has given Me?"

Peter didn't realize Jesus's arrest in the garden was designed to put in motion the prophetic words of Isaiah the prophet. He moved quickly and took matters into his own hands. He committed the sin of presumption, and many believers in Christ commit this sin as well. For David dealt with this himself, for he said, "Keep back Your servant also from presumptuous sin; let them not have dominion over me. Then I shall be blameless, and I shall be innocent of great transgression" (see Psalm 19:13). We can learn a lot from the failures of Peter on how to trust God to work out His plans.

Finally, Peter's fourth failure happened during the Passover also known as the feast of the unleavened bread. It was here that Jesus gave some prophetic counsel to His disciples. It was also during this gathering that Peter got a warning and insight about what was to take place in his personal life and in the days ahead. Jesus told him that "Satan hath desired to have him, that he may sift him as wheat" and that "his faith would not fail" (see Luke 22:31–32).

What a blessing to know that Jesus still intercedes on the behalf of His children to the Father. First Timothy 2:5 (KJV) says, "For there is one God and one mediator between God and men, the man Christ Jesus." Like so many today, Peter's fear of man dictated his actions. Shortly afterward, he denied the Lord three consecutive times, and thus the prophetic word was set in motion.

> Now when they had kindled a fire in the midst of the courtyard and sat down together, Peter sat among them. And a certain servant girl, seeing him as he [Peter]sat by the fire, looked intently at him and said, "This man was also with him" but he denied him, saying woman, I do not say woman, I do not know him. And after a little while another saw him and said, "You also are of them" but Peter said, "Man, I am not." Then after about an hour had passed, another confidently affirmed, saying, "Surely this fellow also was with him, for he is a Galilean. Then after about an hour had passed, another confidently affirmed, saying "Surely this fellow also was with him, for he is a Galilean. But Peter said, "Man, I do not know what you are saying" immediately, while he was still speaking, the rooster crowed. And the Lord turned and looked at Peter, then

> Peter remembered the word of the Lord, how he
> had said to him, "before the rooster crows, you
> will deny me three times" So Peter went out and
> wept bitterly. (Luke 22:52–62)

This was an extremely low point in Peter's life. He had just denied his master, the One he walked close with and taught him many things concerning the kingdom of God. I can just hear Peter saying, "I should have been there for Him" or" How can I have been so foolish?" This was very hard for him seeing Jesus falsely accused and just about to be sentenced to death. Instead of standing up for the Master, he was given over to fear of man and fear for his own life. There are times in the life of the believer when we don't deny the Lord with our mouths; but in our rebellious actions, He is denied.

The good news is the Lord is full of grace and mercy. Psalm 103:3–4 says, "Who forgives all your iniquities, who heal all your diseases. Who redeems your life from destruction, who crowns you with loving-kindness and tender mercies?" Jesus didn't leave Peter hanging in the balance. He prayed that his [Peter's] faith would not fail. Although Peter had failed miserably with any denial of his relationship with the Lord Jesus, God was ready to restore him. He is in the business of restoring people who have fallen from grace, and we're no exception.

During the post-resurrection appearance of Jesus (his third time in which He showed Himself to His disciples), it was at the seashore, eating breakfast, that Peter is graciously restored (see John 21:15–18). We see Jesus doing something familiar that brought back Peter's memory of denial because "as soon as they were come to land, they saw a fire of coals there, and fish laid thereon, and bread" (see John 21:9). This scene was similar to when Peter had denied the Lord Jesus. He refused to acknowledge he knew Jesus around a fire of coals. Perhaps these series of events were Jesus's way of getting Peter's attention. Peter didn't have to go looking for Jesus. He came looking for him.

This is grace and mercy restoring people at its best. Peter did not deserve restoration, but because of God's mercy, grace appeared.

This is a fact that you and I cannot negate. Jesus still leaves the ninety-nine and goes after the one who has fallen from grace. He searches diligently for those who have wandered far from the fold. This was an unusual restoration, seeing Peter was asked the same question three times, "Peter do you love me?" (John 21:15–17). Peter answered yes three times, signifying that his denial of Jesus was reversed, also confirming he was restored back in fellowship and relationship with the Lord.

Grace Cannot Be Measured

In the Gospel of Matthew, Peter asks Jesus a question about forgiveness: "Lord how often shall my brother sin against me, and I forgive him, up to seven times (see Matthew 18:21)?"

Jesus's response is, "I do not say to you, up to seven times, but up to seventy times seven" (v. 22). In other words, never keep a record or count of the injustices done to you. That is God's job, not ours (see Deuteronomy 32:34). God is the Supreme Judge of the universe, and vengeance is reserved for Him only. God forgives us multiple times, and so should we to those who trespass against us (see Psalm 78:38).

So that Peter would gain more understanding on the subject of forgiveness, Jesus shares a parable about a certain king who had taken an account of his servants. After the account of his servants was settled, it was found out that one owed him ten thousand talents (vv. 23–35). The talent was the largest of the silver coins during that time. By Jesus mentioning that it was a volume of ten thousand shows the enormity of the servant's debt and the impossibility of him being able to clear himself.

In comparison, we too had an enormous debt and were unable to clear ourselves of guilt, shame, and sin. The atonement of Jesus cancelled our debts at the cross. Notice the servant carrying out his daily routine, being fully aware of his debt to the king, but was unconcerned until he was confronted. Likewise, sinners are careless about the way they live and the magnitude of their sins until they hear a message that brings them under conviction. Or perhaps a life-threatening illness or when death approaches, they confess, "Wherewith shall I come before the Lord, and bow myself before the high God (see Micah 6:6)?

As it were, the servant was unable to settle his accounts, so the king ordered him, his wife, and children to be sold for payment. In response, he fell down and began to worship the king, asking him to be patient with him, saying he would come up with the payment (see Matthew 18:25). Likewise, sinners feel they can make restitution for the wrong committed without repenting or convinced of their sins but only tears. However, this is not humility nor true repentance. Second Corinthians 7:10 (KJV) says, "For godly sorrow worketh repentance to salvation not to be repented of; but the sorrow of the world worketh death."

Prior to salvation, we came to realize we were unable to pay our sin debts, for they were too great. There was no amount of silver and gold to alleviate our transgressions. The wages of sin were hanging over our heads. Nothing was able to stay the judgment, except the blood of Jesus and the grace of God. When we fall from grace, sacrifices and offerings will not remedy the problem, only a repentant heart. Psalm 51:16–17 (KJV) says, "For thou desirest not sacrifice; else would I give it; thou delightest not in burnt offering, the sacrifices of God are a broken spirit; a broken and contrite heart, O God thou wilt not despise."

According to verse 27, it says, "The Lord of that servant was moved with compassion, and loosed him, and forgave him the debt." Every sin debt we incur against the Lord calls for His mercy.

John 1:9 says, "If we confess our sins, He is faithful and just to forgive us our sins, and to cleanse us from all unrighteousness." That is truly what is meant by receiving God's grace. Romans 5:20 (KJV) says, "But where sin abounded, grace did much more abound."

> But that servant went out and found one
> of his fellow servants who owed him a hundred
> denari and he laid hands on him and took him
> by the throat, saying, pay me what you owe. So
> his fellow servant fell down at his feet and begged

> him saying have patience with me and I will pay
> you all. And he would not but went and threw
> him unto prison till he should pay the debt.
> (Matthew 18:28–30)

When God forgives us of our trespasses, we should have compassion and forgive those who have wronged us. We should not seek to harm or get revenge. The model prayer Jesus taught His disciples included the phrase "And forgive us our debts as we forgive our debtors" (see Matthew 6:12). God honors our prayers when we ask for forgiveness, but he wants us to forgive men their trespasses as well. Matthew 6:14–15 (KJV) says, "For if ye forgive men their trespasses, your heavenly Father will also forgive you, but if ye forgive not men their trespasses, neither will your heavenly father forgive your trespasses."

> So when his fellow servants saw what had
> been done, they were grieved, and came and told
> their master all that had been done. Then his
> master after he had called him, said to him, you
> wicked servant I forgive you all that debt because
> you begged me. Should you not also have had
> compassion on your fellow servant, just as I had
> pity on you. And his master was angry, and deliv-
> ered him to the torturers until he should pay all
> that was due to him. So My Heavenly Father also
> will do to you if each of you, from his heart does
> not forgive his brother his trespasses. (Matthew
> 18:31–35)

It goes without saying that those around us (neighbors, coworkers, etc.) watch how we treat others. We're admonished to "walk in wisdom toward those who are on the outside" (see Colossians 4:5). Considering everything God has done for us, it should provoke us to extend compassion toward others.

The master was very angry at the servant and rightfully so. There are a few things to take into account here. First, we must constantly remind ourselves of the goodness God has bestowed on our lives. Secondly, as a result of being thankful, it should release compassion and love to others. Luke 7:47 says, "Her sins which are many, are forgiven, for she loved much."

There are many people who have fallen from grace and are unwilling to admit their need for forgiveness and restoration. As you have read earlier in this chapter, David knew he needed God to restore him. He made a great appeal to God for restoration. This is what he said again: "Restore unto me the joy of thy salvation" (see Psalm 51:12). God wants us to enjoy once again complete fellowship with him. He wants us to experience a close relationship with his Son Jesus and to feel the abiding presence of His Spirit. If there's unconfessed sin in our lives, we will never enjoy the joy of salvation.

Unlike David who confessed his sin and need for forgiveness, unconfessed sin will drive a wedge between the one who's guilty and God. But thanks to Jesus, we're not left without a remedy. First John 1:8–9 (NIV) says, "If we claim to be without sin, we deceive ourselves and the truth is not in us, if we confess our sins, He is faithful to forgive us our sins and purify us from all unrighteousness." Once forgiven and restored back again, it's natural for an individual to reach out to others with love and compassion.

This is brought home to us concerning a woman whom Jesus had forgiven. In Luke 7:47, Jesus says this about her, "Therefore I say to you, her sins which are many are forgiven, for she loved much, but the same to whom little is forgiven the same loves little." This woman was forgiven of so much it caused her to show compassion and love to others. In this account, Jesus was the target of her love. Only those who comprehend the depth of their sinful life or backslidden condition can recognize the value of God's grace, forgiveness, and restoration as this woman did.

Let's revisit again what David said to God in his earnest request for restoration. Psalm 51:17 says, "The sacrifices of God are a broken spirit; a broken and contrite heart, O God thou will not despise." People who have been restored understand their need for a broken and contrite heart. A broken spirit and contrite heart speak of an inward heart that has been changed. If you have fallen from grace, you can get back up again. God's grace is ready to receive you back when you acknowledge your sins and asked for His forgiveness.

Short Review of Grace that Restores

- It has always been God's objective to restore people back to their rightful place in Him. With the fall of Adam and Eve in the garden, God had a plan of redemption in the person of Christ Jesus.

- Unfortunately, some individuals rather grab instead of receive what the Father has for them. God knows when He's ready to release what He has for us, for He "will not with hold any good thing from them that walk upright" (see Psalm 84:11). He never releases something to us out of His timing or something that would harm us.

- When an individual has fallen from grace (a backslidden condition) or one who has not accepted Jesus as Savior, the end result will invariably be similar to a pigpen situation. In this life, there are people who go through things that are brought on by their own rebellious behavior. The outworking of their transgression produces self-inflicted wounds. We must never confuse the chastisement of God, the penalty brought on by rebellion, with normal trials we face in this life. For Jesus warn us that "in the world, you will have tribulation" (see John 16:33).

- Peter could not discern the prophetic word concerning the Lord Jesus. Matthew 16:21 says, "From that time Jesus began to show to his disciples, that He must go to Jerusalem, and suffer many things from the elders and chief priests and scribes, and be killed, and be raised again the third day." By trying to convince Jesus of canceling His divine purpose and plan, it exposes the fact that he had a preconceived notion about what Jesus was sent on earth to do.

- We see Jesus doing something familiar that brought back Peter's memory of denial because, "as soon as they were come to land, they saw a fire of coals there, and fish laid thereon, and bread" (see John 21:9). This scenario was similar to when Peter had denied the Lord Jesus. He refused to acknowledge he knew Jesus around a fire of coals. Perhaps these series of events were Jesus getting Peter's attention. Peter didn't have to go looking for Jesus; He came looking for him. This is grace and mercy restoring people at its best. Peter did not deserve restoration, but because of God's mercy, grace appeared.

Life's Application

If we fall from grace, we must return to the Lord. It's extremely important to know that God is waiting with loving arms, He's married to the backslider(see Jeremiah 3:14). What's more, He said He would heal our backslidings(see Jeremiah 3:22). Another important thing we must keep in mind is that God will never release something to us out of His timing or something that would harm us, for He "will not with hold any good thing from them that walk upright" (see Psalm 84:11). God's mercy and grace (undeserved favor) are abundant toward all.

Key Scriptures

If we say that we have no sin, we deceive ourselves, and the truth is not in us, if we confess our sins, He is faithful and just to forgive us our sins and to cleanse us from all unrighteousness. (1 John 1:8–9 KJV)

Have mercy upon me, O God, according to your loving-kindness; according to the multitude of your tender mercies, blot out my transgressions. Wash me thoroughly from my iniquity, and cleanse me from my sin, for I acknowledge my transgressions, and my sin is always before me. (Psalm 51:1–3 KJV)

6

AMAZING GRACE

> Amazing Grace! How sweet the sound, that saved a wretch like me! I once was lost, but now am found was blind but now I see. T'was, Grace that taught my heart to fear, and grace my fear relieved; how precious did that grace appear; the hour I first believed![4]

It was John Newton who wrote this famous and beloved hymn, a song that has touched many lives, both Christians and non-Christians alike. This hymn speaks volumes of truth to a reality that happened thousands of years ago and still happens today. That God demonstrated His love toward us in that while we were still sinners, Christ died for us. When you look closely at the lyrics, you see that brother Newton had an encounter with Jesus who was full of grace and truth.

Only the grace and power of God can cause spiritually blind men to see and those who are lost to be found. Jesus sacrificed His life for friends and even those who hated Him. Romans 5:7–8 says, "For scarcely for a righteous man will one die, yet perhaps for good

---

[4] Partial lyrics taken from John Newton "Amazing Grace," Sing His Praise GPH Music, Gospel Publishing House, Springfield, Missouri, 65802–1894, copyright ©1991, p.306.

man someone would even dare to die. But God demonstrates His own love toward us, in that while we were still sinners, Christ died for us."

It is absolutely miraculous how God would make those just who are unjust and forgive those who deserve no favor. That is amazing grace. Can I ask you an important question? Is salvation for the pure and holy who are free from sin? The answer is found by looking at your own life and the lives of your loved ones prior to salvation. It is God who justifies the ungodly and saves the wicked.

> Now to him who does not work but believes on Him who justifies the ungodly, his faith is accounted for righteousness, just as David also describes the blessedness of the man to whom God imputes righteousness apart from works. Blessed are those whose lawless deeds are forgiven, and whose sins are covered, blessed is the man to whom the Lord shall not impute sin. (Romans 4:6–8)

Paul had all the reasons for being thankful for God's grace on his life. First Timothy 1:12–14 says:

> And I thank Christ Jesus our Lord who has enabled me because He counted me faithful, putting me into the ministry. Although I was formerly a blasphemer, a persecutor and an insolent man; but I obtained mercy because I did it ignorantly in unbelief. And the grace of our Lord was exceedingly abundant, with faith and love which are in Christ Jesus.

It looked as if he had experienced more of God's mercy and grace than any New Testament writer. But notice I said "looked as if" because the grace of God has appeared to all men(see Titus 2:11).

Many of us after reading Paul's personal assessment can truly identify with him. It's important to see that even though he acted out of ignorance and rebelled in unbelief, it did not nullify the grace of God upon his life. That's the central point of grace: unearned and unmerited favor. If you're going through a season of hopelessness and despair and feel you deserve nothing but condemnation and judgment, consider the life and conversion of Paul.

There's no limit to God's love for us. From the start, it was His love for us and not our love for Him. First John 4:10 (KJV) says, "In this is love, not that we loved God, but that He loved us, and sent His son to be the propitiation for our sins."

In Pauls' letter to the believers at Ephesus, he explained how God's grace is the source of our salvation. Ephesians 2:8 says, "For by grace are ye saved through faith."

Notice he never said faith was the source or we're saved on the account of our faith. Faith is the channel through which salvation flow and grace is the fountain or stream that flows through that channel.

To put it another way, faith is the aqueduct along which the flood of mercy flows down to refresh our thirsty souls. The aqueduct was a water system in Rome that carried water into the city. It was important that it stayed intact in order to carry the constant flow of water. In comparison, our faith must be true and sound that it may become a solid channel of mercy to our souls. We must bear in mind that faith is only the channel or aqueduct and not the fountainhead. The salvation of the Lord can come to us, even though our faith is that of a mustard seed because the power lies in the grace of God and not in our faith.

Below is a chronological successive list of Paul's rebellion. Perhaps this will give us more insight as to why he was such a strong advocate of grace.

- In the book of Acts, immediately we find Paul (surnamed Saul) consenting to the death of Stephen, a devout man full of faith, power, and the Holy Spirit (see Acts 6:5–8, 8:1).

- Adding to Paul's rebellious résumé prior to conversion the Bible goes on to record that he made havoc of the church, entering every house and dragging off men and women, committing them to prison (see Acts 8:3).
- Paul wasn't finish yet. According to Acts 9:1, he continued breathing out threats and murder against the disciples of the Lord, asking letters from the high priest in order to bring the saints bound to Jerusalem.

By now it's clear what Paul meant when he called himself an insolent man who obtained mercy because of unbelief. As we look further at his life and those who have similarities, we understand that God does not give us what we deserve. He gives us what we don't deserve. What about you, my friend? Do you feel your past failure disqualifies you for God's grace? The answer to that is a resounding no. The Word of God lets us know how important grace is to us.

> But the free gift is not like the offence, for if by the one man's offence many died, much more the grace of God and the gift by the grace of the one man, Jesus Christ, abounded to many, and the gift is not like that which came through the one who sinned. For the judgment which came from one offense resulted in condemnation, but the free gift which came from many offenses resulted in justification, for if by the one man's offense death reigned through the one, much more those who receive abundance of grace and of the gift of righteousness will reign in life through the One, Jesus Christ. (Romans 5:15–17)

I cannot stress enough how we cannot earn God's unmerited favor. Unfortunately, many people believe there's something in them that warrants the approval of God. Romans 3:10 says, "As it is written, there is none righteous no, not one. There is none who understands; there is none who seeks after God. They have all turned aside;

they have they have together become unprofitable; there is none who does good, no, not one." I will now relate a story I read one day showing how God's grace (unmerited favor) cannot be earned. Here's a story according to the *Chicago Tribune* that will shed light on the topic:

> In the summer of 1994, Marcio da Silva, a love-struck Brazilian artist, was distraught over the breakup of a four-year relationship with his girlfriend, Katia de Nascimento. He tried to win back her love by a gesture of great devotion. He walked on his knees for nine miles. With pieces of car tires tied to his kneecaps, the twenty-one-year old man shuffled along for fourteen hours before he reached her home in Santos, Brazil. He was cheered on by motorists and passersby, but when he reached the end of his marathon of love thoroughly exhausted, the nineteen-year-old woman of his dreams was not impressed. She had intentionally left her home to avoid seeing him.[5]

This story is a reminder that every one of us and especially those who are determined to impress God and earn salvation through works is futile. In comparison to the story of the Brazilian artist, God is not impressed when we try to earn salvation. The only thing that brings salvation is God's grace and faith in Jesus Christ, not sacrificial deeds.

Sufficient Grace

And He said unto me, my grace is sufficient
for thee; for my strength is made perfect in weak-

---

[5] Quotation taken from *750 Engaging Illustrations for Preachers, Teachers & Writers*, Craig Brian Larson, "14 Hours and 9 Miles Later, Answer Is Still No" *Chicago Tribune Online*, 28 July 1994.

ness. Most gladly therefore will I rather glory in
my infirmities, that the power of Christ may rest
upon me. Therefore, I take pleasure infirmities,
in reproaches, in necessities, in persecutions, in
distresses for Christ's sake; for when I am weak,
then am I strong. (2 Corinthians 12:9–10 KJV)

No one would contest the fact that Paul was used powerfully in
the work of God. Through the power of Spirit, the sick were healed,
the dead were raised, demons were cast out, and many souls were led
to Christ. Through the power of the Spirit, this was all accomplished
in a short span of time. To add to his spiritual résumé, the Bible says
he was "caught up into paradise and heard unspeakable words, which
it is not lawful for a man to utter" (see 2 Corinthians 12:2).

In God's permissive will, Paul received incredible revelations
that opened the door for him to be attacked by a messenger of Satan.
Verse 7 says, "And lest I should be exalted above measure through the
abundance of the revelations, there was given to me a thorn in the
flesh, the messenger of Satan to buffet me, lest I should be exalted
above measure."

Consequently, this attack on Paul served its purpose because it
produced humility in him. Many people debate as to what kind of
infirmity it was, but nonetheless, Paul wanted this thing removed,
"For this thing I be-sought the Lord thrice that it might depart from
me" (v. 8).

As a result of receiving many revelations, Paul was in danger
of being lifted up with pride. God loves us so much that in His permissive will, He will allow certain things in our lives to keep us from
being exalted above measure. The end purpose in which spiritual tests
are working is to cure the temptation of spiritual pride. The messenger of Satan issued a thorn in Paul's flesh. This must have been a very
painful experience, one that would have frustrated and hindered the
work of the Lord. Nonetheless, God's grace was sufficient.

Romans 8:28 (KJV) says, "And we know that all things to work
together for good to them that love God, to them who are the called
according to His purpose."

Instead of the infirmity becoming a hindrance to him, it actually served as a blessing. Grace played an important role in this trying time as Paul prayed earnestly to God for removal of this irritating and sore grievance. God gives him his answer after three requests to remove the thorn. He tells him, "My grace is sufficient for thee" (v. 9). Even though God accepts our prayer of faith, He doesn't always answer the way we would want. The thing we must bear in mind is it will invariably "work for our good."

In the Garden of Gethsemane, Jesus prays his most important prayer while on earth. Matthew 26:39 says, "He [Christ] went a little farther and fell on His face, and prayed saying O My Father, if it is possible, let this cup pass from Me; nevertheless, not as I will, but as You will."

Jesus first asks "if it is possible," but notice He doesn't press the issue because He goes on to surrender to the will of God and His sufficient grace. Jesus is the blueprint on what it means to submit to the plan and purpose of God.

The Prophet Jeremiah said God has an expected end that will always be in our best interest. Jeremiah 29:11 (KJV) says, "For I know the thoughts that I think toward you, saith the Lord, thoughts of peace, and not of evil, to give you an expected end." When our circumstances are not quickly removed and temptations are present, God gives us a sufficient amount of grace to deal with it. First Corinthians 10:13 says, "No temptation has overtaken you except such as is common to man; but God is faithful, who will not allow you to be tempted beyond what you are able, but with the temptation will also make the way of escape, that you may be able to bear it."

Here's what God's grace will do for us in our hour of despair. First, it strengthens and comforts and gives us a right perspective of God's dealings. Secondly, it cheers up our spirits from all distresses. Finally, God's will is glorified in the time of our sufferings and trials. It's important to see that Paul praised God in the midst of his infirmities. This is very important because he knew the greater the magnitude of his afflictions, the more of God's grace manifested in his life. We know that everything happens to us is not always good, but God is able to turn every circumstance around for our good in the long run.

> And we know that all things work together for good to those who love God, to those who love God, to those who are the called according to His purpose. (Romans 8:28)

> (We are assured and know that [God being a partner in their labor] all things work together and are [fitting into plan] for good to and for those who love God and are called according to [His] design and purpose. (Romans 8:28 AMP)

This promise is not for everyone but is exclusively "for those who love God and are called according to His design and purpose." These individuals have the right perspective and see things from a different angle.

> To give you an illustration of how all things work together for good, let's look at how a cake comes to fruition. A variety of ingredients are placed in a cake batter: flour, baking powder, sugar, butter, oil, vanilla, extract, and salt. Depending on what kind of cake you're baking, you may need to add cinnamon, lemon, chocolate, strawberries, and so on. So as you can see, a cake has many ingredients, however, you cannot eat some of them by themselves—the taste would not be great. You have to mix all the ingredients in a bowl and bake them in the oven. Once the cake is completed in the oven, it is ready for you to taste or eat. All the ingredients worked together to bring a delicious desert. Similar to the illustration concerning the cake, the trials you and I face are not always welcome, but when

they have run their course, they yield within us a peaceable fruit.[6]

Consider Joseph. In the beginning, he was clueless about what was happening to him and that everything he encountered in Egypt was actually working for his good. First, he was hated severely by his own flesh and blood, particularly his brothers (see Genesis 37:4). What's more, they stripped him of the coat his father made for him with intentions of killing him until Reuben stepped in and spared his life (Genesis 37:21–22). Finally, having given up that idea, they decided to sell him to Potiphar, a Midianite, who might have been a slave trader from Egypt (see Genesis 37:27–28).

Straightway after arriving at Potiphar's house, he is placed in charge, but while carrying out his master's duties, he is seduced by his wife. He resists her efforts but still ends up in prison for the next fourteen years. Once again, because of sufficient grace, he's put in charge of the inmates in prison. Finally, he is brought up to interpret Pharaoh's dreams and promoted second in charge. God's grace (unearned, unmerited favor) was in his life in every way and with every circumstance. We must bear in mind it makes no difference what our circumstances are or where we end up at in the case of Joseph. God's grace (unmerited favor) is sufficient, and all things are working together for our good.

The Great Exchange
A Product of Divine Grace

I would like to briefly point out some exchanges that were made as a result of Jesus's sacrificial death. The atonement of Christ paved the way for all believers to enjoy the benefits of grace. Jesus suffered in our place all the dreadful consequences that were due us by justice. As a result, all of our needs are met solely because of and through

---

[6] Quotation taken from Derek Prince, *God's Remedy for Rejection*, copyright ©1993, Whitaker House, New Kensington, Pennsylvania, pp.27, 46.

Him. Philippians 4:19 says, "And my God shall supply all your need according to His riches in glory by Christ Jesus." That includes spiritual, physical, emotional, financial needs, and so on. The most important need God met in our lives is spiritual resurrection.

When Adam sinned, the whole human race spiritually died (see Romans 5:12). As a result of humanity's rebellion, Jesus became a sin offering. Isaiah 53:10 says, "Yet it pleased the Lord to bruise Him; He hath put Him to grief when thou made His soul an offering for sin." There are many exchanges as a result of Christ's obedience which we now have obtained. Let's examine in brief detail what they represent for us.

Jesus was punished that we might be forgiven. Isaiah 53:4 says, "Surely He hath borne our griefs, and carried our sorrows; yet we did esteem Him stricken, smitten of God, and afflicted."

Jesus received the punishment due to our transgressions and iniquities that we, in turn, might be forgiven and have peace with God. This exchange made provision for us to come out of alienation with God and how our relationship with the Father has been restored because of the atonement of Jesus. Romans 5:1–2 says, "Therefore being justified by faith, we have peace with God through our Lord Jesus Christ, by whom also we have access by faith into this grace wherein we stand, and rejoice in hope of the glory of God."

Jesus was wounded that we might be healed. Isaiah 53:5 says, "But He was wounded for our transgressions, He was bruised for our iniquities; the chastisement of our peace was upon Him; and with His stripes we are healed." On the spiritual plane, Jesus received the punishment due us for our transgressions and iniquities that we in turn might be forgiven and have peace with God. On the physical plane, Jesus bore sicknesses and pains that we, through His wounds, might be healed.

An illustration of this exchange is recorded in Matthew 8:16–17:

> When evening had come, they brought to Him many who were demon possessed and He cast out the spirits with a word, and He healed all who were sick, that it might be fulfilled which was

spoken by Isaiah the prophet, saying He Himself
took our infirmities and bore our sicknesses.

Man has a twofold nature. He is both material and a spiritual
being. Both of these natures were affected by the fall. As a result, his
body is exposed to disease and his soul is corrupted by sin. The good
news is the atonement of Christ made provision for both natures.

God is Jehovah-Rapha, which means "the Lord that healeth
thee." I would like to share with you an account of how God (Jehovah-
Rapha) healed me of cancer many years ago. I wrote this in another
book, *Christ Still Heals*, and I deem it's worth sharing again here.

If you had or presently have cancer of any
kind, then you know the physically and mentally
draining effect it can have on your body as well
as your mind. I've experienced it and know the
physical and mental toll it can have on a person.
It is literally a live agent sent from the enemy to
destroy your body (see John 10:10).

I was diagnosed with cancer in August of
1988. At that time, I was twenty-four years of age,
married, and serving in the armed forces. I was
having some problems with the right side of my
neck, so I decided to go to the doctor. Well, after
several visits, medication, and nothing changing,
he decided to do a fine needle aspiration on the
right side of my neck. In case you're unfamiliar
with a "fine needle aspiration," it's when they
take a blood specimen from your mass or tumor.

I can remember being overly anxious about
my situation. After a couple of days, the results
came in. My doctor, who was also in the military,
called me and told me the bad news. I can recall
him saying, "You need to come in as soon as possible. Bring some night clothes with you." After
the shock of the news was over, I gathered myself.

Something inside of me let me know Christ was going to heal me; I just knew it—praise God!

That time and experience was an unforgettable challenge in my life. I went through some intensive treatments. I lost my taste buds; I lost a whole lot of weight to the degree that I was wearing safety pins to hold up my clothes. I was always nauseated, tired, and had problems eating as a result of the loss of my taste buds. I lost half of my hair, and so on.

As time went on, and after many doctors' visits, I was subsequently told that I would have to take another test to see if the cancer was in remission. I will never forget waiting by the phone to hear the report, but once again I knew in my heart Christ had healed me in answer to prayer and what His Word declared. Well, later on the doctor did call, and he told me they could find nothing. I shouted, I cried, I spoke in a heavenly language, and I praised God all that day, and I could not wait to testify in church. When I testified in church, it seemed like the whole church went up in praise. I tell you, we serve an awesome God! Jesus was wounded that we might be healed![7]

It goes without saying that in light of God's divine grace, the great exchange has many benefits, and David reminds us of some of those benefits. Here's one in particular. Psalm 103:2–3 (KJV) says, "Bless the Lord, O my soul, and forget not all His benefits, who forgives all your iniquities, who heals all your diseases." The next time the enemy attacks you or someone you know with some form of illness or disease, be advised that you and your loved ones can claim the

---

[7] Testimony taken from Donald Spellman, *Christ Still Heals*, copyright ©2016, Creation House, a Charisma Media Company, Lake Mary, Florida. Pp. 31–32.

benefit of physical healing because of the great exchange and God's divine grace.

Jesus was made sin with our sinfulness that we might become righteous with His righteousness. Second Corinthians 5:21 (KJV) says, "For He [God] hath made Him [Jesus] to be sin for us, who knew no sin; that we might be made the righteousness of God in Him." The sacrifice Jesus offered was Himself on our behalf, a sin offering. First John 3:5 says, "And you know that He was manifested to take away our sins, and in Him there is no sin." Paul made a valid point to the believers at Corinth. He showed them that we are not credited for any righteousness we can achieve by our own efforts but only by God's own righteousness.

I have been sharing thus far with you that those who operate under religious tradition and legalism try to establish their own righteousness. Our reconciliation to God is only through Jesus Christ and on Him, therefore, we must rely. We must make mention of His righteousness and His only as the Prophet Isaiah bluntly states it, "all our righteous acts [righteousness] are like filthy rags" (see Isaiah 64:6).

Jesus became poor with our poverty that we might become rich with His riches. Second Corinthians 8:9 (KJV) says, "For ye know the grace of our Lord Jesus Christ, that though He was rich, yet for your sakes He became poor, that ye through His poverty might be rich." This Scripture poses an important question that some of us may also have: when did Jesus become poor? In order to answer that, we must first see how He lived on earth. One thing is for sure: unlike many believers today, He understood and embraced His sonship.

It seems as though Jesus had everything He needed at all times. He lived an abundant life, and everything was at His disposal. For example, when He needed money at one point to pay His taxes, He simply told Peter, "Go thou to the sea, and cast an hook, and take up the fish that first cometh up; and when thou hast opened his mouth, thou shalt find a piece of money; that take and give unto them for me and thee" (Matthew 17:24–27).

Another proof of His rich life was His unconventional, supernatural way of acquiring food to feed those who were hungry (see

Luke 9:14–17). Jesus always had an abundance to accomplish His Father's will. So the question remains, when did He become poor that we might become rich? The answer lies within the cross; it is the place in which Jesus endured poverty for our sakes.

- First, He was hungry and thirsty so that "the scripture might be fulfilled, saith I thirst" (see Matthew 19:28).
- Second, His poverty was also shown when He was naked without clothes. John 19:23 (KJV) says, "Then the soldiers, when they had crucified Jesus, took His garments and made four parts to every soldier a part and also His coat; now the coat was without seam, woven from the top throughout."
- Third, he was impoverished of justice, of receiving a fair trial, and a fair verdict.
- Fourth, he was impoverished of the presence of God and communion with God while on the cross.
- Fifth, after His death, He was buried in a borrowed robe and in a borrowed tomb. Luke 23:50–53 (KJV) says, "And behold, there was a man named Joseph, a counselor, and he was a good man, and a just, the same had not consented to the counsel and deed of them, he was of Arimathea, a city of the Jews; who also himself waited for the kingdom of God. This man went to Pilate, and begged for the body of Jesus. And he took it down, and wrapped it in linen, and laid it in a sepulcher that was hewn in stone, wherein never man before was laid."

So you see, while Jesus was living on the earth. He had abundance for every good work, but when He went to the cross, an exchange was made for us that we too might have abundance for every good work. Second Corinthians 9:8 (KJV) says, "And God is able to make all grace abound toward you; that ye always having all sufficiency in all things, may abound to every good work." Divine grace is at the very core of all the good things we receive at the hand of God.

Jesus bore our shame and endured our rejection that we might have acceptance as children of God. Isaiah 53:3 (KJV) says, "He was despised and rejected of men; a man of sorrows, and acquainted with grief; and we hid as it were our faces from him; He was despised, and we esteemed him not."

Shame can surface in people's lives in many ways. One of the ways is by tormenting a person with things that have happened early in childhood or in the past. For example, an individual might have been sexually abused, molested by an adult or family member, and the trauma of it has left them in shame. Another example would be when the devil brings up previous sins, which we have committed prior to salvation.

Only the cross can cure such accusations and guilt brought on by the enemy, whether it's sexual abuse or accusations of the past. Jesus Himself faced and defeated shame on our behalf at the cross. The effects of shame can be described as an acute embarrassment to a sense of unworthiness that cuts a person off from a meaningful fellowship with God or with man.

Consider what Jesus had to endure to set us free. Hebrews 12:2–3 (KJV) says:

> Looking unto Jesus the author and finisher of our faith; who for the joy that set before Him endured the cross, despising the shame, and sat down at the right hand of the throne of God, for consider Him that endured such contradiction of sinners against Himself, lest ye be weary and faint in your minds.

To hang on the cross was the most shameful and humiliating of all kinds of death. It was only reserved for the lowest class of criminals. The person was stripped of his clothes and was exposed naked to people who passed by. The people who looked on would jeer and mock the individuals who were hanging (see Matthew 27:39–42). Everyone can now be delivered and released from their shame because of what Jesus has done. In fact, Jesus put the devil to shame on the cross according to Colossians 2:15 where he made a "public spectacle" of the "powers and authorities."

Jesus endured our rejection that we might have acceptance as children of God. Isaiah 53:3 (KJV) says, "He was despised and rejected of men; a man of sorrows, and acquainted with grief; and we hid as it were our faces from him; He was despised, and we esteemed him not." Rejection usually stems from a range of relationship problems. If we look close enough, we will find there are many examples in our society.

For instance, consider a young person in school who's not accepted in a group or a husband or wife whose spouse has left them, or perhaps a child feeling unwanted by parents or a child whose parents have divorced or separated. This will invariably bring about the spirit of rejection. The late Derek Prince said that:

> Rejection can be a hidden, inner attitude that we carry around. The problem lies in the area of the spirit. Besides an inability to show love, there are other secondary results of rejection. I would say rejection produces three types of people: the person who gives in, the person who holds out, and the person who fights back.[8]

God has made provision for us through the sacrificial death of Christ on the cross. A divine exchange took place, and Jesus was rejected so we could be accepted. Matthew 27:46 (KJV) says, "And about the ninth hour Jesus cried with a loud voice saying, Eli, Eli, lama sabachthani? That is to say, my God, my God why hast thou forsaken me?" Please bear in mind that this was the ultimate rejection. Jesus had always experienced the Father's presence and love, and now having taken on the sins of the world, our sins had separated Him from His Father.

---

[8] Quotation taken from Derek Prince, *God's Remedy for Rejection*, copyright ©1993, Whitaker House, New Kensington, Pennsylvania, pp.27, 46

For the first time in history, Jesus called out to His Father and received no response. This was an extremely painful time in the life of the Savior. My friend, that's why He knows how you feel and what you are experiencing right now. Hebrews 4:15 says, "For we do not have a high priest who cannot sympathize with our weaknesses, but was in all points tempted as we are, yet without sin. Let us therefore come boldly to the throne of grace that we may obtain mercy and find grace to help in time of need."

The great exchange made provision for rejection to be replaced with acceptance from the Father. All we have to do is accept His Son Jesus. This will automatically invoke His grace to intervene.

> Blessed be the God and Father of our Lord Jesus Christ, who hath blessed us with all spiritual blessings in heavenly places in Christ, according as He hath adoption of children by Jesus Christ to Himself, according to the good pleasure of His will, to the praise of the glory of His grace, wherein He hath made us accepted in the beloved. In whom we have redemption through His blood, the forgiveness of sins, according to the riches of His grace. (Ephesians 1:3–7 KJV)

Jesus became a curse that we might be blessed. Galatians 3:13–14 (KJV) says, "Christ hath redeemed us from the curse of the law, being made a curse for us; for it is written, cursed is every one that hangeth on a tree; that the blessing of Abraham might receive the promise of the Spirit through faith."

The curse that came upon Jesus is defined as the curse of the law. It included every one of the curses listed in Deuteronomy 28. Every curse came upon Jesus in all its fullness, therefore allowing us to be recipients of a divine exchange. He took upon Himself the curse and the evil that included in order for us to receive the blessings.

There are many Christians who forfeit their blessings but are tolerating curses instead. Some who get wonderfully saved are under the impression that family or personal curses are automatically broken. One thing we must bear in mind is that just as we had to repent and receive Jesus for salvation, we must invoke and apply the promises of the Bible to break the curses.

For example, if you were ill at the time you got saved, repenting and receiving Jesus brought spiritual healing to your soul. But you had to apply and claim physical healing according to the Bible. The same holds true for someone who believes they have a curse over their family and/or personal life. They must claim and invoke the word for release and breaking of that particular curse. Galatians 3:13 (KJV) says, "Christ hath redeemed us from the curse of the law, being made a curse for us."

The late Derek Prince said that "a curse could be likened to a long, evil arm stretched out from the past. It rests upon you with dark, oppressive force that inhibits the full expression of your personality. You never feel completely free to be yourself. You sense that you have potential within you that is never fully developed. You always expect more of yourself than you are able to achieve."[9]

The main avenue for both blessings and curses is words—words which are spoken or written or spoken inwardly. The Bible has good news concerning this. God has made provision for us to be released from all curses in the person of Christ Jesus. He has made an exchange on our behalf for all the negative consequences of curses. Here's a prayer you can repeat if you're struggling with any of these negative influences over your life (shame, rejection, sickness, sin, poverty, and/or curses).

> Father God, I come to you on the basis of what Jesus did for me at the cross. Jesus, I believe that you're the Son of God. I believe you made a way for me to come back to the Father and that You died on the cross for my sins and rose again form the dead. Based on these facts and the

---

[9] Quotation taken from Derek Prince, Blessing Or Curse You Can Choose, copyright © 2007, Chosen Books a division of Baker Publishing Group, Grand Rapids, Michigan, p.19

exchange You did for me; I believe Satan's claims against me are cancelled. So, now, Lord Jesus, I submit myself to you.

I commit myself to serve and obey You, and with that commitment, I take my stand against every dark evil force that has in any way come into my life, whether it be through my own acts or acts of my family or of my ancestors or something larger than I am part of. Wherever there's any darkness in my life, any evil force, any witchcraft, I renounce shame, rejection, sickness, sin, poverty, and any curse over my life. And I refuse any longer to submit to them.

And in the almighty name of Jesus the Son of God, I take authority over these evil forces. I loose myself from them and all their powers. I drive them from me now in the name of Jesus and invite and invoke the Holy Spirit of God to move in and make my deliverance and liberation fully effective in Jesus's name, Amen!

Undergirding Grace

Every believer in Christ is commissioned to carry out an assigned task or purpose from God. In other words, when God saved us, we were called for a specific purpose and "created in Christ Jesus for good works, which God prepared beforehand that we should walk in them" (see Ephesians 2:10). We have been given everything we need that pertains to life and godliness to carry out this great work. Second Corinthians 9:8 (KJV) says, "And God is able to make all grace abound toward you; that ye always having all sufficiency in all things, may abound to every good work."

Because we are created to do good works, we must be totally dependent upon God's undergirding grace. Let me explain what I mean. The word *undergird* means to support or strengthen. First, everything we undertake for God, we need the guidance and direction of the Holy Spirit. Secondly, we need God to undergird (support, strengthen) us with His grace.

For example, let's say you've been employed with a particular business for many years. But one day, the Holy Spirit says you must resign and begin a full-time ministry. If you walk in disobedience, refusing to quit your job, undoubtedly, this will bring about negative consequences. First, you'll forfeit His grace, and secondly, you're now on your own. What's more, your ability to perform will be greatly affected. Instead of everything flowing, you now suffer and struggle through the day.

Had you obeyed the Lord, He would have undergirded (support or strengthen) and given you the grace for full time ministry. It's important we understand God doesn't give grace for disobedience. James 4:6 (KJV) says, "But He giveth more grace, wherefore he saith God resisteth the proud, but giveth grace unto the humble." He gives grace for what He has purposed, not our efforts mingled with disobedience. Romans 6:1–2 (KJV) says, "What shall we say then? Shall we continue in sin [disobedience], that grace may abound? God forbid."

There are multitudes of people in the body of Christ who are literally burnt out from doing things without God's undergirding grace or, another way to say it, "religious activity." They seek to serve God in this way, but it has become a struggle for them to maintain. We must remember what Jesus said: "My yoke is easy and My burden is light" (see Matthew 11:30). One of the ways to discern if you're operating without His undergirding grace is you're always tired and frustrated. Tiredness and frustration are indications that God's grace is not on what you're trying to accomplish.

Fleshly works is an enemy of God's grace upon our lives. Moreover, they are things we do without God's power flowing through us. They become difficult and drain us, producing no joy, peace, and fulfillment. They are often good things but not God things. There is a spiritual catchphrase which says, "Only what you do for Christ will last." When we operate apart from God's grace, our fleshly works will become evident when revealed by fire. Because wood, hay, and straw are flammable items, fleshly works will not stand against the heat as well.

> For no other foundation can anyone lay than that which is laid, which is Jesus Christ. Now if anyone builds on this foundation with gold, silver, precious stones, wood, hay, straw. Each one's work will become clear; for the day will declare it because it will be revealed by fire; and the fire will test each one's work, of what sort it is. If anyone's work which he has built on it endures, he will receive a reward. If anyone's work is burned, he will suffer loss; but he himself will be saved, yet so as through fire. (1 Corinthians 3:11–15)

The Bible tells us "we can do all things through Christ who strengthens us" (see Philippians 4:13). Although we can claim this important promise, we must bear in mind that Christ wants to strengthen us for those things that glorify the Father. Operating with God's undergirding grace in an area will please the Father and give Him glory. Jesus always positioned Himself to please the Father. John 8:29 says, "For I always do those things that please Him [Father]." Things we do in the flesh will never bring the Father glory.

I stated earlier that it is God "who works in us both to will and to do for His pleasure." It's very offensive and unacceptable for us to operate in the flesh. The reason being it is because God has given us everything we need to accomplish His will in the person of Christ Jesus and the Spirit of Grace. In my understanding, not relying upon the Lord can invoke a curse in our lives. Jeremiah 17:5 (KJV) says, "Thus says the Lord, cursed is the man who trusts in man, and makes flesh his strength."

Nonetheless, God delights in workers in His kingdom, for Paul said, "We are His workmanship created in Christ Jesus for good works, which God prepared beforehand that we should walk in them" (see (Ephesians 2:10). Notice He said good works. These are works in which God predestined for us before the foundations of the world. Therefore, we do not plan our own works without His undergirding grace, but we seek to discover and enter into the work God has given us grace to accomplish. This is why we should pray for guidance of the Holy Spirit to help us with the intent that God would grant us grace to carry out His purpose and plans.

I want to reiterate that tiredness and frustration is an indication that God's grace is not on what we're trying to accomplish. We must keep in mind that God will give us the necessary grace to fulfill and to carry out His purposes. There are individuals in the body of Christ whose lives are characterized by fleshy works. In their desire to please God, they have taken things upon themselves instead of being led by the Holy Spirit. To illustrate this point further, let's now look at a story in Luke's Gospel.

> Now it happened as they went that He entered a certain village; and a certain woman named Martha welcomed Him into her house. And she had a sister called Mary, who also sat at Jesus feet and heard His word. But Martha was distracted with much serving, and she approached Him and said, Lord, you do not care that my sister has left me to serve alone? Therefore, tell her to help me. And Jesus answered and said to her, Martha, Martha; you are worried and troubled about many things. But one thing is needed, and Mary has chosen that good part, which will not be taken away from her. (Luke 10:38–42)

We can only speculate if Martha's intentions and motives were good, but Jesus told her she was troubled about with many things (v. 41). Nonetheless, this is a good example of fleshly works. They are things we supposedly do for the Lord in which we don't have the grace to carry out. We are frustrated in our attempts to fulfill them. However, if we have God's grace on what we're doing, we'll flow and bear much fruit. John 15:5 says, "I am the vine, you are the branches, he who abides in Me [Jesus], and I in him, bears much fruit; for without Me you can do nothing."

An instance of God's grace undergirding, an individual is the story of Queen Esther. Esther 2:17 (KJV) says, "And the king loved Esther above all the women and she obtained grace and favor in his sight more than all the virgins; so that he set royal crown upon her head, and made her queen instead of Vashti."

Esther had become queen, and this would later serve as a blessing to her people. It was extremely important for God to have undergirded her with grace.

First, she had the task of rescuing her people from destruction from a decree made by the king at Haman's request. God's grace upon Esther's life proved to be beneficial to her people as they were delivered out of the hands of wicked Hamon. Second, it wasn't a skip in the park when approaching a king during biblical times, but because grace was upon her life, she was able to go in and out of the king's court. The thing we must remember is that when God undergirds His children, it's always with the end purpose of Him receiving glory.

Short Review of God's Amazing Grace

- Grace must be comprehended in all its fullness. What that simply means is we cannot earn it. What's more, this unmerited favor is available to the sinner for salvation and to the Christian for victorious living in Christ.
- As we look at the life of Paul and those who have similarities, including us, we realize that God does not give us what we deserve. He gives us what we don't deserve.
- Jesus endured in our place all the bad consequences that were due to us. In other words, He took the bad so, in turn, we might receive the blessings.
- The basic problem with mankind that has come out of the fall in the garden is that we all have turned our backs on God, either prior to our conversion or presently now. The most important need God met in our lives is spiritual resurrection.
- Jesus received punishment due to our transgressions and iniquities that we in turn might be forgiven and have peace with God. This exchange made provision for us to come out of alienation with God.
- Man has a twofold nature. He is both material and spiritual being, and both of the natures were affected by the fall. His body is exposed to disease, and his soul is corrupted by sin. The atonement has made provision for both natures.
- The exchanges are as follows: Jesus was punished that we might be forgiven, Jesus was wounded that we might be healed. Jesus was made sin with our sinfulness that we might become righteous with our righteousness. Jesus became poor with our poverty that we might become rich with His riches. Jesus bore our shame and endured our rejection that we might have acceptance as a child of God. Jesus became a curse that we might receive a blessing.
- God has ordered it that the weaker the earthen vessels are, the stronger His power may appear to be and that the trea-

sure should be valued more. God's grace enables us to carry what He has placed in our weak, fragile bodies.

- There are multitudes of people in the body of Christ who are literally burnt out from doing things they have placed on themselves instead of God's undergirding grace; or another way to put it, "religious activity." They seek to serve God in this way, but it has become a struggle for them to maintain. We do well to remember what Jesus said: "My yoke is easy and My burden is light" (see Matthew 11:30).

Life's Application

God has our best interest. He knows that all things work together for our good when we love Him and are fulfilling His purpose. He doesn't always answer us the way we would like, but he answers in a way that will always bring Him glory.

Key Scripture Reference

I thank Christ Jesus our Lord who has enabled me, because He counted me faithful, putting me into the ministry. Although I was formerly a blasphemer, a persecutor and an insolent man; but I obtained mercy because I did it ignorantly in unbelief. And the grace of our Lord was exceedingly abundant, with faith and love which are in Christ Jesus. (1 Timothy 1:12–14 KJV)

7

LEGALISM AN ENEMY OF GRACE

I am astonished that you are so quickly deserting the one who called you by the grace of Christ and are turning to a different gospel, which is really no gospel at all; evidently some people are throwing you into confusion and are trying to pervert the gospel of Christ.

—Galatians 1:6–7 (NIV)

Many Christians who are still under the Old Covenant have not fully embraced the dispensation of grace. Like the believers at Galatia who were turning away from faith to manmade rules and laws, many presently are doing the same. The Galatians were vivacious people who were converted at the preaching of Paul but were bewitched just as quickly by false teachers. Galatians 3:1 says, "You foolish Galatians, who has bewitched you that you should not obey the truth." Paul's letter of rebuke was one of disappointment and disapproval. He had taught them about the grace of Christ.

What's more, during that time, many were teaching that in order to be saved, Gentile believers were told they had to follow Jewish laws and customs, especially circumcision. Unfortunately, they had fell victim to legalism. To better understand more of Paul's displeasure concerning this church, here's a simple definition of legalism: "It is a strict adherence to the Law of Moses or a particular code of rules. It's the attempt to achieve righteousness with God by keeping a set of rules. It is adding to what God has required for righteousness."

The distinction between law and grace is grace writes upon the heart of the "new man" within. The law commands the "old man" from without. That is the core of legalism: a barrage of dress codes and external rules and regulations set forth. But grace allows the spirit to govern the inwards parts. Basically, the law is external. It focuses on the outward man. It says, "That's what I have to do."

Grace focuses on the inward man. It does something inside that results in acting in accordance with what's written on the tablets of our hearts. In short, the Law says, "This is what you have to do and to keep doing all the time." Grace says, "Someone else has done it for you."

There's nothing that upsets religious and legalistic people more than to tell them their religion and legalism do not work. Unfortunately, many Christians are unclear in their understanding of the difference between law and grace. So with an incomplete revelation, no sound teaching, and no understanding, they try to mix the two together. As a result, they struggle to live the kind of life God wants them to have or to enjoy the salvation that He has promised through Jesus. This leaves many walking around with virtually no joy, no peace, and being critical and judgmental. The moment we exercise faith for salvation in Jesus Christ, that ends the Mosaic Law or the ceremonial laws as a means for achieving righteousness.

> For they being ignorant of God's righteousness, and seeking to establish their own righteousness, have not submitted to the righteousness of God, for Christ is the end of the law for righteousness to everyone who believes. (Romans 10:3–4)

> For they don't understand God's ways of making people right with himself, instead

they are clinging to their own way of getting right with God by trying to keep the law. They won't go along with God's way. For Christ has accomplished the whole purpose of the law. All who believe in Him are made right with God. (Romans 10:4 NLT)

In comparison, there are some believers in Christ who are like Peter and Barnabas. Paul had to confront them for being hypocritical concerning the Mosaic Law and grace. Galatians 2:12–13 says:

Before certain men came from James, he [Peter] would eat with the Gentiles; but when they came, he [Peter] withdrew and separated himself, fearing those who were of the circumcision. And the rest of the Jews also played the hypocrite with him, so that even Barnabas was carried away with their hypocrisy.

As I contemplated this Scripture, I thought if an individual was truly set free from the law, but as soon as someone came around them who observed the law and invoked fear in them, then perhaps they may not have been fully set free in the first place (see John 8:32, 36). Paul had to really rebuke Peter concerning this issue, for he told him how he was "not straightforward about the truth of the Gospel" (v. 14).

In order to understand the importance of God's grace is in this dispensation. Let's look at a comparison between the Law of Moses verses, what we have under the grace of God.[10]

---

[10] Quotations taken from Donald Spellman, *Freedom from Spiritual Bondage*, copyright © 2019, by Kingdom House Publishing, Lakebay, Washington, pp. 97–98.

The Old Covenant Under Moses (Law)	The New Covenant Under Christ (Grace)	Scriptural Application
Special sacrifices were made on the behalf of those who were guilty	Sacrificial death of Jesus cleared us of guilt	Galatians 1:4; Ephesians 5:2; 1 Peter 3:18; Hebrews 8:3–4
Focus primarily on a physical and eternal building where they worshipped God	The focal point is supremacy and sovereignty of Christ in the hearts of believers	John 4:24, 14:20; Romans 8:10; Ephesians 3:17–18; Galatians 2.20; 1 John 3:24
Received on tablets of Stone and Ink	The Indwelling of the Holy Spirit	John 14:16–18, 26; 1 Corinthians 6:19–20;
Law of the flesh	Law of the Spirit	Romans 7:5–6, 8:2
Limited and Partial promises (Promised Land)	Unlimited and Boundless promises (a covenant of promises)	Psalm 103:1–4; 2 Corinthians 1:20; Ephesians 1:3–14; Hebrews 8:6
External standards and rules	Internal standards and a new heart	Ezek. 36:26–27; Hebrews 9:7
Ministration of Condemnation	Ministration of Righteousness	2 Corinthians 3:9
Limited Access to God	Unlimited and Unrestricted access to God	John 10:9, 14:6; Romans 5:1–2; Ephesians 2:18
Sin had dominion over us	Sin no longer has dominion over us	Romans 6:14–15; Galatians 5:18
For the Israelites only	For all Men	Deuteronomy 4:7–8, 5:3; Matthew 5:26–28; Titus 2:11
Brings Bondage	Brings liberty	Galatians 4:24–25; 2 Corinthians 3:17

Live by works	Live by faith	Galatians 3:10–11
Ministration of death	Ministration of Spirit and life	2 Corinthians 3:6, 8 2 Corinthians. 3:7
Powerless to save	Saves to the uttermost	Hebrews 7:25, 9:9, 10:4
Exposes sin	Covers sin when we repent	Romans 4:1–8; Galatians 3:19

The Ministry of Life or Death

Who also made us sufficient as ministers of the new covenant, not of the letter but of the Spirit; for the letter kills, but the Spirit gives life. But if the ministry of death, written and engraved on stones, was glorious, so that the children of Israel could not look steadily at the face of Moses because of the glory of his countenance, which glory was passing away, how will the ministry of the Spirit not be more glorious? (2 Corinthians 3:6–8)

Whenever the Mosaic Law is applied, it results in death. But whenever grace is given, it produces life (see 2 Corinthians 3:6–7). The key words concerning law or grace are *condemnation* and *conviction*. The law brought on condemnation while grace brought about conviction in the guilty. Paul makes it clear that the Spirit gives life, but in order for that to take effect, we must surrender to Him.

Unfortunately, in this dispensation, we still have men and women who are ministers of the old covenant, not realizing and taking into account that they are spiritually killing God's people. How? The letter kills, but the Spirit gives life. I stated this earlier and I deemed its worth, saying again there is a vast difference between condemnation *(in which the law brought on)* than conviction *(in which the Holy Spirit produces)*.

In Romans 8:1, Paul showed us how the law causes condemnation:

> There is now no condemnation for those who are in Christ Jesus because through Christ Jesus the law of the Spirit of life set me free from the law of sin and death. For what the law was powerless to do in that it was weakened by the sinful nature, God did by sending His Own Son in the likeness of sinful man.

In summary, the Law of Moses could never set you free from condemnation. It could only bring you under condemnation. As long as you live under the influence of it, you cannot live in liberty.

The word *condemnation* means censure, blame, disapproval, denunciation, and criticism," while *Merriam-Webster's Dictionary* describes *conviction* as the state of being convicted or being found guilty. As you can see, there is a vast difference between condemnation and conviction. The law causes condemnation while the Holy Spirit brings conviction. John 16:8 says, "He [Holy Spirit] will convict the world of sin, and righteousness and of judgment." The law brings death while the Spirit gives life. Second Corinthians 3:6 says, "He has made us competent as ministers of the New Covenant, not of the letter but of the Spirit; for the letter kills, but the Spirit gives life."

Under the old covenant, when a person sinned, an animal sacrifice had to be offered up. Under the new covenant, Christ made the atonement for our sins through His blood shed on the cross (see Hebrews 9:11–10:18). Second Corinthians 3:6 says, "He has made us competent as ministers of a new covenant, not of letter but of the Spirit; for the letter kills, but the Spirit gives life." Ministers of the New Covenant are to be competent of the Spirit rather than of the law. Unfortunately, there are many believers who are under condemnation every Sunday because of what they receive from either their pastor behind the pulpit or their misunderstanding of law and grace.

Many years ago, my wife and I went to a nearby city to visit a church. Regrettably, we didn't know much about this church at the time. We arrived at the church, went in, and sat down. As I began to listen to the message, I realized the pastor was preaching on the subject of love. Initially, it seemed like a good message, but I noticed there was complete silence. No one was affirming the message; you know, the usual "Amen," "Hallelujah," "Praise the Lord" and so on.

At some point during his sermon, he must have noticed the cosmetics my wife had on. She was wearing a little makeup on this particular day. He shifted the message and went legalistic, preaching about women wearing cosmetics and so on. Everyone in the church seemed to come alive with loud affirmations and applause. One lady said, "Pastor tells it like it is!" Another one said, "You're speaking the truth!" and on it went.

I lightly nudged my wife and said, "Let's go." And so we left.

I don't know about you, but I don't waste valuable time listening to nothing which pertains to nothing unless it's the Gospel of Jesus Christ or a message that brings us closer to the Lord. The Spirit of God brings conviction; the law brings condemnation; "the letter (law) kills, but the Spirit gives life" (see 2 Corinthians 3:6). There should always be a reminder that Christ has broken down the middle wall of separation.

Ephesians 2:13–15 says:

> But now in Christ Jesus you who once were far away have been brought near through the blood of Christ, for He Himself is our peace who has made the two one and has destroyed the barrier [middle wall of petition] the diving wall of hostility, by abolishing in His flesh the law with its commandments and regulations. His purpose was to create in Himself one new man out of the two, thus making peace.

In reality, when you are under a religious law, it puts you at enmity with those who are not under the same rules and laws. Why is a denomination at odds with other denominations? More often than not, it is because of religious laws and traditions. People persecute those who do not abide by the same. The trouble with the Church is that most Christians have reerected the middle wall of partition.

The difference now is it's not solely with Jews and Gentiles; we have other labels like Baptists, Catholics, Methodists, Episcopalians, Pentecostals, Charismatics, Evangelicals, or Holiness. When we revert back to the law, we come under the spirit of slavery to fear. Romans 8:14–15 says, "Because those who are led by the Spirit of God are sons of God, for you did not receive a spirit that makes you a slave again to fear, but you receive the Spirit of sonship, and by Him we cry, Abba, Father."[11]

As you have just read, one of the outworking's of legalism is animosity and hostility with those who don't abide by the same. Before Christ (who is full grace and truth) redeemed mankind back to the Father, we were far off. In other words, we had a broken relationship with the Father. But here's what Paul wrote to the Ephesians believers.

> But now in Christ Jesus you who were far off have been brought near by the blood of Christ. For He [Christ] Himself is our peace, who has made both one, and has broken down the middle wall of separation, having abolished in His flesh the enmity, that is the law of commandments contained in ordinances, so as to create in Himself one new man from the two, thus making peace, and that He might reconcile them both to God in one body through the cross, thereby putting to death the enmity. (Ephesians 2:13–16)

---

[11] Quotations taken from Donald Spellman, *Freedom from Spiritual Bondage*, copyright © 2019, by Kingdom House Publishing, Lakebay, Washington, pp. 82–83.

Paul mentions four important things I want draw your attention to. First, Christ is our peace (v. 14). Second, Christ broke down the middle wall of separation (v. 14). Three, Christ abolished in His flesh the enmity (v. 15). Finally, Christ reconciled them both to God in one body through the cross, thereby putting to death the enmity (v. 16). There's an important reason for highlighting these four things. Notice what Paul writes again, "Abolishing in His [Christ] flesh the enmity…and putting to death the enmity."

The word *enmity* is central here because the Jews and Gentiles were at odds with one another. The word *enmity* means hostility, hate, hatred, and animosity. Remember the story about the woman at the well? She mentions how the Jews had no dealings with the Samaritans [Gentiles] (see John 4:9). The separation was a result of the Jews' strict adherence to the Law of Moses. As a result, it brought enmity or hostility between the two.

Those who still follow rules and regulations, the Mosaic Laws, etc., tend to persecute, antagonize, and alienate those who are free in Christ. The Pharisees and Sadducees during Jesus's time on earth would fall in this category. Anyone who wasn't following all the rules and regulations was seen as an outsider and traitor. So in order that the "middle wall of separation" to have been broken down, Jesus abolished in His flesh the enmity, which was "the law of commandments contained in ordinances."

Sanctification through Faith Working by Love

> You have become estranged from Christ, you who attempt to be justified by law; you have fallen from grace. For we through the Spirit wait for the hope of righteousness by faith, for in Jesus Christ neither circumcision availeth anything, nor un-circumcision; but faith which worketh by love. (Galatians 5:4–6 (KJV)

Paul here represents the case for all Christians who through the Spirit wait for the hope of righteousness by faith, which is another way of saying sanctification by faith. This simply implies that we act under the direction and influence of the Holy Spirit. This also means that if we expect to be saved, justified, or sanctified any other way, we will meet with disappointment. There are multitudes of well-meaning Christians who attempt to achieve holiness or sanctification through their flesh combined with the responsibility of living a consecrated life and become discouraged and frustrated.

What's more, many who fall into this category are burdened with the teachings of man-made rules and church bylaws, making it more of an added struggle to attain sanctification. God has given us the necessary resources to conform to the image of His Son, particularly the indwelling of the Holy Spirit. John 16:8 says, "And when He [Holy Spirit] has come, He will convict the world of sin, and of righteousness, and of judgment."

It was A. B. Simpson that said, "It is a principle of human nature that the things which we would not do under necessity we would often gladly do from love." He goes on to share a story which illustrates his point:

> The story is told of two young people who had been predestined to marry because of their father's estates adjoined. They had never met as they were absent at distant schools. But on their way home to be presented to society and each other; they accidently met incognito on the train and became attracted to each other; and the young man before he realized it found himself telling his impromptu friend of the distasteful plan that had been made for him, and his determination not to be forced into marriage of convenience for the sake of uniting two estates. Soon afterwards they met, and to their mutual astonishment found out that they were already in love. That which law and necessity never could have

brought about, but only made the more distasteful, took care of itself when left to the influence of love. So God has seized upon that principle which is the key to every human heart and life, and made it the motive power of holiness and obedience. He gives us liberty to sin if we want to, but He adds, "If you love Me, you will obey what I command" (John 14:15). What a mighty teacher love is! What a perfect disciplinarian love is![12]

Love is the true test of a vital relationship with the Father. When we truly know and love God, we will not sin against Him. First John 2:3–5 says:

> Now by this we know that we know Him, if we keep His commandments, He who says I know Him and does not keep His commandments is a liar and the truth is not in him, but whoever keeps His word truly the love of God is perfected in him. By this we know that we are in Him.

The phrase "whoever keeps His word" speaks of the fact we're to take God's word and apply it in our lives daily. Not just on Sundays or midweek Bible studies but every day and not just sitting under a word but living out the Word. John goes on to say in verse 5, "Truly the love of God is perfected in him." Love is an action word, and the way we live and walk gives us the assurance we love Christ. What that means is we don't need legalistic man-made rules to manage the way we live.

---

[12] Quotation taken from Dr. Albert B. Simpson, *The Christ in the Bible Commentary*, copyright © 2009, by. First Wing Spread Publishers, Camp Hill, Pennsylvania, Book 3, page 362, story No. 6.

Maybe you're struggling to live a holy life and you sit in church week after week feeling frustrated and perplexed. Let me ask you one very important question. What robe are you wearing? The Word of God admonishes us to "put ye on the Lord Jesus Christ, and make no provision for the flesh, to fulfill the lusts thereof" (see Romans 13:14). In other words, instead of the robe of denominational bylaws, put on the Lord Jesus. Instead of the robe of legalistic rules and man-made doctrines, put on the Lord Jesus. Instead of the robe of fleshly struggles, put on the Lord Jesus Christ.

Jesus is the robe we must put on. In other words, when you put on Jesus, you're putting on His attributes and His righteousness. Second Corinthians 5:21 says, "For He made Him who knew no sin to be sin for us, that we might become the righteousness of God in Him." Once we have put on Christ, we immediately identify with His death, burial, and resurrection. Our old lives become buried in Him. Second Corinthians 5:17 says, "Therefore if anyone is in Christ, He is a new creation; old things have passed away; behold all things have become new."

Finally, by putting on Christ, we die to fleshly desires. The Christ that now lives in us now gives us the strength to overcome every temptation and every obstacle the devil throws our way. Galatians 2:20 says, "I have been crucified with Christ; it is no longer I who live, but Christ lives in me; and the life which I now live in the flesh I live by faith in the son of God, who loved me and gave Himself for me."

Short Review of Legalism Is an Enemy of Grace

- To better understand more of Paul's displeasure concerning this church, here's a simple definition of legalism: "It is a strict adherence to the Law of Moses or a particular code of rules. It's the attempt to achieve righteousness with God by keeping a set of rules. It is adding to what God has required for righteousness."

- Basically, the law is external. It deals with the outward man. It says, "That's what I have to do." However, grace deals with the internal man; it will do something inside of us that results in us acting in accordance with what's written on the tablets of our hearts.

- Whenever the Mosaic Law is applied, it results in death. But whenever grace is given, it produces life. The key words we need to understand concerning law or grace are *condemnation* and *conviction*.

- The word *condemnation* means censure, blame, disapproval, denunciation and criticism, while *Merriam-Webster's Dictionary* describes *conviction* as the state of being convicted or being found guilty. As you can see, there is a vast difference between condemnation and conviction. The law causes condemnation while the Holy Spirit brings conviction(see John 16:8).

- When you are under a religious law, it puts you at enmity with those who are not under the same rules and laws. Why is a denomination at odds with other denominations? More often than not, it is because of religious laws and traditions. People persecute those who do not abide by the same. The trouble with the Church is that most Christians have reerected the middle wall of partition.

- The case for all Christians who through the Spirit wait for the hope of righteousness by faith, which is another way of saying sanctification by faith—this simply implies that we act under the direction and influence of the Holy Spirit.

This also means that if we expect to be saved, justified, or sanctified any other way, we will meet with disappointment.

Life's Application

Jesus is the embodiment of truth, and to be liberated from sin, religious tradition, and legalism, we must come to Him. We will never fully be complete if we are in some sort of spiritual bondage. Jesus doesn't give us freedom to sin, but we're free to follow God. To receive the grace of God is to embrace all that is afforded to us through the atonement of Jesus.

This is clearly brought home to us from John's Gospel. John 1:16–17 says, "And of His fullness we have all received, and grace for grace. For the law was given through Moses, but grace and truth came through Jesus Christ." My friend, if you find yourself presently in some kind of spiritual bondage, I pray that Jesus will set you free.

Key Scripture References

Stand fast therefore in the liberty by which Christ has made us free, and do not be entangled again with a yoke of bondage... You have become estranged from Christ, you who attempt to be justified by law; you have fallen from grace. (Galatians 5:1, 4)

You have become estranged from Christ, you who attempt to be justified by law; you have fallen from grace. For we through the Spirit wait for the hope of righteousness by faith, for in Jesus Christ neither circumcision availeth anything, nor uncircumcision; but faith which worketh by love. (Galatians 5:4–6 KJV)

8

GRACE IMPARTED THROUGH THE BELIEVER

> And God is able to make all grace abound
> [thrive, flourish, overflow] toward you, that you
> always having all sufficiency [adequacy, capability] in all things, may have an abundance [plenty,
> wealth, richness, great quantity] for every good
> work.
>
> —2 Corinthians 9:8

As a believer in Christ, we have a responsibility to impart God's grace and mercy that has been given to us to others. Those who have experienced God's grace demonstrate God's grace. The grace that has been given to us is not for us to stockpile or hoard it to ourselves. We are called to be channels through which blessings flow. We can choose to be a channel or a reservoir. In my observation over the years, I've come to realize there are many who choose to be reservoirs as opposed to channels. I'm reminded of what Jesus told His disciples: "Therefore be merciful, just as your Father also is merciful" (see Luke 6:36). If we have experienced God's grace, then it should be natural for us to impart it to others.

The believer is God's creative masterpiece, and according to Paul, "we are His workmanship created in Christ Jesus for good works, which God prepared beforehand that we should walk in them" (see Ephesians 2:10). The Greek word translated "workmanship" is *poiema*. The Latin version is *poema* from which we get the English word *poem*. The Jerusalem Bible uses the phrase "work of art" as just another way of saying we are God's creative masterpiece. When we consider everything God has created, we recognize grace was at work. Aren't you glad you were chosen by God to be materials for His creative masterpiece?

An artist or sculpture takes time in chiseling and cutting away things that take away from his intended product. So it is with God. He works on us, molding and shaping us through the furnace of affliction, and then unveils us to the world. It's at that point we are ready to be of service in His kingdom. Where did God get these materials that are part of His masterpiece? He retrieves them from the body of Christ, the Church, or Ecclesia. He reaches down into the scraps of our lives that have been marred by sin and turns trash into a work of art.

> But God hath chosen the foolish things of the world to confound the wise; and God hath chosen the weak things of the world to confound the things which are mighty; And base things of the world, and things which are despised, hath God chosen, yea and things which are not to bring to naught things that are. (1 Corinthians 1:27–28 KJV)

Throughout the Bible, we're shown examples of God's people created to be useful and functional. It's no secret that God wants to impart through us what He has placed in us. John 15:16 says, "You did not choose Me [Jesus], but I chose you and appointed you that you should go and bear fruit."

With a realization that we're His masterpiece "created for good works," surrendering to His plan for our lives and the impartation of grace to others should be our reasonable service. Isaiah 64:8 (KJV) says, "But now O Lord, You are our Father; we are the clay and thou our potter; and all we are the work of thy hand."

In short, we must be channels of blessings to those who we come in contact with. Whatever God places in us must be given out. I would like to take a minute and ask this question: are spiritual gifts imparted to us for self or to edify our fellow believers in Christ? I believe you would agree we are to edify our brothers and sisters in Christ. Philippians 2:4 says, "Let each of you look out not only for his own interests, but also for the interests of others."

It's important to note that the Greek word for spiritual gifts and gift is *charisma*. The word *charisma* is derived from the basic Greek abstract noun *charis*. The word *charis* is normally translated as grace, the unmerited favor of God toward the undeserving. If we add "ma" to the word *charis* instead of it being an abstract noun, it becomes a specific noun, changing the word *charis* to *charisma,* which means grace made effective. Consequently, spiritual gifts or charisma is a manifestation of the grace of God. It is grace acted out in a particular way. In short, a manifestation of grace that edifies the body of Christ.

What about the ministry gifts (apostle, prophet, evangelist, pastor, and teacher)? According to Paul's letter to the church at Ephesus, these gifts are given to the church for the perfecting of the saints, work of the ministry, and the edification of the body of Christ (see Ephesians 4:11–12). God has bestowed His grace upon us, and we do likewise to those with whom we come in contact with as Paul says, "The love of Christ compels us" (see 2 Corinthians 5:14).

Treasure in Earthen Vessels

God has ordered it the weaker the earthen vessels, the stronger His power may appear to be, and that the treasure should be valued more. God's grace enables us to carry what He has placed in our weak fragile bodies. A "vessel" is a container or receptacle. The vessels that the Hebrew people used were usually earthenware, and it wasn't uncommon for it to be glass, metal, leather, wicker, or stone. The vessels were used to hold everything from documents which the Prophet Jeremiah told the people to place in vessels. They were also used to hold wine, fruit, and oil. This shows you how a vessel can be fragile but yet hold important and valuable things.

In a second letter to the believers at Corinth, Paul said, "We have this treasure in earthen vessels, that the excellency of the power may be of God and not of us" (see 2 Corinthians 4:7). Paul explains to us how the Gospel is compared to a valuable jewel. Jesus alluded to this when He said "the kingdom of heaven is likening unto treasure hidden in a field (Matthew 13:44). God has entrusted our weak fragile vessels to carry the light of the Gospel of Christ to the ends of the earth. This is one of the ways His grace is imparted through us. Since we have His enabling power in us, we're now able to share the light of the Gospel with someone in darkness.

The Holy Spirit has given us this treasure inside that is the word of reconciliation to impart grace to those outside the cross. Second Corinthians 5:18–19 says:

> And all things are of God, who hath reconciled us to Himself by Jesus Christ, and hath given to us the ministry of reconciliation, to wit that God was in Christ, reconciling the world unto Himself, not imputing their trespasses unto them; and hath committed unto us the word of reconciliation.

When Paul referred to the "excellence of the power of God," it highlighted for us the source and left no room to boast. It's no secret that our inabilities and weaknesses make us solely dependent upon the Lord. He has chosen us and ordained us. And not just that alone. He has placed His treasure in us. What a wonderful Savior. Second Corinthians (AMP) says, "Not that we are fit (qualified and sufficient in ability) of ourselves to form personal judgments or to claim or count anything as coming from us, but our power and ability and sufficiency are from God."

Jesus said we're like mere branches that need the support of the vine. As you know, the vine is crucial for branches to receive all the nutrients it needs to survive. The Lord wants us to recognize the importance and value of total surrender and that we're incapable of receiving and accomplishing things apart from Him, for He said, "I am the vine, you are the branches, he who abides in Me, and I in him bears much fruit; for without Me you can do nothing" (see John 15:5). In addition, John the Baptist said, "A man can receive nothing unless it has been given to him from heaven (see John 3:27).

There are times we may applaud and feel good about ourselves for the accomplishments we attain, but none of it would be possible had it not been for the grace of God. Paul understood this more than any of his contemporaries, for he said, "By the grace of God I am what I am; and His grace which bestowed upon me was not in vain" (see 1 Corinthians 15:10). Jesus, while in an earthly body, made this statement: "I can of mine own self do nothing" (see John 5:30). In order for us to make an impact in the lives of people and to reach a lost world, we need God's grace and Spirit to flow in us and through us.

Speech Seasoned with Grace and Salt

Speech that is seasoned with grace is an additional way to impart grace to a fellow believer or the unbeliever. One of ways this happens is when a word of encouragement is shared with someone. Words have power and the capacity to produce life or death (see Proverbs 21:18). I want to ask you this very important question: do the words you speak produce life or death? Do they encourage, exhort, and comfort? Or do they frustrate, humiliate, degrade, or curse? Paul exhorted the believers at Colosse to behave wisely and to guard what they say.

> Let your speech at all times be gracious (pleasant and winsome) seasoned as it were with salt, so that you may never be at a loss; to know how you ought to answer anyone who put a question to you. (Colossians 4:5 AMP)

Our speech is very important when ministering to those who have not received Christ as their Savior. We must always pray for wisdom on how to communicate with them. To say it another way, our lifestyle and walk plays a very important role in our witness among those in darkness, but our speech and conversation is just as important. Proverbs 10:32 says, "The lips of the righteous know what is acceptable." There are many ways our speech can impart grace seasoned with salt to the hearers; something that edifies, influences, affects, and builds up our fellow believers in the Lord.

- Speech that imparts grace to the hearers and seasoned with salt can build up an individual. Proverbs 16:24 says, "Pleasant words are like a honeycomb, sweetness to the soul and health to the bones." These words the writer speaks of are wholesome to the body and sweet to the soul.
- Speech that imparts grace to the hearers and seasoned with salt can affect the life of an unbeliever. Colossians 4:5 (AMP) says:

> Behave yourselves wisely (living prudently and with discretion) in all your relations with those of the outside world (the non-Christians), making the most of the time and seizing (buying up) the opportunity. Let your speech at all times be gracious (pleasant and winsome) seasoned as it were with salt, so that you may never be at a loss; to know how you ought to answer anyone who put a question to you."

- Speech that imparts grace to the hearers and seasoned with salt can be effective if used at the right time. Proverbs 15:23 (NIV) says, "A man finds joy in giving an apt reply and good is a timely word."
- Speech that imparts grace to the hearers and seasoned with salt when used with discernment will have good results.

Proverbs 25:11 says, "A word fitly spoken is like apples of gold in settings of silver."

- Speech that imparts grace to the hearers and seasoned with salt can bring edification and comfort. Ephesians 4:29 says, "Let no corrupt word proceed out of your mouth, but what is good for necessary edification, that it may impart grace to the hearers."

The Grace of Forgiveness

Forgiveness is the cornerstone of our relationship with God and an important part of the Gospel message. Because God has forgiven us through the atonement of Christ, we have an obligation to forgive others. The grace He bestows upon us will birth in us indebtedness, responsibility, and obligation. Jesus placed no limits on the extent to which Christians are to forgive. Luke 17:4 (KJV) says, "And if he trespasses against thee seven times in a day, and seven times in a day turn again to thee, saying, I repent, thou shalt forgive him."

To remain unforgiving shows we misunderstand the grace of God and that we ourselves deeply need to be forgiven. Conversely, when we have a forgiving spirit it shows we are true followers of Christ. God wants us to imitate Christ's compassionate forgiving attitude. He forgave those who rejected and persecuted Him. As you know, Jesus hung on the cross at a place called Calvary, knowing He did nothing that warrant punishment and death, yet He says, "Father forgive them, for they do not know what they do" (see Luke 23:34).

The key to forgiving those who have wronged us is remembering how much God has forgiven us. He is a God of grace and pardon. Daniel 9:9 (KJV) says, "To the Lord our God belong mercies and forgiveness, though we have rebelled against Him." One of the greatest gifts you can give people is the gift of forgiveness. To release an individual from something they committed against you will liberate both of you. What I mean is they will no longer have to carry a burden of guilt, knowing they have hurt or sinned against you or likewise.

> Therefore, as God's chosen people holy and
> dearly loved, clothe yourselves with compassion,
> kindness, humility, gentleness and patience. Bear
> with each other and forgive whatever grievances
> you may have against one another. Forgive as the
> Lord forgave you. (Colossians 3:12–13 NIV)

In a similar letter Paul wrote to the believers at Ephesus, he exhorted them to "be kind to one another, tenderhearted, forgiving one another, even as God in Christ forgave you" (see Ephesians 4:32). There are times when Christians disagree, and if God's grace is upon their lives, it should encourage them to be tenderhearted and forgiving. When we have been wounded, mistreated, and offended, we must forgive. By doing so, we give the offender the grace of forgiveness. Let's now look at two examples of the grace of forgiveness at work in God's servants.

The first example is the betrayal of Joseph by his brothers in the Old Testament. Joseph's brothers had mistreated him in a way that most of us today would have a hard time processing and releasing. In order to appreciate this account of forgiveness, let's look briefly at a few things that took place. First, Joseph's brothers threatened to kill him but afterward decided not to proceed with plans. Secondly, they placed him in a pit and eventually sold him to slave traders on their way to Egypt. For more than fourteen years, Joseph suffered many things. Undoubtedly, this would have brought on bitterness, resentment, and unforgiveness in the lives of many. But Joseph's response was motivated by compassion, mercy, and forgiveness.

> So shall ye say unto Joseph, forgive I pray
> thee now, the trespass of thy brethren, and their
> sin; for they did unto thee evil; and now we pray
> thee, forgive the trespass of the servants of the
> God of thy Father, and Joseph wept when they
> space unto him. And his brethren also went and
> fell down before his face; and they said, behold,
> we be thy servants, and Joseph said unto them,

> fear not, for am I in the place of God? But as for
> you, ye thought evil against me; but God meant
> it unto good, to bring to pass, as it is this day,
> to save much people alive, now therefore fear ye
> not; I will nourish you, and your little ones. And
> he comforted them and space kindly unto them.
> (Genesis 50:17–21 KJV)

What would cause Joseph to readily forgive his brothers? I personally believe He recognized the hand of God was upon him in those critical years. Having experienced the furnace of affliction, he knew that it was the Lord who brought him from the prison to the palace. This birthed in him a willingness to release and not hold any grudges against his offenders. To have done so would have disappointed God. Joseph's forgiveness was complete. He demonstrated how God graciously accepts us, even though we don't deserve it.

The second example of grace of forgiveness at work is found in the New Testament with a man name Stephen. The Bible said Stephen was full of faith, power, and the Holy Spirit. He was chosen as one of the first deacons of the early church. Additionally, he had become well-known as a preacher and a miracle worker (see Acts 6:8). As a result of Stephen being full of the Holy Spirit, he was used of God mightily during the time renewed persecution broke out against the church. Stephen was skilled in Jewish debates and often outwitted people.

But unfortunately, this led to his arrest. Members of certain Jewish synagogues felt Stephen had blasphemed Moses and God. They accused him of being disloyal to the Temple, rejecting Moses, and being hostile toward Judaism. They brought him before the Sanhedrin and Jewish council. False witnesses testified, and charges were placed against him (see Acts 6:13). In his lengthy testimony, he summarized the Old Testament teachings, showing how God had guided his people, Israel, to a specific place in Him. He condemned the council as being stiff-necked, uncircumcised in heart and ears, and accused them of resisting the Holy Spirit (see Acts 7:51). He further charged them for killing Christ, just as their ancestors had killed the prophets and failing to keep their own law (see Acts 7:52–53).

His speech infuriated the Sanhedrin so much that they were cut to the heart, and they gnashed at him with their teeth. At the same time, Stephen had a vision of God in heaven with Jesus on His right hand. As the old catchphrase that says, "The needle that broke the camel's back," this sealed his fate when he shared this vision to his enemies. The crowd rushed upon him, dragged him out of the city, and begin to stone him to death, and as they were stoning him, he cried with a loud voice, saying, "Lord Jesus, receive my spirit and lay not this sin to their charge" (see Acts 7:59–60).

This is perhaps one of the greatest acts of forgiving people while literally being stoned to death. It is parallel or somewhat equivalent to the crucifixion of Jesus who forgave his enemies while dying on the cross. If Jesus and Stephen can forgive men of their trespasses while being falsely accused and dying for the truth, then certainly we can forgive people who have mistreated, wronged, or betrayed us. This is truly what is meant by the grace of forgiveness.

The Ministry Gifts
An Impartation of Grace

As we continue to look at God's grace imparted through the believer, I would like to show you how the ministry gifts are spiritual tools given by the Holy Spirit. This is yet another way grace is displayed through the believer. Paul gives us an explanation of each ministry gift and their function as he writes that "each one of us grace was given according to the measure of Christ's gift" (see Ephesians 4:7). Likewise, just as God has given us a measure of faith, Christ has given each believer a measure or degree of ministry gifts for the "perfecting of the saints, for the work of the ministry, for the edifying of the body of Christ" (see Ephesians 4:12).

Each ministry gift plays an important part in the development and growth of the believer. One of the purposes of God is to bring us to a place of spiritual maturity and wholeness. He accomplishes this through the work of the Holy Spirit and the ascension ministry gifts. Every believer has a measure of faith and different degree of gifts. What's more, every believer has been given at least one minis-try gift or more, but nonetheless, each gift is for the common good of one another. All ministers of the Gospel owe credit to our Lord Jesus, His grace, and His Spirit for the impartation of these ministry gifts.

What are the ministry gifts? Ephesians 4:7 (KJV) says, "And He gave some, apostles; and some prophets; and some evangelists; and some pastors and teachers." There is vast distinction between the ministry gifts and the gifts of the Spirit. In understanding the ministry gifts those who are given a ministry or fivefold ministry gift, become the gift given by Christ to the church. For instance, those who are called to the pastorate, are pastoral gifts to the Body of Christ and so on. Every facet of the total ministry makes up the gift. However, the gifts of the Spirit are given to and through the believer by the Holy Spirit. The gift is a supernatural brief manifestation.

It's important to note that just as the gifts of the Spirit are chan-nels for conveying blessings to others, the ministry gifts operate in the same way. No ministry gift is for self. God's desire is that we be a channel of blessing to others. The central point of the Christian faith is the idea of being a blessing to others. Philippians 2:3–4 (KJV) says, "Let nothing be done through selfish ambition or conceit, but in lowliness of mind let each esteem others better than himself. Let each of you look out not only for his own interests, but also for the interests of others."

Selfish ambition will invariably destroy any relationship, espe-cially in the church, but lowliness of mind (humility) will help build it. When we are putting others interests before our own, we are imparting grace to the recipients. At this point, I want to show you a few examples in the New Testament where there is an impartation of grace through people. The examples I will be sharing with you are the apostolic ministry of Paul, evangelistic ministry of Philip, and the teaching ministry of Apollos. These are just a few believers in whom God used in the ministry gifts. Now let's see how they administered grace to the recipients.

Paul's Apostolic Ministry

It was a glorious occasion after the Holy Spirit's arrival on the day of Pentecost, but it wasn't unusual to find believers scattered abroad who hadn't received Him. Through the power of the Holy Spirit, Paul's apostolic ministry was commissioned to come to the rescue. It's important to know that all nine spiritual gifts were apparent in his ministry. Upon his arrival at Ephesus, the discerning of spirits was very evident in his ministry.

> And it came to pass that while Apollos was at Corinth, Paul having passed through the upper coasts came to Ephesus; and finding certain disciples, He said to them have you received the Holy Ghost since ye believed? And they said unto him, we have not so much as heard whether there be any Holy Ghost. (Acts 19:1–2 KJV)

Paul discerned the disciples did not have the Holy Spirit, so he put forward a question, "Have you received the Holy Ghost since ye believed?"

Their response was, "We have not so much as heard whether there be any Holy Ghost." As a result of their admission, the apostles baptized them in the name of Jesus. Grace was imparted in the form of an act of baptism. Another occurrence of grace being imparted took place at Lystra. Through the power of the Holy Spirit, we see the impartation of gifts of healings and the word of knowledge.

> And there sat a certain man at Lystra, impotent in his feet, being a cripple from his mother's womb, who never had walked; the same heard Paul speak who steadfastly beholding him, and perceiving that he had faith to be healed, said with a loud voice, stand upright on thy feet, and he leaped and walked. (Acts 14:8–10 KJV)

Another occurrence of an impartation of grace was when Paul and Silas were thrown in prison, beaten with their feet fast in stocks. What's more, they were given a jailor to keep charge of them while being placed in the inner prison. But please notice that in spite of these terrible conditions, they were exactly where God wanted them to be, and that is to impart grace (God's unmerited and unearned favor) to a lost soul and his family.

> And at midnight Paul and Silas prayed, and sang praises unto God; and the prisoners heard them. And suddenly there was a great earthquake, so that the foundations of the prison were shaken; and immediately all the doors were opened, and every one's bands were loosed. And the keeper of the prison awaking out of his sleep, and seeing the prison doors open, he drew out his sword, and would have killed himself, supposing that the prisoners had been fled. (Acts 16:25–27 KJV)

Observe God's power and gift of faith in operation as we see the prison shaken by an earthquake, doors opened, and everyone's bands loosed. As a result of this, the keeper of the prison and all his family were saved and baptized. Unquestionably, the Spirit of God manifested grace to this jailer and his family through the ministry of Paul and Silas.

> Then he called for a light, and sprang in and came trembling and fell down before Paul and Silas, and brought them out and said Sirs what must I do to be saved? And they said, believe on the Lord Jesus Christ and thou shalt be saved and thy house, and they spake unto him the word of the Lord, and to all that were in his house. And he took them the same hour of the night and washed their stripes; and was baptized he and all his, straightway. (Acts 16:29–33 KJV)

Apollos's Teaching Ministry

The planting (evangelizing) of the Gospel was that of Paul while the watering (teaching) was that of Apollos. The seed (Word) that God used Paul to spread and plant would have never grown if it was not for the watering (teaching) ministry of Apollos. This ministry gift of grace is very important to the growth of every believer once they have accepted Christ and move forward. Here is the account of Apollos, the teacher in the book of Acts.

> And a certain Jew named Apollos born at Alexandria, an eloquent man and mighty in the scriptures came to Ephesus. This man was instructed in the way of the Lord; and being fervent in the Spirit, he spake and taught diligently the things of the Lord, knowing only the baptism of John, and he began to speak boldly in the synagogue; whom when Aquila and Priscilla had heard, they took him unto them, and expounded unto him the way of God more perfectly. (Acts 18:25–26 KJV)

Although Apollos was later instructed concerning the baptism of the Holy Spirit, he spoke boldly in many synagogues, instructing many in the things of the Lord. God used his teaching ministry to impart grace to the hearers. Verses 27–28 says, "And when he was disposed [willing] to pass into Achaia, the brethren wrote, exhorting the disciples to receive him; who when he was come, helped them much which had believed through grace. For he [Apollos] mightily convinced the Jews, and that publicly, showing by the scriptures that Jesus was Christ."

The teacher gift is an indispensable gift that makes the scriptures simple, real, and applicable for the believer in the body of Christ. This is precisely what Apollos did. He had complete knowledge of the scriptures and was able to convince the Jews and challenged those who opposed the Gospel. Second Timothy 2:25 (KJV) says, "In meekness instructing those that oppose themselves; if God peradventure will give them repentance to the acknowledging of the truth, and that they may recover themselves out of the snare of the devil, who are taken captive by him at his will."

Philip's Evangelistic Ministry

Saul whose name would later be changed to Paul was making havoc of the church and committing believers of Christ to prison. Simultaneously, while this was taking place, Philip the evangelist went down to Samaria and preached Christ to all the people. The people gave heed to everything Philip spoke and upon hearing and seeing the miracles which he did. According to Acts 8:7, it says, "For unclean spirits crying with a loud voice came out of many that were possessed with them; and many taken with palsies and that were lame were healed."

Philip's evangelistic campaign was so successful that a sorcerer name Simon was converted and baptized, a very wicked man who had bewitched the people of Samaria for a very long time. When the ascension ministry gifts are operating through the anointing and power of God's grace, the people are edified and blessed. After Philip had been used of God in many of the villages of Samaria, he was commissioned through an angel to go south unto Gaza, a desert place. It's here he had an encounter with an Ethiopian.

> And he arose and went and behold a man of Ethiopia a eunuch of great authority under Candace queen of the Ethiopians who had the charge of all her treasure and had come to Jerusalem for to worship, was returning and sitting in his chariot read Esaias the prophet. Then the Spirit said unto Philip go near and join thyself to this chariot. And Philip ran thither to him and heard him read the Prophet Esaias and said understandest thou what thou readest?

> Then Philip opened his mouth and began at
> the same scripture and preached unto him Jesus,
> and they went on their way, they came unto a
> certain water and the eunuch said, see here is
> water, what doth hinder me to be baptized? And
> Philip said, if thou believeth with all thine heart
> thou mayest, and he answered and said I believe
> that Jesus Christ is the Son of God and he com-
> manded the chariot to stand still; and they went
> down both into the water, both Philip and the
> eunuch; and he baptized him. (Acts 8:27–30,
> 35–38 KJV)

God uses many avenues to impart grace to those who are in
need of help. Remember, He is "a very present help in times of trouble." We're encouraged also to "come boldly to the throne of grace,
that we may obtain mercy and find grace to help in time of need" (see
Psalm 46:1; Hebrews 4:16). But He also uses His servants to impart
grace in times of need. The ministry gifts are a gift to the church, and
Philip the evangelist was one of those instruments. Those who have
these ministry gifts have an enormous responsibility and opportunity
to make a difference in the lives of people. All it takes is an obedient
heart like that of Philip who surrendered to the guidance and leader-
ship of the Holy Spirit.

The Gifts of the Spirit an Impartation of Grace

Let's look at how spiritual gifts are instruments given by the
Holy Spirit. This is another way grace is imparted through the
believer. But first I want to explain the characteristics of spiritual
gifts and how they affect the body of Christ. In Paul's first letter to
the believers at Corinth, he gives them a list of the gifts of the Spirit.

> For one is given by the Spirit the word of
> wisdom; to another the word of knowledge by

the same Spirit; to another faith by the same
Spirit; to another the gifts of healings by the same
Spirit; to another the working of miracles; to
another prophecy; to another discerning of spirits; to another divers kinds of tongues; to another
the interpretation of tongues. (1 Corinthians
12:8–10, KJV)

The spiritual grace gifts listed above can be divided into three
categories or groups. They are as follows. First, the "Revelation Gifts"
include the word of wisdom, word of knowledge, and discerning of
spirits. Secondly, the "Power Gifts" include the gift of faith, gifts of
healings, and working of miracles. Finally, the "Inspiration Gifts"
include the gifts of prophecy, gift of tongues, and interpretation of
tongues.

The Greek word for spiritual gifts and gift is *charisma*. The word
charisma is derived from the basic Greek abstract noun *charis*. The
word "charis" is normally translated as grace, the unmerited favor of
God toward the undeserving. If you join "ma" to the word *charis,*
instead of it being an abstract noun, it becomes now a specific noun,
changing the word *charis* to *charisma*, which means grace made effective. Therefore, spiritual gifts or charisma is a manifestation of the
grace of God. It is grace acted out in a particular way.

When operating in the gifts of the Spirit, we must be open
and dependent upon God. Notice Paul assumed that everyone has
a gift, although different from each other. In this dispensation each
believer is encouraged to allow the gifts to operate through them,
and every church should expect this manifestation of the Spirit. First
Corinthians 7:7 (KJV) says, "For I would that all men were even as
I myself, but every man hath his proper gift of God, one after this
manner, and another after that."

A spiritual gift is any event, word, or action that embodies and
expresses God's grace. Paul explains by saying, "having then gifts dif-
fering according to the grace that is given to us let us use them"
(see Romans 12:6). The Holy Spirit imparts and empowers us with
spiritual gifts for building up the church and to equip the saints for

ministry until Christ returns (see 1 Corinthians 1:7). The demonstration of gifts of the Spirit is for every believer to benefit from, and when they're used in a discipline and orderly manner, every believer is edified. First Corinthians 12:7 (KJV) says, "But the manifestation of the Spirit is given to every man to profit withal."

Through the power of the Spirit, grace was at work, empowering certain individuals in the Old Testament. Men of renown like Moses, Samuel, Elijah, and Elisha were just a few to name. Prophecy and healing were apparent as Elijah and Elisha touched people's lives. The manifestation was limited to only a few select men, but the Prophet Joel prophesied that God would pour out His Spirit on all flesh in due time. Joel 2:28 says, "And it shall come to pass afterward, that I will pour out my Spirit on all flesh." The gifts are given to us to be exercised and to make us channels for conveying divine blessings and grace to others.

A Word of Wisdom Used to Impart Salvation to Gentiles

Before I share an example of a word of wisdom in action, here's a concise description. A word of wisdom is a supernatural revelation of the mind and purpose of God communicated by the Holy Spirit. It is a miniature portion or fragment of God's total wisdom imparted by the Holy Spirit. Let's now see an example of this gift in action.

On the morrow, as they went on their journey, and drew nigh unto the city, Peter went up upon the housetop to pray about the sixth hour; and he became very hungry, and would have eaten; but while they made ready, he fell into a trance, and saw heaven opened, and a certain vessel descending unto him, as it had been a great sheet knit at the four corners, and let down to earth; wherein were all manners of four-footed beasts of the earth, and wild beasts, and creeping things, and fowls of the air. And there came a voice to him, rise Peter kill and eat. But Peter said not so, Lord; for I have never eaten anything that is common or unclean. And the voice spake unto him again the second time, what God hath cleansed, that call not thou common. This was done thrice: and the vessel was received up again into heaven. (Acts 10:9–16 KJV)

The vision was extremely necessary in order to transform Peter's mindset to minister to the Gentiles with the purpose of bringing them to Christ, being guided by God against his way of thinking and his Jewish background. The transformation of Peter's mindset was seen in the way how he viewed the Gentiles as opposed to his previous stance. For instance, Cornelius was a Gentile, and Peter was a Jew. This information is important because the Jews considered the Gentiles unclean. But Peter wasted no time telling them that "God hath showed me that I should not call any man common or unclean" (see Acts 10:28).

It's important to note that if the manifestation of the word of wisdom had not occurred, Peter's willingness to go with the messengers would not have taken place. Consequently, the outworking of grace imparted through Peter resulted in the Holy Spirit filling those in Cornelius's household after hearing the word. But not just that alone; they heard them speak with tongues and glorify God (see Acts 10:44–46). To put it another way, an impartation of the word of wisdom edified and blessed Peter and Cornelius's household through the Spirit. Let's now look at another manifestation of grace put into effect through the power of the Spirit.

Gifts of Healings Bless Islanders

As with a word of wisdom, I deem it's important to share with you a concise description of the gifts of healings. First, we need to look at the difference between gifts of healings and miracles. Miracles are instantaneous and usually noticeable to the senses, whereas healings are gradual and does not happen in a short period of time. For instance, in the book of Acts, we read about the gifts of healings imparted through the believer by the Spirit of God.

> And when they were escaped, then they knew that the Island was called Melita, and the barbarous people showed us no little kindness; for they kindled a fire, and received us every one because of the present rain, and because of the cold. And when Paul had gathered a bundle of sticks, and laid them on the fire, there came a viper out of the heat, and fastened on his hand. And when the barbarians saw the venomous beast hang on his hand, they said among themselves, no doubt this man is a murderer, whom though he hath escaped the sea, yet vengeance suffereth not to live. And he shook off the beast into the fire, and felt no harm. Howbeit they looked when he should have swollen, or fallen down dead suddenly; but after they had looked a great while, and saw no harm come to him, they changed their minds, and said that he was a god. In the same quarters were possessions of the chief man of the Island, whose name was Publius; who received us, and lodged us three days courteously. And it came to pass, that the father of Publius lay sick of a fever and of a bloody flux; to whom Paul entered in and prayed, and laid his hands on him, and healed him. So when this was done, others also which had diseases in the Island, came and were healed. (Acts 28:1–9 KJV)

What could have turned out a disaster for Paul and his fellow crew members actually worked out for their good. Romans 8:28 says, "And we know that all things work together for good to those who love God, to those who are the called according to His purpose." Notice I said "worked out for Paul's good." The good works according to verse 28 pertains to those who "love God and are called according to His purpose." Undeniably, Paul was called to carry out God's purpose.

The gifts of healings, which operated through him, were an attestation and manifestation of grace. The healing of Publius's father opened the door for others on the island to receive healing and to witness the tremendous power of God. This shows us how the believer receives grace in the form of a gift, then placed in position to impart grace through the power of the Spirit.

A Word of Knowledge Delivers the King of Israel

It's imperative we look at the differences between a word of wisdom and a word of knowledge. Why is it so important? Because both gifts are closely related in the way they operate. The word of wisdom is a supernatural revelation of the mind and purpose of God communicated by the Holy Spirit. On the other hand, the word of knowledge is a supernatural revelation of the existence or nature of the person or a thing or the knowledge of some event. The difference is knowledge gives us facts while wisdom shows what to do about those facts. Let's look at an instance of a word of knowledge in the Old Testament.

Israel and Syria were at war with one another, and the king of Syria formulated a plan to attack them. However, through a word of knowledge, the prophet Elisha warned and gave details about this attack. The warning and details were repeated again and again in the ears of the King of Israel. In short, a word of knowledge was a spiritual instrument used by God to save his people from the Syrians. This supernatural knowledge really exasperated and infuriated the king. Here's his response concerning this revelation.

> Therefore, the heart of the king of Syria was
> sore troubled for this thing; and he called his ser-
> vants, and said unto them, will ye not shew me

which of us is for the king of Israel? And one of his servants said, none, my Lord O king; but Elisha, the prophet that is in Israel, telleth the king of Israel the words that thou speaketh in thy bedchamber. (2 Kings 6:11–12 KJV)

I thought this account was hilarious to me in a good way because the word of knowledge was so effective that it caused the king to be paranoid. He insisted he had a traitor in his camp. After an interrogation of his soldiers, he was informed that his secret plans were being disclosed by the prophet. This even caused an inconvenience for the king, for it caused him to change all his plans. What saved God's people? It was a supernatural word of knowledge spoken through the prophet Elisha. Once more, we see the grace gifts manifest and impart grace through the believer.

In this account, it was the prophet Elisha. Thank God for his grace and mercy, even in the Old Testament. I will now relate a true story of how a word of knowledge, if operated correctly by the Holy Spirit, can impart grace to an individual walking in disobedience.

In Charisma, John Wimber writes about a remarkable manifestation of a gift of the Spirit. "A man of God once related an account of how God used him in the word of knowledge. "I was once on an airplane when I turned and looked at the passenger across the aisle to see the word "adultery" written across his face in big letters. The letters of course, were only perceptible to spiritual eyes. He caught me looking at him (gaping might be more descriptive) and said, what do you want? As he asked that, a woman's name came clearly into my mind. I leaned over the aisle and asked if the name meant anything to him. His face turned white, and he asked if he could talk to me.

It was a large plane with a bar, so we went there to talk. On the way the Lord spoke to me again, saying, "tell him to turn from this adulterous affair, or I am going to take him." When we got to the bar, I told him that God had told me he was committing adultery, the name of the woman, and that God would take him if he did not cease. He juts melted on the spot and asked about what he should do. I led him through a prayer of repentance and he received Christ."[13]

This story is a great illustration that highlights someone using their spiritual gift for the common good. The attestation and manifestation of the gifts of the Spirit was evident. The outworking was a man repenting and his life spared. Not only was his life spared, but the woman's husband and children, if any, were spared also, avoiding the bitter pain of infidelity. When we surrender to the Holy Spirit and allow Him to use us, we become channels for which God's grace and blessings flow. The Lord is glorified, and people's lives are edified and impacted.

Discerning of Spirits Frees Samaria from Witchcraft

As with all the previous gifts, I would like to give you a simple definition of the discerning of spirits. The discerning of spirits is a gift of the Holy Spirit by which an individual is enabled to see into the spirit world (Holy Spirit, good angels, human spirits, fallen angels, rebellious angels, or evil spirits). Let's look at an example of the discerning of spirits in operation through the Spirit of God.

While Philip was preaching in Samaria, he encountered a man named Simon who for a long time dominated the city of Samaria with

---

[13] Quotation taken from *750 Engaging Illustrations for Preachers, Teachers & Writers*, Craig Brian Larson, "In Charisma, John Wimber writes about a remarkable manifestation of a gift of the Spirit," p.705.

witchcraft and sorcery. After Simon heard the message with signs and wonders following, he immediately became a believer. While all of this was taking place, the apostles, without hesitation, sent for Peter and John. Unfortunately, when Simon saw that through the laying on of apostle's hands, the Holy Ghost was given, he decided to offer them money (see Acts 8:18).

The good news is Peter immediately saw through the inward crookedness and wrong motives of Simon's heart, for he tells him:

> Thy money perish with thee because thou hast thought that the gift of God may be purchased with money, thou hast neither part nor lot in this matter; for thy heart is not right in the sight of God. Repent therefore of this thy wickedness and pray God if perhaps the thoughts of thine heart may be forgiven thee. For I perceive that thou art in the gall of bitterness and in the bond of iniquity. (Acts 8:20–23 KJV)

Notice that Philip had an encounter with Simon first, but for some reason, he was unable to discern this deceitful and manipulative spirit. However, when Peter arrives, his discernment quickly kicks in. What was the difference between the two? In my understanding, Philip operated in other various spiritual gifts while Peter had the gift of discerning of spirits among other gifts. Clearly, the gifts of the Spirit are a manifestation of grace operated through the believer. If the gifts function in an orderly manner, they will bring blessings and grace into a person's life or even a whole city. God's magnificent grace is abundant and available to all who accept it.

Forfeiture of Grace Gifts

Thus far, we explored and looked at a few examples as to why we need to embrace all the spiritual gifts. I believe you would agree that the supernatural spiritual ministry gifts are extremely important as well. All of them have at least four things in common. First, they bring glory to God. Second, they are grace gifts. Third, they edify the believer in Christ. Fourth, they wreak havoc against Satan and his kingdom of darkness.

Now that we know the supernatural spiritual and ministry gifts are grace gifts, we should understand also they cannot be earned or worked for. In a legalistic system, the mindset is that everything has to be worked for or earned. Romans 4:4 says, "Now to him who works, the wages are not counted as grace but as debt." One important thing we must take into account is the word *gift*. In the natural, when a person receives a gift, there is nothing they have to do on their part, except receive.

In subsequent days or months to come, they should also put the gift to use. By doing so, it shows their deep appreciation for the gift as well as the giver. So who is He who gives us spiritual gifts? The Holy Spirit is the One who imparts spiritual grace gifts to us. First Corinthians 12:7, 11 says, "But the manifestation of the Spirit is given to each one for the profit of all… But one and the same Spirit works all these things, distributing to each one as He wills."

Although it's the Holy Spirit's role to impart spiritual gifts, He has been delegated that authority from Jesus, and Jesus has been given authority from the Father. John 16:14–15 says, "He [Holy Spirit] will glorify Me [Jesus], for He [Holy Spirit] will take of what is Mine [Jesus] and declare it to you. All things that the Father has are Mine [Jesus]. Therefore I said that He [Holy Spirit] will take of Mine [Jesus] and declare it to you."

With that being said, the gifts of the Spirit are an impartation of heaven's grace to the believer. But once again, we must accept these gifts of grace by faith and with obedience and thanksgiving, and by doing so, we also accept the Gift-giver. Every Christian will tell you they love the Lord. However, I find it to be an oxymoron to say I love the Lord, but I reject His gifts. For example, take a son or daughter who says they love their father but rejects his gifts. How would the father feel about this? Most natural fathers would be hurt and might say things like, "If my gifts are not good enough for you, then perhaps I am not good enough as well."

It's imperative that the body of Christ accept these supernatural spiritual gifts as the apostle wrote to the believers in 1 Corinthians 1:7, "So that you come short in no gift, eagerly waiting for the revelation of our Lord Jesus Christ." Other translations read, "Therefore you do not lack any spiritual gift as you eagerly wait for our Lord Jesus Christ to be revealed" (NIV). Additionally, we read, "So that you are not lacking in any gift, awaiting eagerly the revelation of our Lord Jesus Christ" (NASB).[14]

---

[14] Quotations taken from Donald Spellman, *Freedom from Spiritual Bondage*, copyright © 2019 by Kingdom House Publishing, Lakebay, Washington, pp. 228–230.

Short Review of God's Grace Manifested through the Believer

- As believers in Christ, we have a responsibility to impart God's grace and mercy that has been given to us to others. Those who have experienced God's grace demonstrate God's grace. The grace that has been given to us is not for us to stockpile or hoard for ourselves. We are called to be channels through which blessings flow.

- God has ordered it that the weaker the earthen vessels, the stronger His power is and that the treasure should be valued more. God has entrusted our weak fragile vessels to carry the light of the Gospel of Christ to the ends of the earth. This is one of the ways the grace of God is manifested through us.

- The more perilous the world becomes, the more intense the darkness will be. Second Timothy 3:13 (KJV) says, "But evil men and seducers shall wax worse and worse, deceiving and being deceived." The darker the world becomes, the more Christians should shine as lights.

- Both salt and light are used to affect certain things. Light affects dark places whiles salt enhances the taste of food and serves as a preserver of meat products. The meaning of salt and light in the natural to us in the Spirit is that Christians should affect those around them.

- Our conversation and speech are very important in our witness among those who are unsaved. We must always discern what to say in our speech among those on the outside. Our lifestyle and walk play a very important role in our witness among those in darkness, but our speech and conversation are just as important.

- Forgiveness is the cornerstone of our relationship with God. It is an essential part of the Gospel message. God has forgiven us through the bloodshed of Jesus and His forgiveness of us demands that we forgive others.

- The supernatural spiritual gifts are grace gifts. We should understand also they cannot be earned nor worked for. In a legalistic system, the mindset is that everything has to be worked for or earned. Romans 4:4 says, "Now to him who works, the wages are not counted as grace but as debt." One important thing we must take into account is the word *gift*. In the natural, when a person receives a gift, there is nothing they have to do on their part except receive.
- It's imperative that the body of Christ accepts these supernatural spiritual gifts as the apostle wrote to the believers in 1 Corinthians 1:7, "So that you come short in no gift, eagerly waiting for the revelation of our Lord Jesus Christ." Other translations read, "Therefore you do not lack any spiritual gift as you eagerly wait for our Lord Jesus Christ to be revealed" (NIV). Additionally, we read, "So that you are not lacking in any gift, awaiting eagerly the revelation of our Lord Jesus Christ" (NASB).

Life Application

We must come to accept that we are channels of blessings with the purpose of reaching the lost and building up others in Christ. God has entrusted us to carry the Gospel to the ends of the earth. He has given us all things according to life and godliness and an abundance of grace for every good work. We are stewards of the mysteries of God. What's more, we have spiritual talents and gifts that edify the Church and that God may be glorified!

Scripture Reference

Ye are the salt of the earth; but if the salt have lost his savor, wherewith shall it be salted? It is thenceforth good for nothing, but to be cast out, and to be trodden under foot of men. Ye are the light of the world; a city that is set on a hill cannot be hid, neither do men light a candle, and put it under a bushel, but on a candlestick; and it giveth light unto all that are in the house. Let your light so shine before men, that they may see your good works, and glorify your Father which is in heaven. (Matthew 5:13–16 KJV)

9

THE SPIRIT OF GRACE

> Anyone who has rejected Moses' law dies
> without mercy on the testimony of two or three
> witnesses. Of how much worse punishment, do
> you suppose, will he be thought worthy who has
> trampled the Son of God underfoot, counted the
> blood of the covenant by which he was sanctified
> a common thing, and insulted the Spirit of Grace?
>
> —Hebrews 10:29

The Holy Spirit's role as it pertains to grace is very important, and not to reference Him would be an injustice and insult. He has an enormous effect in and on the lives of God's people. Not only are we afforded great and inexhaustible promises in God's Word, but we have the assurance of the Spirit of Grace. Remember, Jesus said the Holy Spirit would take what is His and declare it to us (see John 16:15). He is the One that helps us understand what has been freely given to us. First Corinthians 2:12 says, "Now we have received, not the spirit of the world, but the Spirit who is from God, that we might know the things that have been freely given to us by God."

The Spirit of God is also called the Spirit of grace, and we're warned not to abuse Him. The threefold indictment the writer makes is this: first, they had contempt for Christ in trampling Him underfoot; secondly, they rejected the blood-bought covenant as worthless and unholy; and finally, they despised the person and work of the Spirit of grace. To go against God's Word and precepts calls for justice, but when we abuse the Spirit of grace, it calls for punishment (v. 29).

It seems that among the Godhead (Father, Jesus, Holy Spirit), there is an unwavering love and adoration for the Holy Spirit. We find this truth in the Old Testament and New Testament as well. For example, at one point, while the children of Israel were wandering through the desert, they rebelled against the Holy Spirit. Isaiah 63:10 says, "But they rebelled and grieved His Holy Spirit, so He [God] turned Himself against them as an enemy, and He fought against them." These were not wicked nations but His people He turned and fought against. I believe this is His estimate of those who treat and violate His Spirit today.

In the New Testament, we see more of how heaven feels about the Spirit of grace. In the Gospel of Matthew, Jesus sends out a stern warning to the Pharisees, the reason being because they were quick to attribute the works of the Holy Spirit to Satan. We must be very careful not to judge or make mockery of the manifestations of the Holy Spirit. If you have been doing these things out of ignorance, my only advice to you is to repent.

> Therefore, I say to you, every sin and blasphemy will be forgiven men, but the blasphemy against the Spirit will not be forgiven men. Anyone who speaks a word against the Son of Man it will be forgiven Him; but whoever speaks against the Holy Spirit it will not be forgiven Him, neither in this age or in the age to come. (Matthew 12:31)

Notice that Jesus says, "Who speaks a word against the Son of Man it will be forgiven Him." But to sin against the Holy Spirit, there is no forgiveness of sin. As I stated before, the Spirit of grace is very essential and indispensable in the life of the believer. And yet, here's another instance of people insulting the Spirit of grace. In the book of Acts, Peter confronts a husband and wife who did not fully understand the seriousness of their deception in the church.

> But a certain man named Ananias with Sapphira his wife sold a possession, and he kept back part of the proceeds, his wife also being aware of it, and brought a certain part and laid it at the apostles' feet, but Peter said Ananias why has Satan filled your heart to lie to the Holy Spirit and keep back part of the price of the land for yourself. While it remained, was it not your own? And after it was sold, was it not in your own control? Why have you conceived this thing in your heart? You have not lied to men but to God. Then Ananias hearing these words fell down and breathed his last. So great fear came upon all those who heard these things, and the young men arose and wrapped him up, carried him out and buried him.
>
> Then Peter said to her, how is it that you have agreed together to test the Spirit of the Lord? Look, the feet of those who have buried your husband are at the door, and they will carry you out. Then immediately she fell down at his feet and breathed her last. And the young men came in and found her dead, and carrying her out, buried her by her husband. (Acts 5:1–7, 9–10)

Notice according verse 3, it wasn't a lie to God or to Jesus but to the Holy Spirit they tried to deceive, "Satan filled your heart to lie to the Holy Spirit." Unfortunately, Ananias and Sapphira paid a tremendous price for their deception. It's beyond disrespectful to sit passively when the Spirit of grace speaks to our hearts to walk in obedience; it's nothing less than an insult to Him. When considering all the blessings that come through the Spirit of Grace, it should cause us to break out in a praise of thanksgiving. I believe that's why Paul often reflected and wrote to the believers about God's grace.

As many of us have come to understand, words could not express or explain the wisdom of God. Romans 11:33 (KJV) says, "O the depth of the riches both of the wisdom and knowledge of God! How unsearchable are His judgments, and His ways past finding out." Yes, God's blessings afforded to us through grace are simply breathtaking! And who do you suppose transfers these blessings and grace to us? If you said the Spirit of grace, you're absolutely right. He conveys the Lord's grace and blessings to us every day. John 16:13 says, "The Spirit will take from what is mine and make it known to you." At this point, let's look at some of these grace blessings in the chart below before we go to our next topic of discussion.

Grace Blessings	Scriptures Reference
Grace brings salvation through Christ	For by grace you have been saved through faith, and that not of yourselves, it is the gift of God. (Ephesians 2:8–9)
Grace has appeared to all men	For the grace of God that brings salvation has appeared to all men. (Titus 2:11)
Grace changes the lives of men	But by the grace of God I am what I am, and His grace toward me was not in vain, but I labored more abundantly than they all, yet not I, but the grace of God which was with me. (1 Corinthians 15:10)
Grace imparts great blessings	And with great power the apostles gave, to the resurrection of the Lord Jesus, and great grace was upon them all. (Acts 4:33)
Grace brings men to repentance	And I will pour on the house of David and on the inhabitants of Jerusalem the Spirit of grace and supplication; then they will look on Me [Christ] whom they pierced. Yes they will mourn for Him as one mourns for his only son, and grieve for Him as one grieves for a firstborn. (Zechariah 12:10)

Grace gives us strength	You therefore, my son be strong in the grace that is in Christ Jesus. (2 Timothy 2:1)
Grace imparts the riches of God	But God, who is rich in mercy, because of His great love with which He loved us, even when we were dead in trespasses, made us alive together with Christ (by grace you have been saved). (Ephesians 2:4–7)
Grace gives those who are called the ability to preach.	To me, who am less than the least of all saints, this grace was given, that I should preach among the Gentiles the unsearchable riches of Christ. (Ephesians 3:8)
Grace brings us hope	Now may our Lord Jesus Christ Himself, and our God and Father, who has loved us and given us everlasting consolation and good hope by grace. (2 Thessalonians 2:16)
Grace imparts great boldness	Nevertheless, brethren I have written more boldly to you on some points, as reminding you, because of the grace given to me by God. (Romans 15:15).
Grace gives us strength for service	But by the grace of God I am what I am, and His grace toward me was not in vain; but I labored more abundantly than they all, yet not I but the grace of God which was with me. (1 Corinthians 15:10)
Grace gives us endurance through circumstances	And He said to me, My grace is sufficient for you, for My strength is made perfect in weakness. Therefore most gladly I will rather boast in my infirmities that the power of Christ may rest upon me. (2 Corinthians 12:9)
Grace helps us in time of need	Let us therefore come boldly to the throne of grace, that we may obtain mercy and find grace to help in time of need. (Hebrews 4:16)

Grace enabled Christ to suffer and die on the cross for us	But we see Jesus, who was made a little lower than the angels, for the suffering of death crowned with glory and honor, that He by the grace of God, might taste death for everyone. (Hebrews 2:9)
Grace helps us to render service in the kingdom	Therefore, since we are receiving a kingdom which cannot be shaken, let us have grace, by which we may serve God acceptably with reverence and godly fear. (Hebrews 12:28)

Sweet Communion

The Holy Spirit longs to commune and fellowship with us. Second Corinthians 13:14 says, "The grace of the Lord Jesus Christ and the love God, and the communion of the Holy Spirit be with you all, Amen." There are five things we can grasp from the word "communion" in relation to the Holy Spirit.

- The word *communion* means presence. John 14:17 says, "The Spirit of truth whom the world cannot receive, because it neither sees nor knows him, for He dwells with you and will be in you."
- The word *communion* means fellowship. In the Old Testament, David recognized and felt the Holy Spirit's presence. Psalm 51:11 says, "Do not cast me away from your presence, and do not take your Holy Spirit from me."
- The word *communion* means participation, which speaks of the Holy Spirit as our partner. An example of this is seen in Acts whereas in the beginning of the church, there rose an issue concerning the Gentile's brethren having to be circumcised. Here's what happened. Acts 15:28 (KJV) says, "For it seemed good to the Holy Spirit and to us, to lay upon you no greater burden than these necessary things." Notice the phrase "the Holy Spirit and us." This

represents the fact they were coworking together or were in participation with.

- The word *communion* means intimacy. You'll never experience a deep love for Christ without the Holy Spirit who brings intimacy. Romans 5:5 says, "Now hope does not disappoint, because the Love of God has been poured out in our hearts by the Holy Spirit who was given to us." It's virtually impossible to love God without the Holy Spirit.
- The word *communion* means friendship. A friend is one who comes alongside and help you. John 14:16 says, "And I will pray the Father, and He will give you another helper (comforter), that He may abide with you forever." You can share your deepest feelings with him, and He will not tell a soul.

One very important question that is often asked is, how can I please God? The answer is simple. We're incapable of pleasing Him in our flesh. Paul said that "those who are in the flesh cannot please God" (see Romans 8:8). In order to please God, we must surrender to the Holy Spirit. There are no other options. In Paul's letter to the believers at Rome, he made this very clear by saying, "There is therefore now no condemnation to those who are in Christ Jesus, who do not walk according to the flesh, but according to the Spirit" (Romans 8:1). There are things you'll never accomplish apart from the Holy Spirit's help, and here are just a few of them.

- It is impossible to know God without the Holy Spirit. Romans 8:16 says, "The Spirit itself beareth witness with our spirit, that we are the children of God."
- It is impossible to know the truth without the Holy Spirit. John 14:26, 16:13 says:

> But the Comforter which is the Holy Spirit, whom the Father will send in my name, He shall teach you all things, and bring all things to your remembrance, whatsoever I have said unto

you… Howbeit when He, the Spirit of truth is come He will guide you into all truth; for He shall hear, that shall He speak, and He will shew you things to come.

- It is impossible to stay free of sin without the Holy Spirit. Romans 8:1–5 says:

  There is therefore now no condemnation to them which are in Christ Jesus, who walk not after the flesh, but after the Spirit, for the law of the Spirit of life in Christ Jesus hath made me free from the law of sin and death… For they that are after the flesh do mind the things of the flesh; but they that are after the Spirit the things of the Spirit.

- It is impossible to pray without the Holy Spirit. Romans 8:26–27 (KJV) says:

  Likewise the Spirit also helpeth our infirmities; for we know not what we should pray for as we ought; but the Spirit itself maketh intercession for us with groanings which cannot be uttered. And He that searcheth the hearts knoweth what is the mind of the Spirit, because He maketh intercession for the saints according to the will of God.

In the initial stages of our walk with God, a change must occur first on the inside. Unfortunately, many Christians are taught to believe that the outside of a person's body has to be transformed first. The truth is the inside has to be cleansed, and then what has occurred will register on the outside, for David said, "Create in me a clean heart, O God; and renew a right Spirit within me" (Psalm 51:10 KJV).

A good illustration is an automobile transmission. I can recall many years ago my pickup truck started jerking while on my way to work. In subsequent days to come, this would be the norm. Finally, I took it to an automobile mechanic, only to find out that the internal mechanisms were going bad. The mechanic told me that in order for the transmission to work again, some of the components must be replaced. So I agreed, and he replaced the parts that were causing the vehicle to skip and jerk.

In comparison, if we're to have a victorious walk in Christ, our heart's condition must be right. In order for this to happen, we must surrender to the Holy Spirit and allow the Word of God to cleanse and purify us. Christ must be evident in our lives. Paul stressed this as he wrote to the believers at Galatia. Galatians 4:19 (KJV) says, "My little children of whom I travail in birth again until Christ be formed in you."

Paul had led the believers to Christ and helped them become spiritually mature. So naturally, his concern for them was that Christ be formed in them. This would only come into fruition by the Holy Spirit imparting righteousness and holiness in them. To have Christ formed in them meant having His character traits, truth, holiness, righteousness, love, compassion, integrity, and so on. It would also include His passion for the lost, and last but not least, His obedience to the Father.

A Royal Adoption

The greatest experience we have in Christendom is the moment we receive Christ as our personal Lord and Savior. At that very moment, we are adopted in the family of God. John 1:12–13 (KJV) says, "But as many as received Him to them He gave the right to become children of God to those who believe in His name, who were born not of blood, nor of the will of man, but of God."

We read also in Ephesians 1:5–6 that says, "Having predestined us to adoption as sons by Jesus Christ to Himself, according to the good pleasure of His will, to the praise of the glory of His grace, by which He made us accepted in the Beloved." We made the commitment, but it's the Spirit of Grace who brings us into adoption.

Adoption is an act of God's grace by which sinful people are brought into His redeemed family. In the New Testament, the Greek word translated adoption literally means placing as a son. It is a legal term that expresses the process by which a man brings another person into his family, endowing him with the status and privileges of a biological son or daughter. My understanding of spiritual adoption points to two great truths; both are transferred through the Spirit of grace.

- First, we are adopted into God's family with all privileges and responsibilities as with a natural family. Romans 8:15–16 (KJV) says, "For ye have not received the spirit of bondage again to fear; but ye have received the Spirit of adoption, whereby we cry, Abba, Father. The Spirit itself beareth witness with our spirit, that we are the children of God."

  In Roman culture, the adopted person lost all rights in his old family and gained all the rights of a legitimate child in his new family. He became a full heir of his father's estate. Likewise, when a person becomes a Christian, he or she gains all the privileges and benefits of a child in God's family.

- Secondly, the adoption points to the transformation of our bodies when we receive the inheritance. Romans 8:23 (KJV) says, "And not only they, but ourselves also which have the first fruits of the Spirit, even we ourselves groan within ourselves, waiting for the adoption, to wit the redemption of our body."[15]

There are times we may not feel like we belong to the family of God, but the Holy Spirit is there to remind us of our adoption.

---

[15] Quotations taken from Donald Spellman, *Freedom from Spiritual Bondage*, copyright © 2019, by Kingdom House Publishing, Lakebay, Washington, pp. 187.

Galatians 4:6 (KJV) says, "And because ye are sons, God hath sent forth the Spirit of His Son into our hearts, crying Abba Father."

Sanctification a Result of the Holy Spirit

Most of us have been taught to believe that our salvation and justification are given through the grace of God and is received by faith alone. Conversely, there are those who believe our sanctification must be worked out by fleshly efforts. What's more, some believe that the scuffle between good and evil in one's life is a long and agonizing road that is worked out by fleshly efforts. This is what the false teachers were leading the Galatians to believe (see (Galatians 3:1–3).

The believers started out in the Spirit but immediately began seeking perfection in the flesh. Paul had taught them the doctrine of grace in their salvation experience. He made this clear as he wrote to the church at Ephesus, admonishing them that "by grace you been saved through faith, and that not of yourselves; it is the gift of God, not of works, lest anyone should boast" (see Ephesians 2:8–9). As I pointed out earlier throughout the book of Galatians, Paul made a strong argument for this claim. He also stressed the fact that sanctification is just as much a gift as their justification and salvation.

Additionally, in his writings to the Galatians, Paul brought out several facts concerning sanctification. One important fact was that sanctification is a part of redemption which was a result of Christ's atoning work at the cross, and therefore, we must see it as a gift of grace. Sanctification is connected to the purchase of Christ's blood and part of our redemption. Hebrews 10:14–16 says, "For by one offering he hath perfected forever them that are sanctified, but the Holy Spirit also witnesses to us; for after He said before, this is the covenant that I will make with them after those days, says the Lord; I will put my laws into their hearts, and in their minds I will write them."

The word perfected in the Greek is *teteleioken*, which means completed. The process of sanctification is a completed work at the cross when Jesus died on our behalf but is worked out in our lives through the Holy Spirit. Jeremiah's covenant prophesies had come to pass. He had prophesied the same thing earlier in regard to how God would change the heart of man. Jeremiah 31:33 (KJV) says, "But this shall be the covenant that I will make with the house of Israel; after those days, saith the Lord, I will put my law in their inward parts, and write it in their hearts; and will be their God, and they shall be my people."

This is precisely what happened when Jesus sent back the Holy Spirit to indwell us. We have the power and assurance within to live holy and acceptable lives before God. Bear in mind this is with the Helper and not our fleshly efforts. By surrendering to God and putting on the Lord Jesus Christ, it's at that moment we're put in position to be delivered from all guilt, power, and punishment of sin. Colossians 1:13 says, "He [Christ] has delivered us from the power of darkness and conveyed us into the kingdom of the Son of His love, in whom we have redemption through His blood, the forgiveness of sins." Jesus now places us in position of being holy and righteous, and note I said Jesus, not us.

It goes without saying that sanctification is through the Holy Spirit and not through struggle and fleshly efforts. The following verse is misunderstood by many who feel it's their task to produce holiness and sanctification. Galatians 5:17–18 (NIV) says, "For the sinful nature desires what is contrary to the Spirit, and the Spirit what is contrary to the sinful nature. They are in conflict with each other, so that you do not do what you want. But if you are led by the Spirit you are not under the law." In some translations, the small "s" in the word Spirit gave the impression that the conflict was between man's flesh and man's spirit.

Let's examine this scripture for a moment and see where the confusion started. In verse 17, Paul said "so you do not do what you want." If we interpret the word *Spirit* in the scripture to mean human spirit instead of Holy Spirit, the statement "you do not do what you want" would leave us doomed to failure. The good news is by replacing the small "s" with a capital "S" shows it's the Holy Spirit who wars against the flesh and not our human spirit.

When we surrender and obey the Holy Spirit, by refusing to submit to the flesh, He automatically fights our battles for us. This would also include temptations in our flesh. We must bear in mind "the battle is not ours but God's" (see 2 Chronicles 20:15). We all know and understand how the enemy comes to suggest things to our minds and tries to convince us to walk in the flesh. I will now give you an example of a suggestion by the devil and what we can do against his deceptions.

For example, let's say Satan speaks a suggestive thought into your ears, saying "You think you are saved, but you're the same as you were some years ago." Or he says to you, "Nothing has changed in your life, and you think you're pleasing God." Finally, he says to you, "You have been deceived." So for a short period, you have accepted these lies. For a short period, you're discouraged and try to fight against your weakness and struggles in your own strength. Then suddenly, you hear the voice of the Spirit telling you, "This is not your battle but the Lord's."

Upon hearing this, you confidently tell Satan that "you're not entertaining his deceptions and lies." You go on to say, "You're casting all your cares on Jesus and placing all your burdens on Him." You rebuke the devil by saying "you have nothing to do with him and that you have given over your weakness, battles, and temptations to Christ." You declare to him that "the Holy Spirit will deal with all his false accusations and conquer all the demonic forces that are against you." That is the essence of surrendering to the Spirit of grace and allowing Him to sanctify and keep and protect you.

The end purpose in which the Spirit of God is working is to not develop in us a set of human virtues or high qualities that we can call our own and have bragging rights but to form Christ in us so that we can be constantly dependent upon Him. Romans 8:29 says, "For whom He [God] foreknew, He also predestined to be conformed to the image of His Son." This was Paul's belief of what sanctification meant in his letter to the Galatians.

He had labored fervently with the believers until Christ was formed in them. Galatians 4:19 says, "My little children, for whom I labor in birth again until Christ is formed in you." The life we live is maintained in union with Jesus. It's not even our faith but the faith of the Son of God, which is manifested in us by virtue of His substitution for us through which He gave Himself to be instead of us. Galatians 2:20 says, "I have been crucified with Christ; it is no longer I who live, but Christ lives in me; and the life which I now live in the flesh I live by faith in the Son of God, who loved me and gave Himself for me." Here's a short story from A. B. Simpson that will help shed light on this.

> A farmer boy, once listening to an exposition of this beautiful promise, "My yoke is easy and my burden is light" (Matthew 11:30), said that his father always fixed the ring in their yoke close to one end, and he put the short end of the yoke on the big ox, and the long end on the weak one. The result was that the big one drew nearly all the load, and the little one just walked along and sort of felt as if he were helping. That is the sort yoke Jesus puts on us. He takes the heavy end and lets us have just enough to feel that we are in the partnership, but the burden rests on Him. Blessed partnership! Blessed Yokefellow! Blessed rest to sing:
>
> Not I, but Christ, my every need supplying,
> Not I but Christ, my strength and Health to be;
> Christ, only Christ, for body, soul and spirit,
> Christ, only Christ, live Thou Thy life in me.[16]

I had stated earlier that most people have been taught to believe sanctification and the struggle between good and evil is a long painful road with an experience of negative circumstances. It does not

---

[16] Quotation taken from Dr. Albert B. Simpson, *The Christ in the Bible Commentary, copyright © 2009,* by. First Wing Spread Publishers, Camp Hill, Pennsylvania, Book 3, page 362, story No. 5.

come through an act of struggling against evil but by receiving and putting on Christ (light of the world) and allowing that light in us to dispel darkness. For example, when we enter a dark room, we quickly flip the switch to turn on the light. We know that once the light is turned on, darkness has to flee.

In other words, the light saturates the entire room. In a similar way, darkness has to vacate our heart and lives when the Spirit of grace enters in. God saves us from the pressure and temptation of sin. He occupies our mind and fills our heart with something stronger and higher, hence by this powerful influence, evil is destroyed, the soul is purified and preserved. Galatians 2:20 (KJV) says, "I am crucified with Christ; nevertheless, I live; yet not I, but Christ liveth in me; and the life which I now live in the flesh I live by the faith of the Son of God, who loved me, and gave Himself for me." To better understand this, I will now share an illustration with you.

> Take a young boy with a dangerous knife in his hand, his mother is unable to convince him to hand it over to her. Afraid that a sudden movement might cause him to hurt himself, she calls for someone to assist her. She tells the person to go to the kitchen and bring back some candy. Walking quietly, he approaches the young boy with the candy to distract him. As the candy come close to his eyes, he starts to reach out his hands for it, and before he knows what happened, the knife dropped unexpectedly out of his hands, and his mother swiftly grabs it and puts it safely away. In turn, the knife that was once in the boy's hand is replaced with sweet candy.

This illustration shows us precisely how sanctification works. God gives us something better, and He overcomes evil with good. Those who have put on Christ have made provision to have the flesh put under subjection. Paul wrote to the believers at Rome, encouraging them to "put ye on the Lord Jesus Christ, and make not provision for the flesh, to fulfill the lusts thereof" (see Romans 13:14).

When an individual is filled with the Spirit of God, he gladly gives up a life of sin, and everything is counted as loss compared to the excellence of knowing Christ Jesus. In addition, this is what Paul meant in Galatians 5:16, "live by the Spirit, and you will not gratify the desires of the sinful nature." The key to sanctification is to put on Christ, to be filled with His presence, His love, His joy, His power, and allow Him to destroy sin through the power of the Holy Spirit. John 16:8 says, "And when He come, He will convict the world of sin, and of righteousness, and of Judgment."

Comforts and Leads Us

The Spirit of grace not only imparts spiritual blessings, convicts of sin, righteousness, and judgment, but He walks alongside us as Comforter. The name "Comforter" denotes "paraclete." A transliteration of the Greek word *parakletos* means "one who speaks in favor of as an intercessor, advocate, or legal assistant." In short, the Holy Spirit is called alongside to help and empower us for carrying out the will of God.

Jesus was fully aware when He departed, the disciples would need some help. He was not going to leave them in the wildness of life to survive on their own. He knew it would have been virtually impossible for them to stand alone in the midst of spiritual serpents and wolves. So He gave them this encouraging promise. John 16:7 (KJV) says, "Nevertheless I tell you the truth; it is expedient for you that I go away; for if I go not away, the Comforter [Holy Spirit] will not come unto you; but if I depart, I will send him unto you."

Likewise, so that we're able to resist sin and endure the perils of life, Jesus understood we needed help as well. He has not left us in this troublesome and unstable world to fight our battles alone. He has made provision by asking the Father to send back the Comforter to live in us who are saved. John 14:16 (KJV) says, "And I will pray the Father, and He shall give you another comforter, that He may abide with you forever."

It's encouraging knowing no matter where God sends us, He will make sure we're in the right place, doing the right things. We don't have to fear or dread, knowing we have the Spirit of God on our side. We have the security and assurance we need. He will not allow us to be shipwrecked. The Comforter played an important role in the ministry Paul and Timothy as they were ministering throughout regions. At one point, they "were forbidden of the Holy Spirit to preach the word in Asia" (see Acts 16:6).

There are a multitude of weary warriors in the body of Christ. Some are depressed, hopeless, oppressed, frustrated, badly wounded, and living with bitterness and unforgiveness. However, there is an answer to their predicament. They must allow the Holy Spirit to govern their lives. Remember, Jesus told the disciples He wasn't going to leave them as orphans. In short, He wasn't going to leave them without help and alone. There are three things we should embrace concerning the role of the Holy Spirit also known as the Spirit of grace.

- First, the Holy Spirit imparts strength we need to persevere and endure. Ephesians 3:16 (AMP) says, "May He grant you out of the rich treasury of His glory to be strengthen and reinforced with mighty power in the inner man by the Holy Spirit Himself indwelling your innermost being and personality."
- Secondly, the Holy Spirit gives us power to carry out God's purpose and plans, primarily to witness and be a witness. Acts 1:8 (KJV) says, "But you shall receive power (ability, efficiency and might) when the Holy Spirit has come upon you, and you shall be my witnesses in Jerusalem and all Judea and Samaria and to all the ends (the very bounds) of the earth." We read also Acts 10:38 (KJV) that says, "How God anointed Jesus of Nazareth with the Holy Ghost and with power, who went about doing good and healing all who were oppressed of the Devil, for God was with him."

- Thirdly, the Holy Spirit gives us power over our circumstances, past experiences, and over all the works of the enemy. In the Gospel of Matthew, the Holy Spirit had just rested on Jesus, empowering Him for service (see Matthew 3:16). The same Holy Spirit that empowered Him for service led Him into the wilderness to be tempted of the devil and, should I say, to defeat the devil (see Matthew 4:1–11). Jesus promised through the power of the Spirit to give victory over the enemy as well. Luke 10:19 (KJV) says, "Behold I give unto you power to tread on serpents and scorpions and over all the power of the enemy and nothing shall by any means hurt you."

It's virtually impossible for the body of Christ to fulfill its purpose if preoccupied with past wounds, cares of life, frustration, discouragement, hopelessness, and so on. This sort of reminds me of the Coast Guard. One of their job descriptions is search and rescue. Unfortunately, it's likely many of the Coast Guard personnel are preoccupied in garrison, fixing broken down vehicles. But what if a distress call comes in while they're distracted with mechanical issues? It would be devastating for those poor souls needing rescue at sea.

In comparison, if we ignore the role of the Holy Spirit and are occupied with personal problems, we're ineffective in our mission to help those in need. Jesus told the disciples that it was "expedient for you that I go away, for if I go not away, the Comforter [Holy Spirit] will not come unto you; but if I depart, I will send him unto you" (see John 16:7). The NIV translation says, "It is to your advantage." What was Jesus saying? Remember, Jesus was in an earthly body and was limited by time and space when he told them this. People could not physically touch him unless they were in His path. However, things have changed as a result of the Holy Spirit indwelling the believer.

Since Jesus sent back the Holy Spirit, we have the privilege of carrying out more work and affecting more lives through the power of the Spirit. John 14:12 says, "Most assuredly I say to you, He who believes in Me, the works that I do he will do also and greater works than these he will do because I go to my Father." Without His power and strength, we're not able to affect lives and carry out ministry assignments. Let me ask you a question. Are you embracing those things the Holy Spirit was sent back here to accomplish? If so, that means you're walking in the Spirit and are cultivating the fruit that comes from Him. Galatians 5:22–23 says, "But the fruit of the Spirit is love, joy, peace, longsuffering, gentleness, goodness, faith, meekness, temperance [self-control]; against such there is no law." The chart below shows the fleshly sins and the outworking of spiritual fruit as a result of the Spirit of grace.

Sins of the Flesh	Spiritual Fruit	Outworking of Spiritual Fruit
Fear, Hatred, Malice Revenge, Un-forgiveness	Love	"For God hath not given us the Spirit of fear, but of Power and of love and of a sound mind" (2 Timothy 1:7 KJV). Love is the bond of perfection (see Colossians 3:14).
Sadness, Wretchedness, Unhappiness	Joy	God has given us joy through the Holy Spirit. The moment we're filled with the Holy Spirit, there is immediate joy which follows. The Spirit has reached down in the crevices of that individual soul and untie knots that has been coiled up for years.
Anxiety, Depression, Frustration, Hopelessness	Peace	To have peace does not mean the absence of problems but the presence of the Holy Spirit and knowing God is in control. We can have peace when we are faced with life's difficulties.

Impatience, Critical, Un-forgiveness Judgmental	Longsuffering	The Holy Spirit has given us longsuffering (a tolerance for others). People in this life who will try our patience with insults and malice. Their mouth will be a constant barrage of criticism and slander. But thanks to the Holy Spirit who gives us the fruit of longsuffering.
Anger, Malice	Gentleness	The Holy Spirit has given us gentleness [kindness]. The original Greek word *chrestos* is translated good, kind, easy and gracious. We are moved with concern and consideration for others. The word *kindness* speaks of compassion, consideration, benevolence, thoughtfulness and helpfulness.
Selfishness, Self-centeredness	Goodness	The Holy Spirit has given us goodness. The Greek noun word is *chretotes* and denotes a sense of kindness of heart or act. It also means the ability to show compassion and generosity toward others (see Philippians 2:3–4). When we are filled with the fruit of goodness, we become people who are generous. Our hearts become open to the cares and sufferings that people face in life.

Instability, Unfaithfulness, Wavering, Uncertainty	Faith	The Holy Spirit has given us the fruit of faithfulness. He helps us to be rooted and grounded in the things of God. We become people who are dependable, loyal and stable. To better understand faithfulness, we must understand how God deals with his children. He is a faithful God!
Harshness, Ruggedness, Unkindness, Insensitivity	Meekness	The Holy Spirit has given us the fruit of gentleness. It Cruelty speaks of kindness, consideration, a spirit of fairness and compassion. Paul in his letter to the believers at Philippi told them to let their, "gentleness be known to all men, the Lord us at hand" (see (Philippians 4:5).
Out of Control, Lust Greed Gluttony	Temperance (Self-control)	The Holy Spirit has given us the fruit of temperance (self-control); able to restrain ourselves in every area of our lives. This also speaks of control of one's actions or emotions by the will. Every believer that has this fruit is governed by God, not by self.

The Holy Spirit's effect upon our lives is very crucial if we are going to have victory over life circumstances. He was sent to heal us of our past, guarantee our future, and liberate us to experience the abundant life. Second Corinthians 3:17 (AMP) says, "Now the Lord is the Spirit and where the Spirit of the Lord is, there is liberty, emancipation from bondage and freedom."

Short Review of the Spirit of Grace

- Not only are we afforded great and inexhaustible promises in God's Word, but we have the assurance of the Spirit of Grace. Remember, Jesus said the Holy Spirit would take what is His and declare it to us (John 16:15).

- Unfortunately, many Christians are taught to believe that the outside of a person's body has to be transformed first. The truth is the inside has to be cleansed, and then what has occurred will register on the outside, for David said, "Create in me a clean heart, O God; and renew a right Spirit within me" (Psalm 51:10 KJV).

- To have Christ formed in us means having His character traits, truth, holiness, righteousness, love, compassion, integrity, and so on. It would also include His passion for the lost and certainly His obedience to the Father.

- The greatest experience we have in Christendom is the moment we receive Christ as our personal Lord and Savior. At that very moment, we are adopted in the family of God. John 1:12–13 (KJV) says, "But as many as received Him to them He gave the right to become children of God to those who believe in His name, who were born not of blood, nor of the will of man, but of God."

- Sanctification is a part of redemption which was a result of Christ's atoning work at the cross, and therefore, we must see it as a gift of grace. Sanctification is connected to the purchase of Christ's blood and part of our redemption. Hebrews 10:14–16 says, "For by one offering he hath perfected forever them that are sanctified, but the Holy Spirit also witnesses to us; for after He said before, this is the covenant that I will make with them after those days, says the Lord; I will put my laws into their hearts, and in their minds I will write them."

- The end purpose in which the Spirit of God is working is to not develop in us a set of human virtues or high qualities that we can call our own and have bragging rights but to form Christ in us so that we can be constantly dependent upon Him. Romans 8:29 says, "For whom He [God] foreknew, He also predestined to be conformed to the image of His Son." This was Paul's ideal of sanctification in which he had addressed the Galatians.

Life's Application

The Spirit of Grace helps us to know who we are in Christ and what we have in Christ. He gives us knowledge of the things freely given to us by God. Without Him, we would not have knowledge of our spiritual inheritance in Christ. What's more, we would not have a revelation about our spiritual armor as well. Jesus sending back the *Holy Spirit* unfolds another important thing we should grasp and understand, and that is He did not leave us powerless and helpless against Satan's attacks or the spiritual equipment to help others. He has given us divine supernatural help through the Spirit of Grace.

Scripture Reference

However, when He [Spirit of grace], the Spirit of truth, has come He will guide you into all truth; for He will not speak on His own authority, but whatever He hears He will speak; and He will tell you things to come. He will glorify Me, for He will take of what is Mine and declare it to you. All things that the Father has are Mine. Therefore, I said that He will take of Mine and declare it to you. (John 16:13–15)

10

THRONE OF GRACE

> Seeing then that we have a great High Priest that is passed into the heavens, Jesus the Son of God; let us hold fast our profession, for we have not an high priest which cannot be touched with the feelings of our infirmities; but was in all points tempted like as we are, yet without sin. Let us therefore come boldly unto the throne of grace that we may obtain mercy, and find grace to help in time of need.
>
> —Hebrews 4:14–16 KJV

Under the Old Covenant, the priests would enter the tabernacle and into the Holy of Holies. Moses had to approach Mount Sinai with all the terror and dread of it. The good news is all of these things are done away with by Christ. Thundering, lightning, voices, and the sound of trumpets have now ceased. What we hear now when approaching the throne of grace is a still small voice. God is accessible and willing to exercise His power in all our circumstances because Jesus is now seated at the throne of grace on His right hand.

Romans 5:1–2 says, "Therefore, having been justified by faith, we have peace with God through our Lord Jesus Christ, through whom also we have access by faith into this grace in which we stand, and rejoice in hope of the glory of God." As a result of Christ entering once again into God's presence, we can now approach the throne of grace. He is able to sympathize with us in all the circumstances of life. Why? Because He was made perfect through His suffering, Hebrews 2:10 says, "For it was fitting for Him [Jesus] for whom are all things, in bringing many sons to glory, to make the captain of their salvation perfect through sufferings."

Do you know our prayers can be hindered when we approach the throne of grace? One way is due to unforgiveness. It can absolutely hinder us from having our petitions granted from God. This is an area many believers in Christ overlook. If our prayers are hindered because of unforgiveness, Jesus has the remedy. Matthew 5:23–24 says, "Therefore if you bring your gift [offering] to the altar, and there remember that your brother has something against you, leave your gift [offering] there before the altar and go your way, first be reconciled to your brother and then come and offer your gift [offering]."

God will not honor our prayers when we have offended our fellow believers and do not ask for forgiveness. He has set forth some conditions we must meet in regard to unforgiveness. In the Gospel of Mark, Jesus gives us this condition, "And whenever you stand praying, if you have anything against anyone, forgive him, that you Father in heaven may also forgive you your trespasses, but if you do not forgive, neither will your Father in heaven forgive your trespasses" (Mark 11:25–26). It's imperative when entering the throne of grace, we have put ourselves in position to receive by not allow anything to hinder us.

One of the greatest privileges as believers is to know when we pray, God will hear and answer us. However, we must know how to approach the Father. Here are four ways we should approach the throne of grace.

- *First, we must approach the throne of grace with godly fear and reverent submission.* When Jesus spent time with the Father in prayer, He always approached Him with godly fear and reverent submission. If Jesus approached the Father with humility, we should follow His example. Hebrews 5:7 says, "Who in the days of His flesh, when He had offered up prayers and supplications, with vehement cries and tears to Him who was able to save Him from death, and was heard because of His Godly fear." The NIV translation says, "During the days of Jesus life on earth, He offered up prayers and petitions with loud cries and tears to the one who could save Him from death, and He was heard because of reverent submission." It's important to note that reverent submission speaks of a willingness to do what God wants and not what we want.

- *Secondly, we must approach the throne of grace in faith.* Hebrews 11:6 (NIV) says, "Without faith it is impossible to please God because anyone who comes to Him must believe that He exists and that He rewards those who earnestly seek Him." It's not enough just to believe only God exists. We must also believe He will reward us when ask from Him. We read also in Matthew 21:22 (KJV) that says, "And whatever things you ask in prayer, believing you will receive."

- *Thirdly, we must approach the throne of grace in Jesus's name.* John 16:23 says, "And in that day you will ask me nothing, most assuredly, I say to you whatever you ask the Father in my name He will give you. Until now you have asked nothing in my name, ask and you will receive that your joy may be full." When we pray in the name of Jesus, we are coming to God on the basis of what Jesus has done on our behalf. Additionally, when we pray to the Father in Jesus's name, we come on the basis of who Jesus is and not who we are. Jesus has made us acceptable to God (Romans 5:1–2).

Moreover, when we come in the name of Jesus, we come with Him as our High Priest and Advocate. First John 2:1 says, "My little children, these things I write to you, so that you may not sin. And if anyone sins, we have an advocate with the Father, Jesus Christ the righteous." The word translated advocate literally means "someone called in alongside to help us and to plead our cause."

- *Fourthly, we must approach the throne of grace boldly.* Hebrews 4:16 says, "Let us therefore come boldly to the throne of grace, that we may obtain mercy and find grace to help in time of need." The NASB translation says, "Therefore let us draw near with confidence to the throne of grace so that we may receive mercy and find grace to help in time of need." Since prayer is our approach to God, we must come with confidence and boldness. When we approach God boldly, it means we are approaching Him with confidence and without condemnation. Confidence and full assurance suggest boldness, based upon the fact that the blood of Jesus has been shed and has been sprinkled in the presence of God. The blood is now speaking on our behalf.
- Finally, we must approach the throne of grace with the right motive. John 14:13–14 (KJV) says, "And whatever you ask in my name, that I will do that the Father may be glorified in the Son. If you ask anything in my name, I will do it." Jesus said, "The Father may be glorified in the Son." The right motive for praying is that the answer to our prayers may bring glory to God. God searches the thoughts and intents of our hearts and discerns our motives. He is not merely concerned with what we ask for when we pray. He is also concerned as to why we want it (see James 4:3).

Jesus Our Great High Priest

Jesus is our High Priest. This encourages and aids in our confidence when we approach the throne of grace. The throne is not just a throne of judgment but a throne of grace and mercy. The throne of grace speaks of hope and encouragement, even to the worst of sinners. When we're in need, we find ourselves often at the throne of grace. Why the throne of grace? We realize our dependency is on God alone, knowing we're not worthy of receiving from Him.

The thing we must bear in mind is God's grace cannot be earned or achieved, only received by faith. We have a High Priest in the heavenlies who stand and act on our behalf. Hebrews 3:1 (KJV) says, "Wherefore, holy brethren partakers of the heavenly calling, consider the Apostle and High Priest of our profession, Christ Jesus." To better understand Christ as our Great High Priest, let's look at the functions of natural high priests.

The high priest is appointed and set apart by God to minister before God and to man. As being a man, he could relate to human weakness and minister to those who go astray. He would offer sacrifices for His own sins as well as those of the people (see Leviticus 4:3–21). In short, a good description that would describe him is one that is totally involved and concerned with the needs of the people. The high priest's special garments represented and symbolized his function as mediator between God and the people.

The high priest was Israel's advocate before God and God's spokesman to the people. The most important responsibility of the high priest was to conduct the service on the Day of the Atonement, the tenth day of the seventh month each year. On this day, he alone entered the Holy Place behind the veil before God. Having made sacrifice for himself and for the people, he brought the blood into the Holy of Holies and sprinkled it on the mercy seat, God's throne. Jesus is compared to this particular ministry of the high priest for us (see Hebrews 9:1–28).

When Jesus became a man of the seed of Abraham, it was at that point He became a faithful and a merciful High Priest. As the Son of God sent into humanity, Christ does not falter nor hesitate from identifying Himself with His own. We are now called His brethren. The defeat of Satan and death shows the atoning work of Jesus was very effective. We now have all the benefits of what a natural high priest offered and more with Christ (see Hebrews 2:11–18).

The ministry of the high priest was specifically in place because of the sins of the people. His responsibility was to open and maintain relations of friendship and fellowship between an offended God and a sinful people. This is seen under the New Covenant provided through the grace of God. Let's look at those for a moment.

- As our Great High Priest, Jesus offered Himself as a sacrifice. The most important work of Jesus Christ was to die in our place. Isaiah 53:6 (KJV) says, "All we like sheep have gone astray; we have turned everyone to his own way; and the Lord hath laid on Him [Jesus] the iniquity of us all." It wasn't righteous or just people He died for but unrighteous, ungodly, and unjust people. First Peter 3:18 (KJV) says, "For Christ also hath once suffered for sins, the just for the unjust, that He might bring us to God, being put to death in the flesh, but quickened by the Spirit."

- The natural high priests offered animal blood that could never take sin away, but Christ died to take away our sins. Hebrews 10:3–4 (KJV) says, "But in those sacrifices there is a remembrance again made of sins every year, for it is possible that the blood of bulls and of goats should take away sins." Jesus offered His own blood. Hebrews 9:11–12 (KJV) says, "But Christ being come an high priest of good things to come, by a greater and more perfect tabernacle, not made with hands, that is to say, not of this building; neither by the blood of goats and calves, but by his own blood he entered in once into the holy place, having obtained eternal redemption for us."

- There were many in the priesthood, but in due course, they died, but Jesus has an eternal priesthood because He lives forever. Hebrews 7:23–24 (KJV) says, "Also, there were many priests, because they were prevented by death from continuing, but He because He continues forever, has an unchangeable priesthood." How blessed we are to be put in right standing with God and to become the righteousness of God in Christ Jesus. However, none of these things would be possible had Jesus not died for us. "For He hath made Him to be sin for us, who knew no sin; that we might be made the righteousness of God in Him" (2 Corinthians

5:21 KJV). Salvation is not merely the forgiveness of the sinner; it is the justification of the sinner" (see Romans 5:4). It is not just forgiving our sins; it's righteousness. It is not just overlooking our account; it's settling our account in full.

- Christ intercedes for us, and over two thousand years, He became our advocate and representative and has been since. His work at the throne of grace is just as unselfish as the work He carried out on earth. Notice He was not on earth for His own pleasure but for our salvation, and even now, He serves as an intercessor for our interests. In a letter to the believers at Philippi, Paul shows us how Christ has a humble servant attitude. Philippians 2:6–8 (KJV) says:

> Who being in the form of God, thought it not robbery to be equal with God, but made Himself of no reputation, and took upon Him the form of a servant, and was made in the likeness of men; and being found in fashion as a man, He [Christ] humbled Himself and became obedient unto death, even the death of the cross.

One of the things we can count on is that Jesus is always close by to help us in a time of need. Hebrews 4:15–16 (KJV) says, "For we have not a high priest which cannot be touched with the feeling of our infirmities; but was in all points tempted like as we are, yet without sin. Let us therefore come boldly unto the throne of grace, that we may obtain mercy, and find grace to help in time of need."

We have far greater privileges than those people who lived during the time of the Old Testament temple worship. They could not enter into the first room of the temple (the holy place), for only the priests could go there. Only the high priest could enter the inner room of the temple. He could only enter there once a year. Hebrews 9:7 (KJV) says, "But into the second went the high priest alone every year, not without blood, which he offered for himself, and for the errors of the people."

Since Jesus is our great high priest, we can come with confidence in prayer to God and believe by faith we have our petitions answered. First John 5:13–15 (KJV) says:

> These things have I written unto you that believe on the name of the Son of God; that ye may know that ye have eternal life, and that ye may believe on the name of the Son of God. And this is the confidence that we have in Him, that if we ask any thing according to His will, He heareth us; and if we know that He hear us, whatsoever we ask, we know that we have the petitions that we desired of Him.

The Lord Jesus's presence in heaven with the Father assures us that our sins have been paid for and forgiven. Hebrews 7:25 says, "Therefore He [Jesus] is able also to save them to the uttermost those who come to God through Him, since He (Jesus) always lives to make intercession for them." Notice that in spite of our limitations and imperfections, He represents us before the throne.

What's more, because of the advocacy of Christ, we can have confidence that no one other than God can condemn us. His advocacy for us is based on the merits He accomplished and His righteousness which we can find continual acceptance. We're kept in constant fellowship and can say with boldness, "Who shall lay anything to the charge of God's elect? It is God that justifieth. Who is he that condemneth? It is Christ that died, yea rather, that is risen again, who is even at the right hand of God, who also maketh intercession for us" (Romans 8:33–34 KJV).

A Sympathetic and Compassionate High Priest

Christ is able and willing to sympathize with us in all our temptations. He has experienced the pain, strain, and the confrontations of the powers of darkness. There is no manner of temptation which he has not experienced. That's why He's capable of aiding and comforting those in their time of struggle. Hebrews 2:17–18 (KJV) says:

> Wherefore in all things it behooved Him to be made like unto His brethren, that He [Jesus] might be a merciful and faithful High Priest in things pertaining to God, to make reconciliation for the sins of the people, for in that He Himself hath suffered being tempted, He is able to succor (support, help) them that are tempted.

Christ is able and willing to sympathize with us in our weaknesses. He knows what it means to be extremely vulnerable to temptation. Jesus was at risk when He fasted forty days, exhausted and hungry. The devil knew this and was trying to tempt Him in three areas (lust of the flesh, lust of the eyes, and the pride of life (see Matthew 4:1–11; 1 John 2:16). So when you are hard-pressed, troubled on every side, distressed, persecuted, and vulnerable to evil influences, understand that Jesus "was in all points tempted as we are, yet without sin" (see Hebrews 4:15).

As we take into account the sufferings of Christ, the book of Hebrews gives us an encouraging word. Hebrews 12:2–3 (KJV) says:

> Looking unto Jesus the author and finisher of our faith; who for the joy that was set before Him endured the cross, despising the shame, and is set down at the right hand of the throne of God. For consider [reflect on, contemplate] Him that endured such contradiction of sinners against Himself, lest ye be wearied and faint in your minds.

Christ is able and willing to sympathize with us even in our failures. When we stumble and make mistakes, we can repent and ask for forgiveness and grace to help. 1 John 1:9 says, "If we confess our sins, He [Christ] is faithful and just to forgive us our sins and to cleanse us from all unrighteousness." For instance, during Jesus crucifixion, when He needed Peter the most, He would deny Jesus three consecutive times. Although Peter failed Jesus miserably, he was restored back into fellowship. After David had also fallen, he knew the Lord was merciful, for he said, "Restore to me the joy of Your salvation, and uphold me by Your generous Spirit... The sacrifices of God are a broken spirit, a broken and a contrite heart—these O God, you will not despise" (Psalm 51:12, 17).

Christ is able and willing to sympathize with us in our sorrows. If you have cried over situations, Jesus understands as He shed tears for His friend, Lazarus, at Bethany. Have you felt the pain of a friend who abandoned you in time of need? Jesus did when Peter denied Him three times prior to His crucifixion. Has a friend ever kissed you on the face, only to betray you for money? Jesus had when Judas Iscariot betrayed him for thirty pieces of silver. Have you ever been deserted by a love one? Jesus felt the most agonizing sorrow of His earthly life when His own Father deserted Him on the cross (see Matthew 27:46).

With an understanding of His role as our Great High Priest, we can approach the throne of grace with confidence and receive the help we need. He's ready to give us instant help. The following example gives us more understanding of the throne of grace. It's when the throne of grace is bombarded with the prayers of the righteous and God's mercy is given.

Peter's Liberation from Prison

There was a time in which King Herod wanted to aggravate and harass certain individuals in the church. So he started by killing James with the sword. Herod took great pleasure in pleasing the Jews. So by killing James, he satisfied not only their demands but the Roman Emperor as well. It wasn't a matter of right or wrong in Herod's eyes. His objective and motive was to please the Jews. The Jews were angry against Christ and the apostles but at times worshipped the God who they served. On another occasion, Herod proceeded to take hold of

Peter also and placed him in prison, another attempt to gain favor of the Jews.

> And when he had apprehended him, he put him in prison, and delivered him to four quaternions of soldiers to keep him; intending after Easter to bring him forth to the people. Peter therefore was kept in prison but prayer was made without ceasing of the church unto God for him. And when Herod would have brought him forth, the same night Peter was sleeping between two soldiers, bound with two chains; and the keepers before the door kept the prison. And behold the angel of the Lord came upon him, and a light shined in the prison; and he smote Peter on the side, and raised him up, saying arise up quickly. And his chains fell off from his hands. And the angel said unto him, gird thyself and bind on thy sandals. And so he did, and he saith unto him, cast thy garment about thee, and follow me. And he went out and followed him; and wist not that it was true which was done by the angel; but thought he saw a vision. When they were past the first and the second ward, they came unto the Iron Gate that leadeth unto the city; which opened to them of his own accord; and they went out and passed on through one street; and forthwith the angel departed from him. (Acts 12:4–10 KJV)

Peter was in dire straits held in check by a quaternion of soldiers, but even plenty soldiers were not sufficient enough to block the prayers of the church petitioning the throne of grace. Peter was in desperate need, and the only solution was the intercessory prayer of the righteous saints. There may be times when we are in distressed conditions and might not be able to pray for ourselves. Those are the times we need someone to intercede for us. James 5:16 says, "The effectual [powerful] fervent [passionate] prayer of a righteous man availeth much."

Notice again that "prayer was being made without ceasing" (v. 5). A very simple principle read in that scripture is that when trouble comes our way, and it will, pray without ceasing. Luke 18:1, 7 says, "And He [Jesus] spoke a parable unto them to this end, that men ought always to pray, and not to faint… And shall not God avenge His own elect, which cry day and night unto Him, though He bear long with them?"

A Midnight Need

> And He said unto them, which of you shall have a friend, and shall go unto him at midnight, and say unto him, friend lend me three loaves; for a friend of mine in his journey is come to me, and I have nothing to set before him. And he from within shall answer and say, trouble me not; the door is now shut, and my children are with me in bed; I cannot rise and give thee. I say unto you, though he will not rise and give him, because he is his friend, yet because of his importunity he will rise and give him as many as he needeth. And I say unto you, ask and it shall be given you; seek and ye shall find; knock and it shall be opened unto you. For everyone that asketh receiveth; and he that seeketh findeth; and to him that knocketh it shall be opened. (Luke 11:5–10 KJV)

This story symbolizes God's grace and mercy in response to the prayers of those in need. Note the loaves of bread are not for the one who comes at midnight but for a friend. In comparison, there are times when we petitioned the throne of grace not for our personal needs but for the needs of others. This is not your average ordinary need but a need that required prompt assistance. This is clear because he comes at midnight while his friend and children are in bed.

It's comforting to know that no matter when we come to the throne of grace, God is awake and ready to help. Psalm 121:1–4 (KJV) says:

> I will lift up mine eyes unto the hills, from whence cometh my help. My help cometh from the Lord, which made heaven and earth, he will not suffer thy foot to be moved; he that keepeth thee will not slumber. Behold he that keepeth Israel shall neither slumber nor sleep.

This is no stranger or neighbor that he asks help from but a familiar friend. Likewise, Jesus is our friend, and we can come to Him for help anytime. John 15:13–15 (KJV) says:

> Greater love hath no man than this that a man lay down his life for His friends. Ye are my friends, if ye do whatsoever I command you. Henceforth I call you not servants; for the servant knoweth not what his lord doeth; but I have called you friends; for all things that I have heard of my Father I have made known unto you.

The friend is very persistent and will not give up until he gets help. Luke 11:8 says, "Though he will not rise and give him, because he is a friend, yet because of his importunity he will rise and give him as many as he needeth." We are also encouraged to be persistent and expectant when we pray to the Father. God moves when we operate in faith and with an unrelenting determination. In the Gospel of Luke, Jesus shares a story about a widow who acted similar to this friend. She was very persistent and determined to see her adversary brought to justice (see Luke 18:1-8).

God is able and willing to help us not only in season but out of season. He operates completely different from the way man does, for He sets on the outside of time, and time itself is not an issue. So therefore, it makes no difference as to what time of day we petition Him. Although we are undeserving of His intervention, His grace and mercy steps in to see us through. Unlike the unjust judge who was troubled by the widow continually coming, God wants us to come to him and to receive from Him as well. Hebrews 4:16 (KJV) says, "Let us therefore come boldly unto the throne of grace, that we may obtain mercy, and find grace to help in time of need."

It's wonderful to read about the generosity of the friend as he says he will give "as much as he needs" (see Luke 11:8). His friend only asks for three loaves of bread, but he's willing to exceed the amount that was necessary. In comparison, God is willing to do more than what we ask Him for when we approach Him in faith. Ephesians 3:20 (KJV) says, "Now unto Him that is able to do exceeding abundantly above all that we ask or think, according to the power that worketh in us."

Finally, the man displayed an example of bold faith in that he accepted a traveler or stranger while he knew he had nothing to offer him (see Luke 11:6). It was a reciprocal act of faith because the traveling friend had an unwavering trust in his friend to come through for him.

In approaching the throne of grace, God wants us to have that same unwavering trust in Him. We must have confidence in His willingness to provide for us or those connected with us.

We should always pray in faith and according to His will. Yes, I said according to His will. It is His will for us to be a blessing to others, and He will not disappoint us in our prayers. First John 5:14–15 (KJV) says, "And this is the confidence that we have in Him, that if we ask any thing according to His will, He heareth us; and if we know that He hear us, whatsoever we ask, we know that we have the petitions that we desired of Him."

An Emergency System

The 911 emergency systems are a state-of-the-art system. All that is required is to dial the numbers, and you'll be immediately connected to a dispatcher. In comparison, when we dial (in prayer) to the throne of grace, we are immediately connected to God. Psalm 3:4 (KJV) says, "I cried unto the Lord with my voice and He heard me out His holy hill, Selah." Yet here's another scripture showing us that we're connected to the throne of grace when we pray. Psalm 18:6 (KJV) says, "In my distress I called upon the Lord, and cried unto my God; He heard my voice out of His temple, and my cry came before Him, even into His ears."

In front of every dispatcher, there is a read-out list with our telephone numbers, address, and the name by which the call is connected with that address. Likewise, God knows us by name, and as Paul told the Athens men, God "has determined their preappointed times and the boundaries of their dwellings" (see Acts 17:26). Jesus said He knows those who are His sheep and ready to answer their petition in prayer. Psalm 34:15, 17 says, "The eyes of the Lord are upon the righteous, and His ears are open unto their cry... The righteous cry, and the Lord heareth, and delivereth them out of all their troubles."

When someone communicates with a dispatcher, there are others who are listening as well: police, fire department, and the paramedics. Likewise, the Father, the Son, and Holy Spirit are listening and ready to assist us in our troubles. Ephesians 2:18 (KJV) says, "For through Him [Jesus] we both have access by one Spirit unto the Father." There is time when an individual calls into a dispatcher and is unable to explain their problem. It could be someone or a spouse who may be having a heart attack and cannot speak calmly with the dispatcher. But in spite of the circumstances that are present, the dispatcher doesn't need the person to say a lot or speak clearly because they're able to see where the call is coming from. With this type of technology, those who need help know help is on the way.

In comparison, there will be times in our lives when we're in a desperate situation that requires 911 prayers to be dialed to the throne of grace. Maybe we're panic-stricken and don't know how to pray under those circumstances. Many people in times of testing struggle to say the right things when praying to Father, but the Holy Spirit knows what to pray. Romans 8:26 (KJV) says, "Likewise the Spirit also helpeth our infirmities; for we know not what we should pray for as we ought, but the Spirit itself maketh intercession for us with groaning which cannot be uttered."

It's comforting to know that Jesus is our Great High Priest. We can always approach the throne of grace. Psalm 46:1 (KJV) says, "God is our refuge and strength, a very present help in trouble."

The Faithfulness of God

It's important to know when times of troubles arise, we can call on God. He is faithful, even when we are faithless. First Corinthians 1:9 (KJV) says, "God is faithful, by whom ye were called unto the fellowship of His Son Jesus Christ our Lord." Notice Paul does not say "we are faithful" because the faithfulness of man is very unreliable. On the contrary, he says, "God is faithful" because if we are found faithful, it will be because God is faithful. The whole burden of salvation and our deliverance rests on the faithfulness of our gracious God. Here are five known facts concerning the faithfulness of God.

- Fact one: He is faithful to His purpose. He does not begin a work and then leave it undone. Philippians 1:6 (KJV) says, "Being confident of this very thing, that he who hath begun a good work in you will perform it until the day of Jesus Christ."
- Fact two: He is faithful in His love. First John 3:16 says, "By this we know love, because He [Jesus] laid down His life for us, and we ought to lay down our lives for the brethren."
- Fact three: He is faithful to his Son Jesus and will not allow His precious blood to be spilled in vain. Colossians 1:20 says, "And by Him to reconcile all things to Himself, by

Him, whether things on earth or things in heaven, having made peace through the blood of His cross."

- Fact four: He is faithful to His people to whom He has promised eternal life and He will keep His word. John 5:24 says, "Most assuredly, I say to you, he who hears my word and believes in Him who sent Me has everlasting life, and shall not come into judgment, but has passed from death into life."

It's comforting to know God's mercies and compassions will never fail us. Having this understanding causes us to come to the throne of grace with expectation. Lamentations 3:22–23 says, "Through the Lord's mercies we are not consumed, because His compassions fail not. They are new every morning; great is Your faithfulness." It's important to bear in mind that God's mercies and compassions are not limited to the past but are new every morning.

Short Review of the Throne of Grace

- As a result of Christ entering once again into God's presence, we can now approach the throne of grace. He is able to sympathize with us in all the circumstances of life. Why? Because He was made perfect through His suffering (see Hebrews 2:10).

- Do you know our prayers can be hindered when we approach the throne of grace? One of the ways this happens is through unforgiveness. It can absolutely hinder us from having our petitions granted from God. This is an area in many Christian's lives that is sometimes overlooked. Matthew 5:23–24 says, "Therefore if you bring your gift [offering] to the altar, and there remember that your brother has something against you, leave your gift [offering] there before the altar and go your way, first be reconciled to your brother and then come and offer your gift [offering]."

- We must approach the throne of grace with Godly fear and reverent submission. When Jesus spent time with the Father in prayer, He always approached the Father with Godly fear and reverent submission. If Jesus approached the Father with such humility, we should follow His example (see Hebrews 5:7).

- The Lord Jesus's presence in heaven with the Father assures us that our sins have been paid for and forgiven. Hebrews 7:25 says, "Therefore He [Jesus] is able also to save them to the uttermost those who come to God through Him, since He (Jesus) always lives to make intercession for them."

- There were many in the priesthood but in due course died, but Jesus has an eternal priesthood because He lives forever. Hebrews 7:23–24 (KJV) says, "Also there were many priests, because they were prevented by death from continuing, but He because He continues forever, has an unchangeable priesthood."

- For over two thousand years ago, Jesus has been our advocate and representative. His work at the throne of grace is just as unselfish as the work He carried out on earth. He was not on earth for His own pleasure but for our salvation, and He serves as an intercessor for our interests.

- Christ is able and willing to sympathize with us in all our temptations. He has experienced the pain, strain, and the confrontations of the powers of darkness. There is no manner of temptation which he has not experienced. That's why He's capable of aiding and comforting those in their time of struggle (see Hebrews 2:17–18).

- Peter was in desperate need, and the only solution was the intercessory prayer of the righteous saints. There may be times when we are in distressed conditions and might not be able to pray for ourselves. Those are the times we need someone to intercede for us. James 5:16 says, "The effectual [powerful] fervent [passionate] prayer of a righteous man availeth much."

Life Application

As a result of Jesus's bloodshed at the cross, we have been given access to the throne of grace. Our prayers now can be heard. Whenever we are in distress and are in any kind of need (spiritual, emotional, and physical), we can come boldly before the throne and obtain grace and help from the Father. The key to unlocking all of our benefits is to see Christ's role as High Priest who can feel our pain, understand our sorrow, and sympathize with our weaknesses. Jesus stands between us and the Father as a mediator. We now have the assurance of victory over all our circumstances. Praise God!

Scripture References

Seeing then that we have a great High Priest
that is passed into the heavens, Jesus the Son
of God; let us hold fast our profession, for we
have not an high priest which cannot be touched
with the feelings of our infirmities; but was in all
points tempted like as we are, yet without sin. Let
us therefore come boldly unto the throne of grace
that we may obtain mercy, and find grace to help
in time of need. (Hebrews 4:14–16 KJV)

11

WHAT MANNER OF LOVE

> Beloved what manner of love the Father has bestowed on us, that we should be called children of God! Therefore, the world does not know us, because it did not know Him...
>
> In this the love of God was manifested toward us that God has sent His only begotten Son into the world that we might live through Him. In this is love, not that we loved God, but that He loved us and sent His Son to be propitiation for our sins.
>
> —1 John 3:1, 4:9–10

The times in which we live are very unstable and unpredictable. As a matter of fact, Paul describes them as perilous times in his letter to Timothy. Second Timothy 3:1 (KJV) says, "This know also, that in the last days perilous times shall come." The good news is there are some things we take comfort in: the grace of God and the love of God. In his letter to the believers at Rome, Paul points out that God loved us that even while we were rebelling against Him, God still sent his Son Jesus to die for us (Romans 5:8).

Love is an indispensable attribute of God. But even more, it's a very important part of His nature. This is evident in what He said concerning His people, the Israelites.

> The Lord did not set His love upon you, nor choose you because ye were more in number than any people; for ye were the fewest of all people, but because the Lord loved you, and because He would keep the oath which He had sworn unto your fathers, hath the Lord brought you out with a mighty hand, and redeemed you out of the house of bondmen, from the hand of Pharaoh king of Egypt. (Deuteronomy 7:7–8 KJV)

Most people confuse or misunderstand the phrase "God is love or love is God." To say that God is love or love is God is to characterize Him as we would define love, and most people's definition of love is not biblical or correct. We would also be making God equal to love, and we know no one or thing is equal or above God except Jesus and the Holy Spirit. First John 5:7 says, "For there are three that bear witness in heaven; the Father, the Word [Christ], and the Holy Spirit, and these three are one."

God has many attributes or aspects that are a part of Him, and love is definitely one of them. It is an expression of His attributes in the God head. So is holiness, mercy, faithfulness, and truth. From looking at God's other attributes, we may learn a great deal about His love. For example, we know that because God is self-existent, His love has no beginning. He is eternal. Another way of saying it is His love has no end because He is infinite (never-ending). It has no limit because He is holy. It is the embodiment or personification of all spotless purity. He is immeasurable or vast, and His love is incomprehensible.

God's mercy can be defined as divine goodness because it has a special reference to the unworthy and the powerless. There's something in God that can love the unlovely, handcuff those who are wrong, and by the power of His grace, turn wrong into right and curses into blessings. God's mercy is the part of love which deals with the unworthy, the needy, and the most undeserving. It explains how His love can pardon, accept, and bless where no other could do. The Apostle Paul, in writing about his past experiences and obtaining God's love, mercy, and grace described it this way.

> Who was before a blasphemer, and a persecutor, and injurious; but I obtained mercy, because I did it ignorantly in unbelief. And the grace of our Lord was exceedingly abundant with faith and love which is in Christ Jesus. This is a faithful saying, and worthy of all acceptation, that Christ Jesus came into the world to save sinners, of whom I am chief. Howbeit for this cause I obtained mercy, that in me first Jesus Christ might shew forth all longsuffering, for a pattern to them which should hereafter believe on Him to life everlasting. (1 Timothy 1:13–16 KJV)

Another quality of God's love reveals to us that He is friendly. He is our friend and longs for us to be friends with Him. In the book of Genesis, Abraham did not call God first his friend, but God said that Abraham was His friend. The disciples did not call Jesus their friend or claim friendship with Christ, although Jesus said, "Henceforth I call you not servants; for the servant knoweth not what his Lord doeth; but I have called you friends; for all things that I have heard of my Father I have made known to you" (John 15:15 KJV). In short, Jesus called them his friends.

Jesus said He is our friend. It is absolutely flabbergasting to be called a friend of Christ. John 15:13 (KJV) says, "Greater love hath no man than this, that a man lay down his life for his friends." God is eternal, holy, and infinite, yet He has allowed His heart and love to connect with us. First John 4:10 (KJV) says, "Herein is love, not that we loved God, but that He loved us, and sent His Son to be the propitiation for our sins."

God is delighted in His creation and enjoys what He created. Most people think God is disappointed at what He made. That is unbiblical and not true. However, He is upset with sin and rebellion but not with what He created. Genesis 1:31 says, "Then God saw everything that He had made, and indeed it was very good." He loves us so much that He said we were created for His glory (see Isaiah 43:7).

David recognized God's gracious hand upon his life and was provoked within to give praise for all of God's providence. Psalm 139:14 says, "I will praise thee; for I am fearfully and wonderfully made; marvelous are thy works; and that my soul knoweth right well." God loves us tremendously, and His love for us is unconditional. There are two distinct Greek words meaning "to love" which comes into view in the Bible. The word *phileo* means to have passionate devoted affection and feeling. The word *agapao* means to have high esteem or high regard. This is an attribute term used in Christianity. Agapao is used more than a few times and several different ways in the Bible. Let's look at some of these terms.

- Agape love reveals the nature and love of God toward His beloved Son. John 17:26 (KJV) says, "And I have declared unto them thy name, and will declare it; that the love wherewith thou loved me may be in them, and I in them." God's love toward people in the world shows the gracefulness and beauty of His love that He would give not just His Son but His only Son. He gave him to suffer and die on a cross for humanity.

  John 3:16 (KJV) says, "For God so loved the world, that He gave His only begotten Son, that whosoever believeth in Him should not perish, but have everlasting life." Agape love points out His love toward those who believe on the Lord Jesus Christ. John 14:21 (KJV) says, "He that hath my commandments, and keepeth them, he it is that loveth me; and he that loveth me shall be loved of my father, and I will love him, and will manifest myself to Him."

- Agape love communicates the will of God to His children about their disposition toward one another. Our love for our fellow brothers and sisters in Christ is genuine proof to the world about of our discipleship with Christ. John

13:34–35 (KJV) says, "A new commandment I give unto you, that ye love one another, as I loved you, that ye also love one another, by this shall all men know that ye are my disciples, if ye have love one to another."

- Agape love also expresses a very important indispensable nature of God. First John 4:8 (KJV) says, "He that loveth not knoweth not God; for God is love." Love can be known only from the actions it prompts. This is seen in God's love in the gift of His Son. First John 4:9–10 (KJV) says, "In this was manifested the love of God toward us, because that God sent His only begotten Son into the world, that we might live through Him, herein is love, not that we loved God, but that He loved us, and sent His Son to be the propitiation for our sins." Love found its perfect expression in the Lord Jesus at the cross. Christian love is the fruit of the Spirit in the believer (see Galatians 5:22).

Jesus, Our Good Shepherd

Another aspect or characteristic of God's love for us is seen in His role as the Good Shepherd. You and I are symbolically compared to natural sheep, and as sheep, we have certain rights and privileges. David had this idea in mind when he wrote Psalm 23, familiar biblical verses that we all love and turn to in times of trouble. The grace, provision, protection, and love of God can be seen clearly throughout these scriptures. Let's look at them in depth.

> The Lord is my Shepherd; I shall not want. He maketh me to lie down in green pastures; He leadeth me beside still waters. He restoreth my soul; He leadeth me in the paths righteousness for His name sake. Yea, though I walk through the valley of the shallow of death, I will fear no evil; for thou art with me; thy rod and thy staff they comfort me. Thou preparest a table

before me in the presence of mine enemies; thou anointest my head with oil; my cup runneth over. Surely goodness and mercy shall follow me all the days of my life; and I will dwell in the house of the Lord forever. (Psalm 23:1–6 KJV)

When I was in the military in the late eighties, I was stationed near a city called Stuttgart, Germany. Occasionally, it wasn't uncommon to see shepherds with their flocks. One thing that stood out about the sheep was their calmness, so to speak, in the midst of an autobahn highway. If you're not familiar with the autobahn, it's a freeway where vehicles are moving at an extreme fast pace, very intense driving, and is noisy. I'm familiar with that type of road because my wife and I traveled it frequently while stationed in Germany.

Although loud sounds were coming from the autobahn, the sheep were grazing peaceably in a nearby field. The shepherd was standing closely in the event wild animals might attack or any sheep would wander off. It was as though the sheep knew they were protected and secure. I realize they're just domestic farm animals, but it seems like there was an unspoken trust in their shepherd for guidance, provision, and security. In my understanding, this is precisely what Jesus meant when He said, "I am the good shepherd, the good shepherd gives His life for the sheep" (John 10:11).

In writing Psalm 23, from the start, David acknowledges God as his Shepherd. "The Lord is my Shepherd" (v. 1). In the natural, shepherds of the Middle East love and care for their flocks. They know them, live with them, love them with tender affection, and sacrifice everything for them. The shepherd would stand between the sheep and everything that would be a threat or harm them. In addition, the shepherds would move the sheep from place to place. This was necessary in order to guard and secure them from wild animals and robbers.

Out of all creatures, the sheep are the most defenseless and helpless animals. They are completely vulnerable and unable to help and defend themselves. They must rely on the shepherd for everything. And just like natural shepherds who know, love, and protect their flocks, the Lord does the same for us who are the sheep of His pasture. The trouble with many of God's precious people is they try to be their own shepherds. How quickly we forget the Lord is our Shepherd. Jesus makes this clear to us in the Gospel of John.

> I am the Good Shepherd; the Good Shepherd gives his life for the sheep, but he that is an hireling, and not the Shepherd, whose own the sheep are not, seeth the wolf coming, and leaveth the sheep and fleeth; and the wolf catcheth them and scattereth the sheep. The hireling fleeth, because he is a hireling and careth not for the sheep. I am the Good Shepherd and know my sheep and am known of mine, as the Father knoweth me, even so know I the Father and I lay down my life for the sheep.
>
> My sheep hear my voice, and I know them and they follow me. (John 10:11–15, 27 KJV)

In revisiting Psalm 23:1, David says, "I shall not be in want." This covers every possible need of human life whether it's for this life or the life to come. Since the Lord is our Shepherd, we can claim the fullness of His supply and say, "My God shall supply all my needs according to His glorious riches in Christ Jesus" (Philippians 4:19 KJV). We can also declare, "O taste and see that the Lord is good; blessed is the man that trusteth in him. O fear the Lord, ye His saints; for there is no want to them that fear Him. The young lions do lack, and suffer hunger; but they that seek the Lord shall not want any good thing" (Psalm 34:8–10 KJV).

Second, David says, "He makes me lie down in green pastures" (*v. 2*). Notice he did not say one pasture but many pastures as it is worded in plural form. What's more, they are all green. The shepherd's task was to find fresh grass every day for the sheep. In comparison, the Lord does the same for us. He does not feed us on the stale bread of past experiences but gives us fresh supplies every day. Lamentations 3:22–23 (KJV) says, "It is of the Lord's mercies that we are not consumed because His compassions fail not. They are new every morning; great is thy faithfulness."

Please note that even though the herds in the Middle East rest amidst tall green grass and are full, however, they could eat more if they so choose. This speaks to the fact that our God is a God of more than enough, and as David says, "my cup runs over" (v. 5). Let's now look at some of the benefits of being a sheep in God's pasture.

- He has blessed us with abundant life. John 10:10 says, "The thief does not come except to steal, and to kill and to destroy; I come that they may have life and that they may have it more abundantly." In contrast to the devil that comes to take life, Jesus gives us abundant life. A life that has richness and fullness.
- He has blessed us with abundant sufficiency. Second Corinthians 9:8 says, "And God is able to make all grace abound toward you, that you always having all sufficiency in all things, may have an abundance for every good work."
- He has blessed us with abundant power for service. Ephesians 3:20 says, "Now unto Him that is able to do exceeding abundantly above all that we ask or think, according to the power that worketh in us."
- He has blessed us with abundant provision and supply for our needs. Philippians 4:19 (KJV) says, "And my God shall supply all your need according to His riches in glory by Christ Jesus." No matter what it is that we may need in this life, God will always supply.

Third, David said "He leads me besides still waters" (v. 2). We could call them "the waters of rest" because there is not one stream but many. They are waters. This speaks of the Holy Spirit role as Divine Comforter as He brings us into the deepest rest of Jesus. He also gives us that peace that surpasses all understanding in Christ. It's only when we follow Jesus, the Chief Shepherd, and are led by the Holy Spirit that we find quiet waters or still waters. Quiet and still waters speak of "rest for our souls." Jesus said we must come to Him to obtain this rest. Matthew 11:28–29 (KJV) says, "Come unto me all that labor and or heavy laden, and I will give you rest, take my yoke upon you, and learn of me; for I am meek and lowly in heart, and ye shall find rest unto your souls."

Fourthly, David said "He restores my soul" (v. 3). The Hebrew meaning of this statement could mean "He restores my life." This speaks of His physical redemption and healing for life. He quickens our life, our bodies, as well as the soul. If can be honest with ourselves, sometimes we go astray or stumble along the way. The Lord is a tender compassionate Shepherd who is merciful and gentle. He restores a lost sheep who has wandered away from the flock.

An example of this would be the Prophet Elijah. He was on the run from Jezebel after a massive victory over her false prophets and then finds himself hidden in a cave. First Kings 19:9 (KJV) says, "And he came thither unto a cave and lodged there; and behold the word of the Lord came to him and he said unto him, What doest thou here Elijah?" Following a conversation with Elijah, God gives him rest, food, and restores him. This is what David meant when he said, "He restoreth my soul" (see Psalm 23:3).

Fifth, David says, "He guides me in paths of righteousness" (v. 3). Not only does He give us rest, He sanctifies, cleanses, and keeps us. Jude 24 says, "Now to Him who is able to keep you from stumbling, and to present you faultless before the presence of His glory with exceeding joy." Our righteousness is as filthy rags (Isaiah 64:6). It's only when we submit to Christ that His righteousness becomes ours. This is solely based on His shed blood for us. Second Corinthians 5:21 says, "For He made Him who knew no sin to be sin for us, that we might become the righteousness of God in Him."

Sixth, David said that "though I walk through the valley of the shadow of death, I will fear no evil" (v. 4). After we have become the Lord's servant, it's now at this point we are called to pass through the most painful of circumstances. We are tested sometimes in the most excruciating ways (see Acts 14:22; 1 Peter 4:12). The good news is when we obey God's voice, He guarantees we are protected in whatever we are facing. Proverbs 1:33 (KJV) says, "But whoever listens to me will dwell safely, and will be secure without fear of evil."

Seventh, David encourages us with this word "For you are with me, your rod and your staff they comfort me" (v. 4). A shepherd in the Middle East with a rod in his hand would deal with a wondering sheep that would not listen to his call. He would take a sling combined with a stone and hurl it at the wandering sheep feet. The sheep would fall and get up and hobble back to the fold but would escape the perils of the wilderness solely because of the rod. God has a way of getting our attention as well. He knows the best rod to use. David had a revelation about God's rod. He said, "Before I was afflicted, I went astray, but now I keep your word… It is good for me that I have been afflicted, that I may learn your statues" (Psalm 119:67, 71 KJV).

Not only does His rod comfort us, but His staff comforts us even more. God has two hands. One presses us down, and the other pulls us up. It's the right hand that holds us up. In the book of Peter, we see an illustration of these rods by Peter showing us two hands of God. First Peter 5:6 says, "Humble yourselves, therefore under God's mighty hand." This is the hand (rod) that presses us down. Then Peter says, "Cast all your cares [anxiety] on Him because He cares for you" (1 Peter 5:7). This is the hand (staff) that holds us up. In short, this is the staff that comforts us when the rod had smitten us.

Eighth, David says, "You [Lord] prepare a table before me, in the presence of mine enemies" (Psalm 23:5). David had plenty of enemies on every side, yet God blessed him abundantly in the midst of them. Please understand that while we're being provided for, the Lord is protecting us. In comparison to a natural sheep while eating, he knows the shepherd is guarding him with safety from every enemy. We can sit and enjoy what God has for us without worrying about our enemies or demonic forces overtaking or destroying us. We can feast on the goodness of God, knowing we're protected.

Ninth, David says, "You anoint my head with oil, my cup runs over" (v. 6). This speaks of the Holy Spirit who infuses us with joy and gladness, a symbol of healing and sweet fragrance. In the Middle East, when a traveler comes in from his journey, he is stained and wet from perspiration. His feet are washed to take away the dust of the road, his head is anointed with oil, and sweet perfume removes the odor of heat and perspiration. Afterward, he sits down all refreshed and restored at the table of his host.

The "cup runs over" speaks of abundance because the Lord is in the business of overflow and will not give us anything less. Ephesians 3:20 says, "Now unto Him that is able to do exceedingly abundantly above all that we ask or think." In the same way, a traveler is refreshed and restored, the Lord anoints our head with oil, fills us with gladness, sweetens us with fragrance, and brings us in fellowship with Himself. All of this is owing to the Lord and carried out through the Holy Spirit, and as Paul said, "The grace of the Lord Jesus Christ, and the love of God and the communion of the Holy Spirit" (see 2 Corinthians 13:14).

Tenth, David says, "Surely goodness and mercy will follow me all the days of my life" (v. 6). Not only do we have the Lord's abiding presence supplied; we receive His goodness as well. Goodness covers every temporal need while mercy covers every spiritual need. Goodness includes every gift of His love, mercy, and provision for our sinfulness while mercy keeps us holy and guards us from even our unworthiness.

Finally, David gives us one last encouragement "I will dwell in the house of the Lord forever" (v. 6). Similar to a natural sheep who always has the assurance of the shepherd nearby, we too will have the Chief Shepherd in our midst forever. Second Corinthians 5:1 (KJV) says, "For we know that if our earthly house of this tabernacle were dissolved, we have a building from God, a house not made with hands, eternal in the heavens."

Loved and Accepted

In the world at large, rejection is a growing problem for many. All through life, many fight an uphill battle of trying to fit in. They want to be part of something, for people to like them, love, respect, and accept them. What's more, there are those who crave validation and recognition for their accomplishments. This is the end purpose in which they strive to be accepted. In addition, many fall victim to gangs, secret societies, and carnal things simply because they want acceptance. But thank God through Christ Jesus, we don't have to lose our identity to gain acceptance because we have been accepted in the beloved.

> Blessed be the God and Father of our Lord Jesus Christ, who hath blessed us with all spiritual blessings in heavenly places in Christ. According as He hath chosen us in Him before the foundation of the world, that we should be holy and without blame before Him in love. Having predestinated us unto the adoption of children by Jesus Christ to Himself, according to the good pleasure of His will, to the praise of the glory of His grace, wherein He hath made us accepted in the beloved. (Ephesians 1:3–6 KJV)

God's amazing grace was central in us being accepted in Christ Jesus. He is the beloved of His Father. Matthew 3:17 says, "And suddenly a voice came from heaven, saying this is my beloved Son in whom I am well pleased" (Matthew 3:17). It is absolutely a great privilege to be accepted and loved of God in His care and brought into His family (see John 1:12). Let's examine each of these gracious privileges and benefits.

- First, God has accepted us not on the basis of who we are, the people we know, or how educated we are but on the basis of Jesus's death and resurrection. First John 3:1 says, "Behold what manner of love the Father hath bestowed upon us, that we should be called the sons of God."
- Second, God has placed us under His care. First Peter 5:7 (AMP) says, "Casting the whole of your care, all your anxieties, all your worries, all your concerns, once and for all on Him, for He cares for you affectionately and cares about you watchfully." We read also Psalm 55:22 (AMP) says, "Cast your burden on the Lord releasing the weight of

it and He will sustain you; He will never allow the consistently righteous to be moved, made to slip, fall or fail." If anyone needed to be loved and accepted on earth and had a case for it, it was Jesus. Isaiah 53:3 says, "He was despised and rejected and forsaken by men, a man of sorrows and pains and acquainted with grief and sickness; and like one form whom me hide their faces, He was despised and we did not appreciate His worth or have any esteem for Him."

- Third, God has brought us into His family. Many unbelievers and backsliders feel God has no room for them; they are afraid of being rejected. The story of the prodigal son is a good example of a father who fully accepts the return of His rebellious Son. Luke 15:21–23 (NIV) says: The son said to him, father I have sinned against heaven and against you. I am no longer worthy to be called your son. But the father said to his servants, quick! Bring the best robe and put it on him, put a ring on his finger and sandals on his feet. Bring the fatted calf and kill it, let's have a feast and celebrate." God's grace (unearned, unmerited favor) has opened the door for us to be accepted in the beloved (Jesus). We are no longer enemies or alienated from the Father. Romans 5:1–2 (KJV) says, "Therefore being justified by faith, we have peace with God through our Lord Jesus Christ. By whom also we have access by faith into this grace wherein we stand and rejoice in hope of the glory of God."

God's Compassionate Love

There have been and are multitudes of people who have been forsaken and abandoned by earthy relationships. For instance, a mother or father may have walked out and abandoned the family. Then there's a child who has been abandoned by his or her parents. Perhaps you fit in one of these categories. I have good news for you. God has always promised those who place their trust in Him that He would never leave us nor forsake us (see Hebrews 13:5).

The question you might be contemplating is how can God bequeath such amazing grace and love on a wretched and dejected sinner? For the answer to that question, let's read what Paul said to Timothy. First Timothy 1:13–14 says, "Although I was formerly a blasphemer, a persecutor, an insolent [disrespectful, rude] man; but I obtain mercy because I did it ignorantly in unbelief, and the grace of our Lord was exceedingly abundant, with faith and love which are in Christ Jesus."

Right from the start, we quickly recognize Paul's appreciation and recognition of God's grace (unearned and unmerited favor) and love upon his life. Please understand that it makes no difference as to what you have done. Jesus said all manner of sin is forgiven, except blasphemy of the Holy Spirit (Matthew 12:31–32). God's grace and love is available to every sinner on the face of the earth. It makes no difference what family lineage you come out of or what people think or say about you. You're a candidate for his mercy and grace. Titus 2:11 (KJV) says, "For the grace of God that brings salvation has appeared to all men."

Unfortunately, there are many well-meaning people who try to earn God's salvation and love by doing something morally good and right. They have a misconception that everything that proceeds from Him has to be worked for. So with that rationale, they give up, realizing their strength and efforts have failed them. "All have sinned and fallen short of the glory of God." A moment of truth has set in that "all our righteousness are like filthy rags" (see Isaiah 64:6).

God sent His one and only Son to take our place at the cross. Can you envision or comprehend how much love He has for us? To experience all that pain for people who He knew would ridicule and reject Him, that is genuine love. This love He has for us is reciprocal or shared. John 3:35 says, "The Father loveth the Son, and hath given all things into His hand." The Son loves the Father, for Jesus says "that the world may know I love the Father" (see John 14:31).

The Father and the Son love us, and as a result of their love for us, we should love each other. John 13:34–35 (KJV) says, "A new commandment I give unto you, that ye love one another; as I have loved you, that ye also love one another, by this shall all men know that ye are my disciples, if ye have love one to another." How do we know love if we have never seen it? God showed us first what love is. He first loved us. First John 4:19 (KJV) says, "We love Him, because He first loved us." What can separate us from this love? Paul gives us the answer to this important question.

> Who shall separate us from the love of Christ? Shall tribulation, or distress, or persecution, or famine, or nakedness, or peril, or sword? As it is written, for thy sake we are killed all the daylong; we are accounted as sheep for the slaughter, nay in all these things we are more than conquerors through Him that loved us, for I am persuaded that neither death, nor life, nor angels, nor principalities, nor powers, nor things present, nor things to come, nor height, nor depth, nor any other creature, shall be able to separate us from the love of love, which is Christ Jesus our Lord. (Romans 8:35–39 KJV)

The things that are mentioned in this scripture would intimidate many people, but none of them are able to stand between God's love and the soul of a mature believer in Christ. The things we experience are the very things that develop spiritual maturity in us. Instead of those things separating us from Him, they should bring us closer to Him (see Philippians 3:10). Paul's assessment in Romans 8:35–39 reiterates and confirms God's love for His people. God reassures us how great His love is for us and how we are totally secure in Him.

Fear hath torment, and the Bible says perfect love casts out all fear. First John 4:18 (KJV) says, "There is no fear in love; but perfect love casteth out fear because fear hath torment. He that feareth is not made perfect in love." When we love God, we are unafraid of what may happen in the future, eternity, or God's judgment. We can always be cognizant of the fact that God loves us, and it's based on His Word. He has favored His people by revealing Himself by several names that offers exceptional insight into His love and grace. Let's look at some of His names and define their meanings. They will give more insight into His love for us.

- Jehovah/Yahweh is one of the most important names of God in the Old Testament. Yahweh or Jehovah comes from the verb "to be," meaning simply "He is." The full meaning is "I am who I am" or "I will be who I will be." Exodus 3:14 (KJV) says, "And God said unto Moses, I AM that I AM; and He said thus shalt thou say unto the children of Israel, I AM hath sent me unto you." It was here that God spoke to Moses at the burning bush. The endless bush burning speaks of God everlasting love for His people. Jeremiah 31:3 (KJV) says, "Yea, I have loved thee with an everlasting love; therefore, with loving-kindness have I drawn thee." I AM that I AM speaks of God being eternal and unchangeable and always the same yesterday, today, and forever. He will be what He will be and what He is. Revelation 1:8 (KJV) says, "I am Alpha and Omega, the beginning and the ending saith the Lord, which is and which was and which is to come, the Almighty." He is faithful in all His promises and unchangeable in His nature. The attribute of love being part of His unchangeable nature gives us the understanding that He does not change or alter His love for us. God doesn't lie, and if He told you He loves you, He means exactly what He says. Hebrews 6:18 says, "It was impossible for God to lie."

- Jehovah-Jireh means the "The Lord will provide," commemorating the provision of the ram in place of Isaac for Abraham's sacrifice. Genesis 22:13–14 (KJV) says, "And Abraham lifted up his eyes, and looked and behold behind him a ram caught in a thicket by his horns; and Abraham went and took the ram, and offered him up for a burnt offering in the stead of his son, and Abraham called the name of that place Jehovah-Jireh; as it is said to this day, in the mount of the Lord it shall be seen." It's important for us to know that Abraham didn't pray for God's intervention, but the Lord stepped in his hour of testing (see Genesis 22:15).

God loves us so much that He will make sure we are provided for; He will never allow His children to be in want. Psalm 23:1 says, "The Lord is my Shepherd; I shall not want." Abraham knew that God was His Shepherd, and many believers have come to this moment of truth as well. He's our Shepherd and He loves us. We also can say "I shall not be in want." No matter what the provision calls for, God will provide. Philippians 4:19 (KJV) says, "But my God shall supply all your need [spiritually, emotionally and physically] according to his riches in glory by Christ Jesus."

- Jehovah-Nissi means "The Lord is my banner." This is in honor of God's defeat of the Amalekites. Exodus 17:14–15 (KJV) says, "And the Lord said unto Moses, write this for a memorial in a book, and rehearse it in the ears of Joshua; for I will utterly put out the remembrance of Amalek from under heaven, and Moses built an altar, and called the name of it Jehovah-Nissi." We can always lift up our banners so to speak because of the knowing God who loves us, and He will always fight our battles. Psalm 20:5–6 says, "We will rejoice in thy salvation, and in the name of our God we will set up our banners; the Lord fulfill all thy petitions, now know I that the Lord saveth his anointed; he will hear him from his holy heaven with the saving strength of his right hand."

No matter what the enemy brings against God's people, the Lord is ready to avenge our adversaries. Isaiah 54:17 (KJV) says, "No weapon that is formed against thee shall prosper; and every tongue that shall rise against thee in judgment thou shalt condemn. This is the heritage of the servants of the Lord, and their righteousness is of me, saith the Lord."

- Jehovah-Shalom means "The Lord is peace." This is the name that Gideon gave the altar he built in Ophrah. Judges 6:24 (KJV) says, "Then Gideon built an altar there unto the Lord, and called it Jehovah-shalom; unto this day it is yet in Ophrah of the Abiezrites." In Paul's letter to the believers at Ephesus, he shows us how the Lord has brought in peace between believers in Christ. Ephesians 2:14 (KJV) says, "For He is our peace, who hath made both one, and hath broken down the middle wall of partition between us." Christ has made this reconciliation between God's people possible by the blood he shed.

Gideon and his people were in dire straits because of the Midianites, but the Lord assured him of a victory against his enemies. So instead of them being afraid, they had the assurance of the peace of God. We too can have true peace, no matter what the situation is or how horrendous our circumstances are. If we trust God, we have peace. John 14:27 (KJV) says, "Peace I leave with you, my peace I give unto you; not as the world giveth, give I unto you. Let not your heart be troubled, neither let it be afraid."

- Jehovah-Shammah: this phrase expresses the truth that "The Lord is there." Referring to the city which the Prophet Ezekiel saw in his vision, Ezekiel 48:35 (KJV) says, "It was round about eighteen thousand measures; and the name of the city from that day shall be, the Lord is there." This prophetic word gives us comfort in knowing God loves us enough to have given us a future home in heaven, a city where He is there. To be in His midst is to have the security that cannot be described. John 14:1–3 (KJV) says, "Let not your heart be troubled; ye believe in God, believe also in me. In my Father's house are many mansions; if it were not so, I would have told you. I go to prepare a place for you, and if I go and prepare a place for you, I will come again, and receive you unto myself; that where I am there ye may be also."

- Jehovah-Rapha means "the Lord that healeth thee." It is seen when Israel is assured that God, their healer, will prevent the diseases of Egypt from affecting them. Exodus 15:26 (KJV) says, "I will put none of these diseases upon thee, which I have brought upon the Egyptians; for I am the Lord that healeth thee." When sickness comes upon our bodies or our loved ones, we can be assured that God with His unconditional love and compassion is willing to heal us when we believe. Psalm 103:1–3 (KJV) says, "Bless the Lord, O my soul; and all that is within me, bless his holy name. Bless the Lord, O my soul and forget not all his benefits; who forgiveth all thine iniquities; who healeth all thy diseases."

The atonement of Christ made provision for the healing of souls as well as our bodies. Isaiah 53:5 (KJV) says, "But he was wounded for our transgressions, he was bruised for our iniquities; the chastisement of our peace was upon him; and with his stripes we are healed." Jesus is the same yesterday, today, and forevermore. Remember that just as he went about healing all who were sick in biblical times, He does the same today. Matthew 8:16–17 (KJV) says:

> When the evening was come, they brought unto him many that were possessed with devils; and he cast out the spirits with his word, and healed all that were sick; that it might be fulfilled which was spoken by Esaias the prophet, saying Himself took our infirmities, and bare our sicknesses.

By Grace through Faith

God has made it a point since the beginning of time and creation of man not to make us like robots. He has given us free will to make our own choices, to live for Him or to live for ourselves. Here are a few questions that you might ask: why do we have to be born again? Why is it so important? And how can God declare us guilty for something Adam did thousands of years ago? Perchance, these might be questions on your mind right now. I will attempt to answer them from the Bible, so let's begin.

Some of you might be saying is it fair for God to judge us because of Adam's sins? The answer is found in Romans 5:12–14 (KJV) says:

> Wherefore as by one-man sin entered into the world, and death by sin; and so death passed upon all men, for that all have sinned, for until the law sin was in the world; but sin is not imputed when there is no law, nevertheless death reigned from Adam to Moses, even over them that had not sinned after the similitude of Adam's transgression, who is the figure of him that was to come.

It isn't fairness that the sinner man needs; it's God's mercy and grace that's needed. Yet here's another question people ask: can I be saved and inherit eternal life by good works and deeds? Another way of asking that question would be, can good works and deeds save me? The answer is found in Titus 3:5. It says, "Not by works of righteousness which we have done, but according to His mercy He saved us, through the washing of regeneration and renewing of the Holy Spirit."

We are saved by God's grace through faith, not as a result of any works we have achieved (see Ephesians 2:8–9). For example, when someone gives you a gift, do you ask them how much you owe them? You just receive the free gift. That's what salvation is. It is God's unmerited favor, a free gift given to you from God based primarily on what Jesus accomplish at the cross.

> But God, who is rich in mercy, for His great love wherewith He loved us, even when we were

dead in sins, hath quickened us together with Christ (by grace ye are saved), And hath raised us up together, and made us sit together in heavenly places in Christ Jesus; that in the ages to come He might shew the exceeding riches of His grace in His kindness toward us through Christ Jesus. For by grace you been saved through faith, and that not of yourselves; it is the gift of God, not of works, lest anyone should boast. (Ephesians 2:4–9 KJV)

Notice the phrase Paul uses, "you been saved." This proves that it's possible to be saved in this present life and recognize it. In short, we can be saved here and now. It is the gift of God's grace, which is God's free unearned favor toward the sinful and undeserving. The gift of salvation is received through faith, whereby faith is the channel, and grace is the stream or water flow. The gift is received entirely through the channel of faith "not of works, lest anyone should boast" (v. 9).

If we could do something to earn our salvation, we would boast about what we have done. We would not give God any credit but would owe it to our own good works and fleshly efforts. Grace only saves us when we cease trying to save ourselves and entrust ourselves to Jesus Christ and His finished work on the cross for our sins. I will now give you an illustration of the folly and tragedy of trying to save ourselves.

For instance, take a 300-pound high school teenager who is a football player. He jumps from a boat into the water to retrieve a ball. The unanchored boat drifts away from him, and as an inexperienced swimmer, he begins to panic. A friend nearby tries to save him but is pulled down by the aggressive efforts of the teenager trying to save himself. Unfortunately, the football player never gave up the fight to save himself. Instead, he drowned in the water.

Unlike the illustration of the teenager who never surrendered to a friend who tried to help, if we give up and allow God's grace to pull us to shore, we can be saved. Ephesians 2:8–9 (KJV) says, "For by grace you been saved through faith, and that not of yourselves; it is the gift of God, not of works, lest any man should boast." If we desire salvation, it cannot be upon the merit of any works of righteousness we have done but completely upon the basis of God's mercy.

> But after that the kindness and love of God our Savior toward man appeared, not by works of righteousness which we have done, but accord-ing to His mercy He [God] saved us, through the washing of regeneration and renewing of the Holy Spirit, which He shed on us abundantly through Jesus Christ our Savior, that being justified by His grace, we should be made heirs according to the hope of eternal life. (Titus 3:4–7 KJV)

When you receive Jesus as your Lord and Savior, things will change. In other words, the way you see things will be different. He'll change your old ways (habits) and give you eternal life. Second Corinthians 5:17 says, "Therefore if anyone is in Christ, he is a new creation; the old has gone the new has come." At this point, you may be asking some very important questions. "Why must I be born again? How can I be born again? Or how can I become a new creation?"

Why must we be born again is a very good question. It gives us insight and appreciation for Jesus redeeming us back to the Father. As you know, in the beginning, there was no sin in the world, and God "saw everything that He had made, and behold it was very good" (Genesis 1:31). It was only until Adam ate the forbidden fruit in the garden that sin entered the world. Sin had previously entered the world through fallen angels. Many of them revolted from their alle-giance and left their first estate. But it never entered into the world of mankind until Adam sinned.

So many who are born after Adam have sinned. First Corinthians 15:22 (KJV) says, "For in Adam all die, even so in Christ shall all be made alive." In his letter to the believers at Rome, Paul said, "The wages of sin is death" (see Romans 6:23). So when Adam sinned, it brought forth spiritual death. God had warned him that if he disobeyed the commandment, he would die. To whom we give credit to for sin and death? No other than Adam, and as God had said, "O Adam! What hast thou done?"

So the primary reason we must be born again is Adam sinned, thus making us sinful by nature. Romans 5:12–14 says:

> Therefore, just as through one-man sin entered the world, and death through sin, and thus death spread to all men, because all have sinned; for until the law sin was in the world; but sin is not imputed when there is no law. Nevertheless, death reigned from Adam to Moses, even over them that had not sinned after the similitude of Adam's transgression who is the figure of him that was to come.

Now that we know Adam sinned and our sins separated and alienated us from God, we must repent. What Peter said to the people doing his sermon at Pentecost speaks volumes to what you must do. Acts 2:28 says, "Repent, and be baptized every one of you in the name of Jesus Christ for the remissions of sins, and ye shall receive the gift of the Holy Ghost"

It's important to understand that repentance is not an emotion; it's a decision. It does not come from the emotions; it comes from the will. The Greek word in the secular language is always translated "to change your mind"—change the way you think. It is simply changing your mind about the way you have been living. The Hebrew word for "repentance" involves a result; the word literally means "to turn around." In other words, you been facing one way with your back turned against God. You must turn 180 degrees around and face God and say, "Here am I." If you put the Greek and Hebrew definitions together, you come up with a complete definition of repentance. It is a decision followed by action.

You cannot truly believe unless you have first repented. The first command that came out of Jesus's mouth concerning salvation was "repent, for the kingdom of heaven is at hand" (see Matthew 4:17). Repentance means going to the Father who loves you and saying "I made a mess of my life. I need you to take control of my life. Thank you for your mercy and grace." Everything that's good starts with God. We must recognize we must always be dependent on the grace of God. Psalm 80:3 says, "Restore us, O God; cause Your face to shine, and we shall be saved."

The second thing we must do is receive Jesus as our personal Lord and Savior. John 1:12–13 KJV says, "But as many as received Him, to them, He gave the right to become children of God, to those who believe in His name; which were born, not of blood, nor of the will of the flesh, nor of the will of man, but of God."

The new birth is a supernatural thing and is not to be confused with a natural birth. The Jews (Israel) are called in scripture God's firstborn son; everyone else is considered Gentiles. We who are Gentiles become children of God when we place our faith and trust in Christ. Galatians 3:26–27 (KJV) says, "For ye are all the children of God by faith in Christ Jesus, for as many of you as have been baptized into Christ have put on Christ."

Notice He gave us this power and not in our own strength (v. 12). People are not born Christians but are given the right and the grace to become children of God. First John 3:1 says, "Behold, what manner of love the Father hath bestowed on us, that we should be called the children of God." All credit belongs to Christ who has given us this great privilege to call God our Father. The Son of God became the Son of man that the sons and daughters of men might become the sons and daughters of God.

The third thing we must do is confess with our mouth and believe in our heart. Romans 10:9–10 (KJV) says:

> But what saith it? The word is nigh thee, even in thy mouth, and in thy heart; that is the word of faith, which we preach. That if you confess with your mouth the Lord Jesus and believe in your heart that God has raised Him from the dead, you will be saved. For with the heart one

believes unto righteousness, and with the mouth
confession is made unto salvation.

The word is nigh thee; it's in our mouth and in our hearts. It is
the Word of God proclaimed by the servants of God.

Christ made it possible by going to the cross, and just before
He gave up the ghost, He declared it was finished, signifying the way
of salvation was made possible. Through a covenant that God had
previously made with Israel, He promised it would be in our mouths.
Isaiah 59:21 (KJV) says, "As for me, this is my covenant with thee,
and my words which I have put in thy mouth, shall not depart out
of thy mouth, nor out of the mouth of thy seed, nor out of thy seed's
seed, saith the Lord, from henceforth and forever."

The Prophet Jeremiah prophesied how God had placed His
word in the hearts of the people. God had made a covenant with the
house of Israel, but the same principle applies to us who are Gentiles
who repent and believe. Jeremiah 31:33 (KJV) says, "But this shall
be the covenant that I will make with the house of Israel; after those
days, saith the Lord, I will put my law in their inward parts, and
write it in their hearts; and will be their God, and they shall be my
people."

Believing is word of motion. By faith, we believe unto salvation.
It's not simply taking an intellectual position. You can have intellectual faith and never change. You can embrace all the doctrines of the
Bible with head knowledge and remain completely the same. But
when you have faith in your heart, it leads to salvation. The Gospel
message objective is to offer the plan of salvation. The promise made
to us is if we repent, confess, and believe, we shall be saved from guilt
and wrath. We are to confess Jesus openly before men.

Jesus stressed the importance of an open confession. Matthew
10:32–33 (KJV) says, "Whosoever therefore shall confess me before
men; him will I confess also before my Father which is in heaven.
But whosoever shall deny me before men, him will I also deny before
my Father which is in heaven." Paul was very adamant about the fact
he was, "not ashamed of the gospel of Christ" (see Romans 1:16).
Having a confession and not being ashamed of Christ will show our

hatred for sinful things in this world, and as Paul confessed, "The world is crucified unto me, and I unto the world" (see (Galatians 6:14).

Perhaps you have come to realize and recognize how much God loves you and that "the grace of God that brings salvation has appeared to all men" (see Titus 2:11). A good illustration of the Lord Jesus saving us in our wretched state is the story of the Good Samaritan. There are lessons in this story that I deem noteworthy and must be given some thought.

> Then Jesus answered and said, A certain man went down from Jerusalem to Jericho, and fell among thieves, who stripped him of his clothing, wounded him, and departed, leaving him half dead. Now by chance a certain priest came down that road. And when he saw him, he passed by on the other side. Likewise, a Levite, when he arrived at the place, came and looked, and passed by on the other side. But a certain Samaritan, as he journeyed, came where he was. And when he saw him, he had compassion. So he went to him and bandaged his wounds, pouring on oil and wine; and he sat him on his own animal, brought him to an inn and took care of him. (Luke 10:30–34)

First, the man was wounded and half dead (v. 30). In comparison, this is a vivid description of those who are not saved. They "are still without strength…and dead in trespasses and sins" (Romans 5:6; Ephesians 2:1).

Secondly, the Good Samaritan came where the wounded man was (v. 33). In other words, he gave of his time and resources for a complete stranger. Is not this what our Father in heaven has done? He gave His Son Jesus for us, and because of sin, we were alienated from Him. John 3:16–17 (KJV) says, "For God so loved the world that He gave His only begotten Son, that whoever believes in Him should not perish but have everlasting life. God sent not his Son into the world to condemn the world; but that the world through Him might be saved."

Thirdly, the Good Samaritan saw him and had compassion on him (v. 33). We see an example of Jesus doing something similar in Matthew 9:35–36 (KJV) that says:

> And Jesus went about all the cities and villages, teaching in their synagogues, and preaching the gospel of the kingdom and healing every sickness and every disease among the people. But when He saw the multitudes, He was moved with compassion on them, because they fainted and were scattered abroad as sheep having no shepherd.

Jesus sees us the same way in this dispensation. Finally, the Good Samaritan went to the man, bound up his wounds, poured oil and wine on him, set him on his beast, brought him to an inn, and took care of him (v. 34). In comparison, this is what Christ did for us. Romans 5:6 (KJV) says, "For when we were yet without strength, in due time Christ died for the ungodly."

The Good Samaritan gives us a glimpse of what God through Christ is willing to do for us who are the offspring of Adam, who because of one man's offense were made sinners. You say, "I don't know if I'm ready to receive Christ." I would respond by saying, "You cannot afford not to." There are only two places we can spend eternity, either heaven or hell. God's grace and the atonement of Christ give us the strength that is necessary to make the appropriate changes in your lives. Jesus said He came to heal sick souls; do you need a physician?

> And when the scribes and Pharisees saw Him eat with publicans and sinners, they said unto His disciples, how is it that He [Jesus] eateth and drinketh with publicans and sinners? When

Jesus heard it, He saith unto them, they that are whole have no need of the physician, but they that are sick. I came not to call the righteous, but sinners to repentance. (Mark 2:16–17 KJV)

In order to give you more understanding, I will now share something that took place many years ago. In years past, the physicians made house calls. The home visits were strictly for those who were sick. It would have been unlikely for the physician to have gone to a house that didn't have a sick person to attend. The physician did not go to those who were whole but to those that were sick and confined to their homes. Jesus is still making house calls, and if you're sin sick, He will come and visit you when you call on Him. It is my prayer that you have made a decision to receive Jesus into your life as Savior and Lord, and if so, please pray this prayer.

Short Review of What Manner of Love

- There are some things we take comfort in: the grace of God and the love of God. In his letter to the believers at Rome, Paul points out that God loved us; even while we were rebelling against Him, God still sent his Son Jesus to die for us (see Romans 5:8).

- Most people confuse or misunderstand the phrase "God is love or love is God." To say that God is love or love is God is to characterize Him as we would define love, and most people's definition of love is not biblical or correct. We would also be making God equal to love, and we know no one or thing is equal or above God except Jesus and the Holy Spirit. First John 5:7 says, "For there are three that bear witness in heaven; the Father, the Word [Christ], and the Holy Spirit, and these three are one."

- David says, "I shall not be in want." This covers every possible need of human life whether it's for this life or the life to come. Since the Lord is our Shepherd, we can claim the fullness of His supply and say, "My God shall supply all my needs according to His glorious riches in Christ Jesus" (Philippians 4:19 KJV).

- God wants our love, and He will not be satisfied until He gets it. He's eternal and holy. He's infinite, yet He has allowed His heart and love to connect with us. First John 4:10 (KJV) says, "Herein is love, not that we loved God, but that He loved us, and sent His Son to be the propitiation for our sins."

- There are many well-meaning people who try to earn God's salvation and love by doing something morally good and right. They have a misconception that everything that proceeds from Him has to be worked for. So with that rationale, they give up, realizing their strength and effort has failed them. "All have sinned and fallen short of the glory of God." A moment of truth has set in that "all our righteousness are like filthy rags" (see Isaiah 64:6).

- The Father and the Son loves us, and as a result of their love for us, we should love each other. John 13:34–35 (KJV) says, "A new commandment I give unto you, that ye love one another; as I have loved you, that ye also love one another, by this shall all men know that ye are my disciples, if ye have love one to another."
- Out of all creatures, the sheep are the most defenseless, helpless, and foolish of animals. They are completely vulnerable and unable to help and defend for themselves. They must rely on the shepherd for everything. And just like natural shepherds who know, love, and protect their flocks, the Lord does the same for us who are the sheep of His pasture. The trouble with many of God's precious people is they try to be their own shepherds.
- God does not feed us on the stale bread of past experiences. He gives us fresh supplies every day. Lamentations 3:22–23 (KJV) says, "It is of the Lord's mercies that we are not consumed, because His compassions fail not. They are new every morning; great is thy faithfulness."

Life Application

God has gone out of His way to show us how much He loves us. He sent His Son, Jesus, to die in our place. His love is unconditional that even while we were deep in sin and without strength, Christ died for us. It's now our choice to respond to His love, and our response should be to accept His Son, Jesus. Now that we have made a decision to accept His Son, our love for God should reciprocate in our obedience to Him. Jesus told us if we love Him, we would keep His commandments. Now that the Holy Spirit is shed abroad in our hearts, we can love God and love our fellow brothers and sisters.

Scripture Reference

In this was manifested the Love of God toward us, because that God sent His only begotten Son into the world, that we might live through Him. Herein is love, not that we loved God, but that He loved us, and sent His Son to be the propitiation for our sins, beloved if God so loved us, we ought also to love one another. (1 John 4:9–11 KJV)

12

RESPONDING TO GOD'S GRACE

For if we are beside ourselves, it is for God;
or if we are of sound mind, it is for you. For the
love of Christ compels us, because we judge thus;
that if One died for all, then all died; and He
[Christ] died for all, that those who live should
live no longer for themselves, but for Him who
died for them and rose again.

—2 Corinthians 5:13–15

In this last chapter, I want to focus on how we should respond to God's grace. Grace rejects our human merit, but it demands our acceptance and responsibility. Do you know we are spiritual millionaires? God has opened a spiritual account for us in His bank of grace. Faith is the withdrawal slip, and grace is our account number, figuratively speaking. We didn't earn it or deserve it. All of what we have is owing to the atonement of Christ. And as John the Baptist said, "no one can receive anything unless it be given from above."

Paul's response was one of appreciation, gratitude, and indebtedness to God's grace upon his life. He had not forgotten where he came from, so in his first letter to the believers at Corinth, he wrote, "But by the grace of God I am what I am; and His grace which was bestowed upon me was not in vain; but I labored more abundantly than they all; yet not I but the grace of God which was with me" (1 Corinthians 15:10 KJV). What was his previous state prior to receiving Christ? In his letter to Timothy, he shows us.

> I thank Christ Jesus our Lord who has enabled me, because He counted me faithful, putting me into the ministry. Although I was formerly a blasphemer, a persecutor and an insolent man; but I obtained mercy because I did it ignorantly in unbelief. And the grace of our Lord was exceedingly abundant, with faith and love which are in Christ Jesus. (1 Timothy 1:12–14 NIV)

In comparison to many people in this generation, Paul knew what it meant to value the grace of God. He knew it wasn't anything he had done to deserve it, so he wasted no time showing his love and appreciation for it. Here's a man, an insolent man and chief among sinners, but who obtained mercy and grace from God. Paul says all his sins were acted out in unbelief and ignorance. Let me point out that ignorance of God will alienate us from a walk with God.

Paul at one point walked in ignorance, and this qualified him to give spiritual advice to the believers at Ephesus. Ephesians 4:18 says, "This I say, therefore and testify in the Lord, that you should no longer walk as the rest of the Gentiles walk, in the futility of their mind, having their understanding darkened, being alienated from the life of God because of the ignorance that is in them because of the blindness of their heart." It is a fact that those who have suffer many things are experienced and competent to give others advice and counsel. As a result of receiving God's grace, Paul was devoted to the Gospel. It was evident in many things he wrote in his epistles. Here are just a few of them.

> For if I preach the gospel, I have nothing to boast of, for necessity is laid upon me; yes, woe is me if I do not preach the gospel! For if I do this willingly, I have a reward; but if against my

will, I have been entrusted with a stewardship. (1 Corinthians 9:16–17)

But God forbid that I should glory, save in the cross of our Lord Jesus Christ, by whom the world is crucified unto me, and I unto the world...
From now on let no one trouble me, for I bear in my body the marks of the Lord Jesus. (Galatians 6:14, 17 KJV)

For this reason, I, Paul, the prisoner of Christ Jesus for you Gentiles if indeed you have heard of the dispensation of the grace of God, which was given to me for you...of which I became a minister according to the gift of the grace of God given to me by the effective working of His power. To me, who am less than the least of all the saints, this grace was given, that I should preach among the Gentiles the unsearchable riches Christ. (Ephesians 3:1–2, 7–8)

Yet indeed I also count all things for the excellence of the knowledge of Christ Jesus my Lord, for whom I have suffered the loss of all things, and count them as rubbish, that I may gain Christ... Brethren, I do not count myself to have apprehended, but one thing I do, forgetting those things which are behind and reaching forward to those things which are ahead, I press toward the goal for the prize of the upward call of God in Christ Jesus. (Philippians 3:8, 13–14)

Paul's response to God's grace was evident in many other scriptures as well. You and I should not waste valuable time or treat God's kingdom lightly or with contempt. Ephesians 5:15–16 says, "See then that you walk circumspectly, not as fools but as wise, redeeming the time because the days are evil." Although we can never repay God for what He has done for us through His grace, having it should compel us to walk in love and obedience.

Hannah's Song of Thanksgiving

Elkanah had two wives, Peninnah and Hannah. Peninnah brought forth children, but Hannah was barren (1 Samuel 1:1–6). Hannah was in dire straits because the Lord had closed her womb. During biblical times, for a woman not to bear children brought on shame. But in spite of Hannah's circumstance, she accompanied her husband yearly to worship and sacrifice in Shiloh. In subsequent years that followed she would go up to the house of God, weep, and sometimes go without eating because of her barrenness. First Samuel 1:10 says, "She was in bitterness of soul and prayed unto the Lord and wept sore."

To add to Hannah's sorrows, she was constantly provoked by Peninnah who contribute to her afflictions. As I stated earlier because of Hannah's barrenness, Peninnah despised and intimidated her every time they visited the house of God. Why did Peninnah provoke Hannah particularly when they went to the temple? The Bible said that when the sons of God came to present themselves before the Lord, Satan often showed up as well (see Job 1:6). In my opinion, Peninnah allowed the enemy to use her against Hannah, for "we do not wrestle against flesh and blood, but against principalities..." (see Ephesians 6:12).

It was a time Hannah visited Shiloh to worship and offer sacrifices that she made a vow to the Lord, saying, "If thou wilt indeed look on the affliction of thine handmaid, but wilt give unto thine handmaid a man child, then I will give unto the Lord all the days of his life, and there shall no razor come upon his head" (see 1 Samuel 1:11). She was sincere concerning her vow and prayer, and as a result, Eli the priest "answered and said, go in peace and the God of Israel grant thee thy petition that thou hast asked of Him" (v. 17). In the course of time, God granted Hannah's request and she conceived and bore a son name Samuel (v. 20).

Once more, Hannah and her husband were supposed to visit Shiloh to offer sacrifices to God, but this time, she would remain home until Samuel was weaned. Afterward, she would bring him to appear before the Lord forever. I think it was important to share from Scripture some of Hannah's background and circumstances. The reason is because God's grace was apparent on her life as the Scripture below shows.

> And she said, O my Lord as your soul lives, my Lord, I am the woman who stood by you here, praying to the Lord. For this child I prayed, and the Lord has granted me my petition which I asked of Him. Therefore, I also have lent him to the Lord; as long as he lives he shall be lent to the Lord, so they worshipped the Lord there. (1 Samuel 1:26–28)

Hannah received the grace of God at a time when she needed it the most. It wasn't anything she did that qualified her to receive it. What was her response to God's mercy and grace? She responded with a beautiful song of thanksgiving.

> And Hannah prayed and said my heart rejoiceth in the Lord mine horn is exalted in the Lord; my mouth is enlarged over mine enemies; because I rejoice in thy salvation.
>
> There is none Holy as the Lord for there is none beside thee; neither is there any rock like our God.
>
> Talk no more exceeding proudly; let not arrogance come out of your mouth; for the Lord is God of Knowledge, and by Him actions are weighed.

The bows of the mighty men are broken,
and they that stumbled are girded with strength.

They that were full have hired themselves
for bread; and they that were hungry ceased; so
that the barren hath born seven; and she that
hath many children is waxed feeble.

The Lord killeth and maketh alive; He bringeth down to the grave and bringeth up.

The Lord maketh poor and maketh rich;
He bringeth low and lifted up.

He raiseth up the poor out of the dust, and
lifteth up the beggar from the dunghill, to set
them among princes and to make them inherit
the throne of glory; for The Pillars of the Earth
are the Lord's and He hath set the world upon
them.

He will keep the feet of His saints, and the
wicked shall be silent in darkness; for by strength
shall no man prevail.

The adversaries of the Lord shall be broken to
pieces; out of heaven shall He thunder upon them;
the Lord shall judge the ends of the earth; and He
shall give strength unto His King, and exalt the
horn of His anointed. (1 Samuel 2:1–10 NIV)

David's Response to God's Grace

David's response to God's forgiveness, mercy, and grace in his life
was in a most dramatic way. He had fallen from grace by committing
adultery with Bathsheba, and to cover his sin, he procured the death
of her husband, Uriah (see 2 Samuel 11:1–17). As a result, David was
not only guilty of adultery but murder as well. In this dispensation,
the sins for which he was guilty would not have been taken lightly
nor thought of without detestation. His sin with Bathsheba was an
entrance into which all other sins followed thereafter.

Moreover, it was a forbidden door that allowed him to be in trouble with God. However, as I have stressed throughout this book, God is full of grace and mercy. David's response to God's grace begins with a sincere prayer of repentance. Psalm 51:1–3 (KJV) says, "Have mercy upon me, O God, according to your loving-kindness; according to the multitude of your tender mercies, blot out my transgressions. Wash me thoroughly from my iniquity, and cleanse me from my sin, for I acknowledge my transgressions and my sin is always before me." As a result of God's grace stepping in to rescue David, in his heart of gratitude, he made these statements.

> Restore unto me the joy of thy salvation; and uphold me with Thy free Spirit. Then I will teach transgressors thy ways; and sinners shall be converted unto thee. (Psalm 51:12–13 KJV)

> I will freely sacrifice unto thee; I will praise thy name, O Lord for it is good, for He [God] hath delivered me out of trouble; and mine eye hath seen His desire upon mine enemies. (Psalm 54:6–7 KJV)

> I will praise thee, O Lord my God, with all my heart; and I will glorify thy name for evermore, for great is thy mercy toward me; and thou hast delivered my soul from the lowest hell. (Psalm 86:12–13 KJV)

What is your response to God's grace and mercy upon your life? Are you filled with a heart of thanksgiving? Or do you treat the grace of God with contempt? Only you can honestly answer that question. If you have not been grateful, now is a great time to begin thanking God for His undeserved and unmerited favor upon your life. First Thessalonians 5:18 (KJV) says, "In everything give thanks; for this is the will of God in Christ Jesus concerning you." As I mentioned earlier, grace demands acceptance and responsibility from the benefactor. Paul's letter to the believers at Ephesus explains this in an irrefutable way.

> That in the ages to come He might shew the exceeding riches of His grace in His kindness toward us through Christ Jesus, for by grace are ye saved through faith; and that not of yourselves; it is the gift of God, not of works, lest any man should boast, for we are His workmanship, created in Christ Jesus unto good works, which God hath before ordained that we should walk in them. (Ephesians 2:7–10 KJV)

Paul shows us the riches of God grace through the bloodshed of Jesus (v. 7–8). In addition, he shares how we're saved to carry out our preordained purposes (v. 10). Clearly, works do not save us but are necessary after salvation for useful service in the kingdom. And the good news is God will give us the grace to perform them. Philippians 2:12–13 (KJV) says, "Wherefore my beloved as ye have always obeyed, not as in my presence only, but now much more in my absence, work out your own salvation with fear and trembling, for it is God which worketh in you both to will and to do of His good pleasure."

Woman with the Alabaster Box

> And behold a woman in the city which was a sinner, when she knew that Jesus sat at meat in the Pharisee's house, brought an alabaster box of ointment, and stood at his feet behind Him weeping and began to wash His feet with tears and did wipe them with the hairs of her head and kissed His feet and anointed them with the ointment. Now when the Pharisee which had bidden him saw it, he spake within himself saying, this

man if he were a prophet would have known who and what manner of woman this is that toucheth Him; for she is a sinner... And he turned to the woman and said unto Simon, seest thou this woman, I entered into thine house, thou gavest me no water for my feet; but she hath washed my feet with her tears and wiped them with the hairs of her head. Thou gavest me no kiss; but this woman since the time I came in hath no ceased to kiss my feet. Thou gavest me no kiss; but this woman since the time I came in hath not ceased to kiss my feet. My head with oil thou didst not anoint; but this woman hath anointed my feet with ointment. Wherefore I say unto thee, her sins which are many are forgiven; for she loved much, but to whom little is forgiven, the same loveth little. (Luke 7:37–39, 44–47 KJV)

This account gives us a good illustration of what it means to be grateful for God's mercy and grace. Here's a story of a woman who was delivered as her faith leads her to worship and minister to Jesus. Jesus sees her humility as she was willing to kiss and wash His feet with her tears, something the other guests would never do. Why did she respond in such a way? The answer lies in the forgiveness of her many sins. She did not forget as many do that special encounter with Jesus the day she was forgiven of so much. She had all the right reasons to respond the way she did.

According to the Old Testament, it was customary or normal for someone who acted as a handmaid or a servant to wash the guest's feet (see 1 Samuel 25:41). She took on a servant attitude. It was natural for her to serve the One who had changed her life. Many people can learn a lot from this woman for she was remorseful and shed tears for the sins she committed. Second Corinthians 7:10 (KJV) says, "For godly sorrow worketh repentance to salvation not to be repented of; but the sorrow of the world worketh death."

Her love for Jesus was genuine. This is confirmed when He took note of it "she loved much" (v. 47). She wanted to honor Him and used what was available to accomplish it. In comparison, when God's grace rescues us in our wretched state, we are to respond with much humility and worship as well. Although we can never repay the Lord for what He's done for us, we can love Him, worship Him, and serve Him. Second Corinthians 5:15 says, "And He [Christ] died for all, that those who live should live no longer for themselves, but for Him who died for them and rose again."

The more we express our sorrow for sin and our love for Christ, the clearer evidence we have of the forgiveness of our sin. For it is by an understanding of a work of grace produced in us that we possess humility for the grace wrought for us. In other words, we respond to grace in a similar way as that woman who was forgiven. This is one of many ways we can show our gratitude for His amazing grace in our lives.

The Apostles Response to Grace

Shortly after the Holy Spirit came upon the believers at Pentecost, which was an act of God's grace (unearned, unmerited favor), they were all commissioned. Jesus told them they "would receive power after that the Holy Ghost is come upon you; and ye shall be witnesses unto me both in Jerusalem, and in all Judea and in Samaria and unto the uttermost part of the earth" (Acts 1:8). Upon receiving the Holy Spirit straightway, they became ambassadors for Christ.

Peter, as you know, denied Jesus during His most vulnerable time, but after being restored by Christ, the Holy Spirit wrought mightily in his ministry. For example, in Acts chapter 2, he preached to a crowd of three thousand explaining what happened after the believers were filled with the Holy Spirit. When he had finished speaking, the results were remarkable.

> Then Peter said unto them, repent and be
> baptized every one of you in the name of Jesus
> Christ for the remission of sins, and ye shall

receive the gift of the Holy Ghost, for the promise is unto you, and to your children, and to all
that are afar off, even as many as the Lord our
God shall call. And with many other words did
he testify and exhort, saying, saying yourselves
from this untoward generation, then they that
gladly received His word were baptized; and the
same day there were added unto them about
three thousand souls. (Acts 2:38–40 KJV)

People responded with great zeal and urgency. Immediately
following the outpouring of God's grace through the Holy Spirit,
things begin to happen. The response to God's grace was phenomenal, healings were frequent, and people were set free from demonic
oppression, the dead were raised to life, and the church grew exponentially (Acts 2:46–47). What a powerful manifestation of God's
grace. However, none of this would have occurred if the believers
were indifferent or unresponsive to the Spirit of grace.

Simultaneously, while this was taking place, a man named
Ananias along with his wife, Sapphira, who kept back part of the
money through deception, while the believers were making good on
their personal contributions to the work of the ministry, this couple
had other plans (see Acts 5:1–2). The Apostle Peter got a word of
knowledge from the Holy Spirit, telling them how "Satan had filled
their hearts to lie to the Holy Ghost" (v. 3). Unfortunately, after this
supernatural insight and rebuke from the Holy Spirit, both Ananias
and Sapphira fell dead.

This manifestation of the Spirit through the apostles brought
about great fear upon the church (v. 11). In addition, it opened the
door for many more believers to be added to the church (v. 14).
What's even more, this magnificent work of grace provoked a powerful move of God:

Insomuch that they brought forth the
sick into the streets, and laid them on beds and
couches, that at the least the shadow of Peter pass-

ing by might overshadow some of them, there came also a multitude out of the cities round about unto Jerusalem, bringing sick folks and them which were vexed with unclean spirits; and they were healed everyone. (Acts 5:15–16 KJV)

This move of God provoked anger and indignation in the high priests (v. 17). Shortly later, the apostles were put in prison for a brief period but were soon delivered by an angel of the Lord who opened the prison doors. However, regardless of everything surrounding their circumstances (thrown in prison, beaten, etc.), it did not foster bitterness or anger in them because, "they departed from the presence of the council, rejoicing that they were counted worthy to suffer shame for His name" (see Acts 5:41–42).

The apostles acknowledged how God had tremendously bestowed grace upon their lives and ministries. Although they endured an onslaught of persecution, it did not prevent them from serving Him see (1 Peter 4:12–13, 16). There's a lesson we can learn in this when we're persecuted and insulted for Christ. Just remember, He went through the same things and more, even giving up His life as a ransom. Hebrews 12:3 says, "For consider Him [Jesus] who endured such hostility from sinners Himself, lest you become weary and discouraged in your souls."

The Leper Who Returned

And it came to pass, as He [Christ] went to Jerusalem that He passed through the midst of Samaria and Galilee, and as He entered into a certain village, there met Him ten men that were lepers, which stood afar off; and they lifted up their voices and said Jesus Master have mercy on us. And when He saw them, He said unto them go shew yourselves unto the priests, and it came to pass that as they went they were cleansed. And one of them when He saw that He was healed, turned back and with a loud voice glorified God, and fell down on His face at His feet, giving Him thanks and He was a Samaritan. And Jesus answering said were there not ten cleansed? But where are the nine? There are not found that returned to give glory to God save this stranger. And He said unto Him, arise go thy way; thy faith hath made thee whole. (Luke 17:11–19 KJV)

This is a very important question by Jesus: "Were there not ten cleansed, but where are the nine? There are not found that returned to give glory to God save this stranger" (v. 17–18). There are innumerable times in which God bestows His grace upon individuals in their most desperate circumstances. The stupidity of it is they soon forget and never return to give Christ thanks for His gracious acts in their lives.

The leper who responded to God's grace and mercy received something in addition to his healing. He received not just a healed body but a healed soul. In short, Jesus gave him wholeness. He received the complete package deal. In comparison to the other nine who didn't return to give God glory, many find themselves with a half of a blessing instead of God's complete package. Just think about a child after receiving a gift, returns to their parents with a heart of gratitude. That gesture of thanks shown will provoke the parents to want to do more.

Why It's Important to Respond to God's Grace

The Lord is benevolent and compassionate with His children, for the psalmist said He "would not withhold any good thing from them that walk upright" (see Psalm 84:11). When we think on the goodness of God and all He has done for us, we realize "Every good gift and every perfect gift is from above, and cometh down from the

Father of lights, with whom is no variableness neither shadow of turning" (see James 1:17).

In the book of Psalms, David at various times pointed out many of God's benefits. If you're like me, I'm encouraged during moments of testing after reading the book of Psalms. In it, we read about countless promises and benefits. For instance, Psalm 103:1–5 gives us a list of benefits that strengthens and encourages.

> Bless the Lord, O my soul; and all that is within me, bless His holy name, bless the Lord, O my soul, and forget not all His benefits; who forgiveth all thine iniquities; who healeth all thy diseases; who redeemeth thy life from destruction; who crown thee with lovingkindness and tender mercies; who satisfieth thy mouth with good things; so that thy youth is renewed like the eagle's. (Psalm 103:1–5 KJV)

We must never forget we did not deserve any of these gracious blessings, but possessing them should provoke a praise that never ceases. Psalm 34:1–2 (KJV) says, "I will bless the Lord at all times; His praise shall continually be in my mouth. My soul shall make her boast in the Lord; the humble shall hear thereof and be glad." This could be a reference to the time when King David and all the house of Israel brought up the Ark of the Covenant. David was so excited about the Ark coming to Jerusalem that he danced and praise the Lord in front of the people.

He was not a shame to respond with praise and thanksgiving. As David approached Jerusalem with the Ark, he danced before the Lord with all his might (see 2 Samuel 6:14). His praise was so immense with leaping and dancing that Michal, his wife, despised him in her heart as she looked through a window. Second Samuel 6:20 (KJV) says, "How glorious was the King of Israel today, who uncovered himself today in the eyes of the handmaids of his servants, as one of the vain fellows shamelessly uncovereth himself!"

It's important that when God bestows blessings upon us, we're not ashamed to show a sense of gratitude in spite of who's around or looking out the window, or in some cases, our enemies, for God will "prepare a table before me in the presence of my enemies" (see Psalm 23:5). David's reply to Michal's insult reveals his response and that he wasn't ashamed of his Lord.

> And David said unto Michal, it was before the Lord which chose me before thy Father, and before all his house, to appoint me ruler over the people of the Lord, over Israel; therefore, will I play before the Lord, and I will yet be more vile than thus, and will be base in mine own sight, and of the maidservants which thou hast spoken of, of them shall I be had in honor. (2 Samuel 6:21–22 KJV)

Reflecting back on life, I can see clearly a work of God's grace covering me every step of the way from boyhood to manhood. His grace was and is sufficient in my life. Maybe you haven't come to understand how God's grace has been a vital part of your life. Perhaps you're not a born-again believer at this moment and have not recognized His goodness in your life. I have some good news for you, and that is His grace is patiently waiting for you to come to the end of yourself.

> For when we were yet without strength, in due time Christ died for the ungodly. For scarcely for a righteous man will one die; yet peradventure for a good man some would even dare to die. But God commendeth His love toward us, in that while were yet sinners, Christ died for us. (Romans 5:6–8 KJV)

> The Lord is not slack concerning His promise, as some men count slackness; but is longsuffering to us-ward, not willing that any should perish, but that all should come to repentance. (2 Peter 3:9 KJV)

When people do not have to work for something or earn it, there's a tendency to take for granted the thing(s) they have acquired. For example, when a parent gives a child a vehicle as a gift, some children tend to be irresponsible in how he or she treats the vehicle. What I'm implying is they never wash or make sure the maintenance is performed on the vehicle. By not having to make payments, many take on an "I don't care" attitude or "I didn't have to pay for it."

As we know, God's grace is unearned and unmerited. Every so often, we take for granted all He has given us through the atonement of Christ. Paul said, "His grace which was bestowed upon me was not in vain" (see 1 Corinthians 15:10). He did not take God's grace for granted and neither should we minimize it as well. There are multiple ways we can receive God's grace in vain. A distorted assessment of God's grace will cause us to be ungrateful and indifferent. It will cause us to forfeit all the spiritual blessings imparted to us through the Holy Spirit.

Short Review of Our Response to God's Grace

- Do you know we are spiritual millionaires? God has opened a spiritual account for us in His bank of grace. Faith is the withdrawal slip, and grace is our account number, figuratively speaking. We didn't earn it or deserve it. All of what we have is owing to Christ Jesus's death on the cross.
- Grace demands a responsibility from the benefactor, the epistle Paul wrote to the church at Ephesus illustrates this in an irrefutable way, Ephesians 2:7–10 says:

> That in the ages to come He might shew the exceeding riches of His grace in His kindness toward us through Christ Jesus, for by grace are ye saved through faith; and that not of yourselves; it is the gift of God, not of works, lest any man should boast, for we are His workmanship, created in Christ Jesus unto good works, which God hath before ordained that we should walk in them.

- Immediately following the outpouring of God's grace through the Holy Spirit, things begin to happen. The response to God's grace was phenomenal, healings were frequent, and people were set free from demonic oppression. The dead were raised to life, and the church grew exponentially (see Acts 2:46–47).
- In comparison, when God's grace rescues us in our wretched state, we are to respond with much humility and worship as well. Although we're unable to repay the Lord for what He's done for us, we can love Him, worship Him, and serve Him. Second Corinthians 5:15 says, "And He [Christ] died for all, that those who live should live no longer for themselves, but for Him who died for them and rose again."
- There are innumerable times when God bestows His grace upon us, but we soon forget to return and give Him thanks

for what He has done in our lives. One of the lepers that returned received something extra or more than the others because he responded with thankfulness to God's grace on his life. He received not just a healed body but a healed soul; in short, Jesus gave him wholeness.

- The leper who responded to God's grace and mercy received something in addition to his healing. He received not just a healed body but a healed soul. In short, Jesus gave him wholeness. He received the complete package deal. In comparison to the other nine who didn't return to give God glory, many find themselves with a half of a blessing instead of God's complete package.

Life's Application

When people do not have to work for something or earn it, they tend to take for granted the thing(s) they have acquired. Since God's grace is unearned and unmerited, there are times we take for grant all He has given us through the death of Jesus on the cross. Paul said that God's grace, which was bestowed upon him, was not in vain. Likewise, we should value everything the Lord has done for us.

Scripture Reference

For if we are beside ourselves, it is for God; or if we are of sound mind, it is for you. For the love of Christ compels us, because we judge thus; that if One died for all, then all died; and He [Christ] died for all, that those who live should live no longer for themselves, but for Him who died for them and rose again. (2 Corinthians 5:13–15)

13

THE CONCLUSION

Salvation is not deserved or earned by works but is the bestowment of God's sovereign grace. No one is good enough to save him or herself. We must be totally dependent on Christ's atoning work at the cross. Rather, you committed horrible sins in the past or present or were an honest hardworking citizen or carried out good deeds in the community; "all have sinned, and come short of the glory of God" (see Romans 3:22–23).

In a letter written to the believers at Colossi, Paul wrote, explaining how they "were sometime alienated and enemies in your mind by wicked works, yet now hath He [Jesus] reconciled, in the body of flesh through death, to present you holy and unblameable and unreproveable in his sight" (see Colossians 1:21–22). One very important reason we can claim salvation is by an admission we are sinners in need of God's grace and mercy. The good news is God's grace has made salvation available to everyone.

> Now it happened as He [Jesus] went to Jerusalem that He passed through the midst of Samaria and Galilee. Then as He entered a certain village, there met Him ten men who were lepers, who stood afar off. And they lifted up their voices and said, Jesus, Master, have mercy on us! So when He saw them, He said to them,

go show yourselves to the priests. And so it was
that as they went, they were cleansed. And one of
them, when he saw that he was healed, returned
and with a loud voice glorified God, and fell
down on his face at His feet, giving Him thanks,
and He was a Samaritan. So Jesus answered and
said, where there not ten cleansed? But where are
the nine? Were there not any found who returned
to give glory to God except this foreigner? And
He said to him arise, go your way your faith has
made you well. (Luke 17:15–18)

Jesus is giving an account of ten men from Galilee who had a
dreadful disease called leprosy. So that you understand God is no
respecter of persons, you need to know a little history about this man
who returned. First, he was a leper. Leprosy is a slow-progressing and
incurable disease.

This man and his friends more than likely had a severe type of
psoriasis that is associated with the disease. The infectious disease is
characterized by sores, scabs, and white shining spots beneath the
skin. Because of the need to control the spread of the disease for
which there's no cure, the law required that the leper be isolated from
the rest of society (see Leviticus 13:45–46). The law also stated that
any contact with lepers defiled the persons who touched them.

Secondly, he was a Samaritan, a mixed race despised by the Jews
as idolatrous half-breeds that were produced when the Jews from
the northern kingdom intermarried with Syrians, Assyrians, and
Babylonians after Israel's exile. Moreover, being they were a mixed
race, they were contaminated by false worship. According to his-
torians, the Samaritans were opportunists. When the Jews enjoyed
prosperity, the Samaritans were quick to acknowledge their blood
relationship. But when the Jews suffered hard times, the Samaritans
disowned any such kinship, declaring that they were descendants of
Assyrian immigrants.

Jesus was fully aware of his history, yet His purpose was to save
men from their sins. Matthew 18:11 (KJV) says, "For the Son of man

is come to save that which was lost." It's important to note when this leper returned, he received more than just a healing; he was made whole "thy faith hath made thee whole." In other words, he got a full spiritual package (spiritually, emotionally, and physically). How is this possible? In the atonement, it provides for the whole man.

Another example of salvation is seen in the Old Testament concerning Noah and his family. Salvation is seen many times in the Old Testament as deliverance from danger, deliverance of the weak from an oppressor, and deliverance from blood guilt and its consequences. The salvation here I am referring to is deliverance from wrath and sin. The Apostle Peter viewed Noah's and his family deliverance as a pattern of salvation we receive in Christ. Here's what Peter wrote concerning this.

> For Christ also hath once suffered for sins, the just for the unjust, that he might bring us to God, being put to death in the flesh, but quickened by the Spirit. By which also he went and preached unto the spirits in prison. Which sometime were disobedient, when once the longsuffering of God waited in the days of Noah, while the ark was a preparing, wherein few that is, eight souls were saved by water, the like figure whereunto even baptism doth also now save us (not putting away of the filth of the flesh, but the answer of a good conscience toward God) by the resurrection of Jesus Christ. Who is gone into heaven, and is on the right hand of God; angels and authorities and powers being made subject unto him. (1 Peter 3:18–22 KJV)

This clearly shows us that Christ's good news of salvation and victory is not limited, and the word of salvation has been preached in the past as well as in the present. What's more, it shows us the Word was preached to the dead as well as the living. God's grace has given everyone the opportunity to come to him, but this does not imply a second chance for those who reject Christ in this life. Noah's salvation through the water symbolized baptism, a ceremony involving water. In baptism, we identify with Jesus Christ who separates us from the lost and gives us new life. However, it's not the ceremony that saves us but faith in Christ's death and resurrection. It is a transformation in the hearts of those who believe. Galatians 3:27 (KJV) says, "For as many of you as have been baptized into Christ have put on Christ."

Salvation is purchased through the atonement of Christ's blood. Please bear in mind that while we are free, it cost Jesus His life. He was willing to cover the cost and pay all debts on our behalf with His blood. He literally took our place. First Peter 1:18–19 (KJV) says, "Forasmuch as ye know that ye were not redeemed with corruptible things, as silver and gold, from your vain conversation received by tradition from your fathers; but with the precious blood of Christ, as of a lamb without blemish and without spot."

When we are brought into remembrance of what it cost Jesus and the ransom He paid on our behalf, it gives us a motivation to holiness. First Corinthians 6:19–20 (KJV) says, "What? Know ye not that your body is the temple of the Holy Ghost which is in you, which ye have of God, and ye are not your own? For ye are bought with a price; therefore, glorify God in your body, and in your spirit, which are God's." Three powerful things happened as a result of Christ redeeming us with His precious blood.

First, as a result of Christ's atonement, He freed us from the oppressive bondage of slavery to sin. John 8:34–36 (KJV) says, "Jesus replied, I tell you the truth, everyone who sins is a slave to sin. Now a slave has no permanent place in the family, but a son belongs to it forever. So if the Son sets you free, you will be free indeed." Read again where Jesus said *"free indeed."* Is this the case with many Christians? Are they free indeed? Many have left behind a world of sin (bondage) and joined a church full of spiritual bondage *(legalism, religious tradition, dogma, and so on)*. So they have left one type of bondage only to embrace another form of bondage.

Let's look at the word *indeed.* This will help us understand what Jesus meant. Indeed means to be sure; without a doubt; certainly; undeniably and definitely. Allow me to share an example of being in bondage to only go to another form of bondage. In one particular prison, I was told by an inmate they have three levels *(high, mid, low levels)*. For instance, the prison moved the inmates based on time left from one level to another. The thing we must see in this example is the individual is never free. They weren't free indeed.

This is what Jesus meant when He said, "Therefore if the Son makes you free, you shall be free indeed." To be truly free meant the individual wasn't just going from one confinement level to another but is actually walking out free. In comparison, this is the condition of many believers in the body of Christ. They aren't free indeed. They have moved from one spiritual location to another. They have been liberated from sin to a church of spiritual bondage (legalism, religious tradition, dogma and etc.).

The Apostle Paul said that "being made free from sin, ye become the servants of righteousness" (Romans 6:18). Sin has a way of controlling, dictating, and dominating people lives. Jesus has made provision for everyone who is bound by any form of spiritual bondage. He paid an enormous price with His blood.

Second, as a result of Christ's ransom He has freed us from the bondage of the law. Galatians 4:4–5 (KJV) says, "But when the fullness of the time was come, God sent forth His Son, made of a woman, made under the law, to redeem them that were under the law, that we might receive the adoptions of sons." We read also Galatians 4:9 (KJV) says, "But now after that ye have known God, or rather are known of God, how turn ye again to the weak and beggarly elements, whereunto ye desire again to be in bondage?"

They were called elements because they belong to the legalistic religion of Judaism and not to Christianity, and to those who were not mature in the faith. It was important that Christ was born of a virgin in order to fulfill the law to redeem His people from the bondage and curse of the law. Galatians 3:13–14 (KJV) says, "Christ hath redeemed us from the curse of the law, being made a curse for us; for it is written, cursed is everyone that hangeth on a tree, that the blessing of Abraham might come on the Gentiles through Jesus Christ; that we might receive the promise of the Spirit through faith."

Third, as a result of as a result of the atonement of Christ, we have been liberated from the oppression of fear and power of death. Hebrews 2:14–15 (KJV) says, "Forasmuch then as the children are partakers of flesh and blood, He also Himself likewise took part of the same; that through death He might destroy Him that had the power of death, that is, the devil; and deliver them who through fear of death were all their lifetime subject to bondage." In order for Jesus to destroy the power of death and the fear of death, He had to be born a human (flesh and blood). This was necessary in order for Him to die and rise again. Moreover, it was crucial because only then could Christ deliver individuals who lived in constant fear of death so they can live for Him.

As you come to the end of this book, I want to ask you a very important question. Are you saved or to put it another way, are you a born-again believer in Christ? And I have one more question. Are you trying to gain salvation through your own efforts? In other words, are you attempting to save yourself by carrying out good deeds (church attendance, serving, giving, etc.), believing that will save you? If you answer yes to any of these questions, I'm sorry to say these are good things but will not save you.

God has sent forth His Son, Jesus, to die for us any attempt of trying to save ourselves is fruitless and futile. Paul makes this clear in his letter to the believers at Ephesus. Ephesians 2:8 (KJV) says, "For by grace are ye saved through faith; and that not of yourselves; it is the gift of God, not of works, lest any man should boast." The Lord Jesus is long-suffering and willing that none should perish. He is waiting for you to receive Him as your personal Lord and Savior.

Romans 5:6–8 (KJV) says, "For when we were yet without strength, in due time Christ died for the ungodly, for scarcely for a righteous man will one die; yet peradventure for a good man some would even dare to die, but God commendeth His love toward us, in that while we were yet sinners, Christ died for us." When you receive Him, you are given the right to become His child. John 1:12–13 (KJV) says, "But as many as received Him, to them, He gave the right to become children of God, to those who believe in His name;

which were born, not of blood, nor of the will of the flesh, nor of the will of man, but of God."

Although I made it my objective to share with you the depth and riches of God's grace, it is extremely important you receive Jesus into your life. If you have made that decision to do so, why not pray this prayer?

> Lord God, thank You for sending Your Son, Jesus, to die for me. I know without Him, I would be separated from You forever. I invite You, Jesus, into my life as my personal Lord and Savior. Lord Jesus, baptize me with the Holy Spirit so that I can live for You and serve You. Lord God, direct me to a church family that I may grow in grace and in the knowledge of my Lord and Savior Jesus Christ. Now take full, complete control of my life in Jesus's name. Amen!

WORKSHEET STUDY QUESTIONS

P lease circle or check all correct answers. The correct answers are found on "Worksheet Study Answers" page.

1. Who did grace and truth come through (John 1:17)?
    (a) Moses (b) Jesus Christ (c) apostle Paul (d) New Testament

2. What is one key attributes of God according to Exodus 34:6?
    (a) Supernatural (b) Gracious (c) Creator (d) Redeemer

3. What is the definition of Grace?
    Grace is favor or kindness shown...
    Grace is justice and love shown...

4. To who has the grace of God appeared (Titus 2:11)?
    (a) Jews (b) All Men (c) Disciples (d) Gentiles

5. Who is the Mediator between God and man (1 Timothy 2:5)?
    (a) Peter (b) Old Testament (c) Christ Jesus (d) High Priests

6. How should we approach the throne of Grace (Hebrews 4:16)?
    (a) Cautiously (b) Timid (c) With fear (d) Boldly

7. Jesus obtained an excellent ministry and covenant that was established on what (Hebrew 8:6)?
    (a) Discipleship (b) Holy Spirit (c) Better promises (d) Salvation

8. What scripture lets us know we are justified by faith, have peace with God and have access by faith?
   (a) Romans 5:1–2. (b) 1 Corinthians 2:1–2. (c) Romans 5:5– 7. (d) James 3:1–2.

9. What is the first successive stage in adding to our faith (2 Peter 1:5)?
   (a) Temperance (b) Love (c) Virtue (d) Diligence

10. Can an individual receive the grace of God in vain (2 Corinthians 6:1)?
    (a) At times (b) Yes (c) Sometimes (d) No

11. Can we frustrate and set aside the grace of God (Galatians 2:21)?
    (a) Yes (b) At times (c) Sometimes (d) No

12. What is Universal Grace?
    Universal Grace is undeserved blessings...
    Universal Grace is deserved blessings...

13. Is Universal Grace part of the salvation plan (Matthew 5:45)?
    (a) No (b) At times (c) Yes (d) Sometimes

14. Will grace set aside all sentences for future sins (John 5:14)?
    (a) No (b) At times (c) Yes (d) Sometimes

15. Can we continue in sin that grace may abound (Romans 6:1–2)?
    (a) Yes (b) At times (c) No (d) Sometimes

16. Will grace allow God to forgive unconfessed sins (1 John 1:8–10)?
    (a) No (b) Sometimes (c) Yes (d) At times

17. What could Peter not discern; when he tried to convince Jesus of canceling His divine purpose and plan (Matthew 16:21)?
    (a) The End Times (b) The Prophetic Word (c) The Anti-Christ (d) Judas plot

18. Who was formerly a blasphemer, a persecutor and an insolent man; but obtained mercy?
    (a) Peter (b) James (c) Paul (d) John the Baptist

19. The promise according to Romans 8:28 "that all things work together" is exclusively "for who?"
    "Those who love God and are called according to His design and purpose."
    "Those who carry out the kingdom purpose and plan."

20. What is the meaning of Jehovah-Rapha?
    (a) The Lord that healeth thee. (b) The Lord is my deliverer. (c) The Lord is my comfort.

21. Which one below is a simple definition of legalism?
    "It's a hindrance from fulfilling the call of God upon one's life…"
    "It is a strict adherence to the Law of Moses or a particular code of rules…"

22. What is one simple distinction between law and grace?
    Grace writes upon the heart of the "new man" within. The law commands the "old man" from without.
    Grace writes upon the heart of the "new man" without. The law commands the "old Man" from within.

23. Is there a vast difference between conviction and condemnation?
    (a) Yes (b) No (c) Same

24. What is a simple definition of the word conviction?
    Conviction is the state of being convicted or being found guilty.
    Conviction is shame brought on by religious tradition.

25. Who was it that said, "I am the vine; you are the branches"?
    (a) Israel (b) Jesus (c) Moses (d) John

26. What are two indications that God's grace is not on what you're trying to accomplish?
    (a) Sadness and Anger (b) Tiredness and Frustration (c) Depression and Withdrawal

27. When you are under a religious law, it puts you at enmity with those who are not under the same rules and laws.
    (a) True (b) False

28. What is one of the main avenues for both blessings and curses?
    (a) Words (b) Accusations (c) Lies (d) Jealousy

29. Who said, "My yoke is easy and My burden is light"?
    (a) Paul (b) Angels (c) Jesus (d) Apollos

30. Is it a fact that the word "enmity" means hostility, hate, hatred, and animosity?
    (a) True (b) False

31. Did Jesus make this statement, "I can do all things myself" while in an earthly body?
    (a) True (b) False

32. "The letter (law) _____, but the Spirit gives life" (2 Corinthians 3:6).
    (a) Strengthens (b) Revives (c) Kills (d) Damage

33. What barrier has been destroyed as a result of the blood of Christ?
    (a) Temple Curtain (b) Racism (c) Middle Wall of Petition (d) Sin

34. How are we encouraged to the throne of grace?
    (a) Come Fearful (b) Come Boldly (c) Come Loving (d) Come Angry

35. Who imparts spiritual grace gifts to us?
    (a) Heaven (b) Angels (c) Holy Spirit (d) The Church

36. Charisma is a manifestation of the grace of God. It is grace acted out in a particular way.
    (a) True (b) False

37. Since the supernatural spiritual gifts are grace gifts, can they be earned or worked for?
    (a) Yes (b) No

38. Who is it that said "by the grace of God, I am what I am?"
    (a) Jesus (b) John the Baptist (c) Paul (d) Stephen

39. What are two possible ways to achieve righteousness if you are born again through the blood of Christ?
    One is by the works of the law and the other is by grace through faith.
    One is by following all the rules and the other is by good works.

40. Jesus said blasphemy against whom could not be forgiven?
    (a) Godhead (b) Himself (c) The Holy Spirit (d) Angels

41. What is one of the most important reasons for the existence of God's grace?
    (a) Believers (b) Sinners (c) Jews (d) Ministers

42. Who house was blessed for the sake of Joseph in the Old Testament?
    (a) Hezekiah (b) Potiphar (c) David (d) the Priests

43. What was the end purpose in which spiritual tests were working, when the messenger of Satan issued a thorn in Paul's flesh?
    (a) To cure the temptation of spiritual pride (b) To strengthen him

44. The sacrificial death of Jesus cleared us of what?
    (a) Satan (b) Guilt (c) Giving (d) Devil

45. What is the act of God's grace by which sinful people are brought into His redeemed family?
    (a) Salvation (b) Redemption (c) Adoption (d) Deliverance

46. To what city did the Lord send Jonah and showed mercy and grace?
    (a) Nineveh (b) Jerusalem (c) Jericho (d) Samaria

47. When Christ went to the cross, what was it He conquered?
    (a) Pride (b) Death (c) Universe (d) Demons

48. What end purpose is the Spirit of God is working in us?
    (a) To form Christ in us (b) To make us religious (c) To be faithful in Church

49. According to Romans 6:1, shall we continue in sin that grace may abound?
    (a) God forbid (b) Yes (c) Occasionally (d) In weakness

50. The Greek word *parakletos* means "one who speaks in favor of as an intercessor, advocate. Who is this referring to?
    (a) John the Baptist (b) Holy Spirit (c) High Priests (d) Kings

WORKSHEET STUDY ANSWERS

1. Jesus Christ. *"For the Law was given through Moses, but grace and truth came through Jesus Christ" (John 1:17).*
2. Gracious. *Exodus 34:6* says, *"The Lord God is "merciful and gracious, longsuffering and abounding in goodness and truth."*
3. Grace is favor or kindness shown…receives it and in spite of what that person deserves.
4. All men. *Titus 2:11* says, *"For the grace of God that brings salvation has appeared to all men."*
5. Christ Jesus. *1 Timothy 2:5* says, *"For there is one God and one mediator between God and men, the man Christ Jesus."*
6. Boldly. *Hebrews 4:16* says, *"Let us therefore come boldly unto the throne of grace, that we may obtain mercy, and find grace to help in time of need."*
7. Better promises. *Hebrews 8:6–7* says, *"But now hath He obtained a more excellent ministry, by how much also He is the mediator of a better covenant, which was established upon better promises…"*
8. Romans 5:1–2. *"Therefore being justified by faith, we have peace with God through our Lord Jesus Christ; by whom we also have access by faith into this grace wherein we stand, and rejoice in hope of the glory of God."*
9. Virtue. *2 Peter 1:5* says, *"And beside this, giving all diligence, add to your faith virtue."*
10. Yes. *2 Corinthians 6:1* says, *"We then, as workers together with Him, beseech you also that ye receive not the grace of God in vain."*
11. Yes. *Galatians 2:21* says, *"I do not set aside the grace of God, for if righteousness comes through the law, then Christ died in vain?"*
12. *Universal Grace is undeserved blessings that God gives to all people, both believers and unbelievers alike.*

13. No. It is the grace of God by which He gives people count-less blessings that are not part of salvation. *Matthew 5:45* says, *"That you may be sons of your Father in heaven; for He makes His sun rise on the evil and on the good, and sends rain on the just and on the unjust."*

14. No. Grace will not set aside all sentences for future sins unless one repents. Jesus made this very clear to an impo-tent man. *John 5:14 (KJV)* says, *"Afterward, Jesus findeth him in the temple, and said unto him, 'Behold, thou art made whole; sin no more, lest a worse thing come unto thee.'"*

15. No. *Romans 6:1–2* says, *"What shall we say then? Shall we continue in sin, that grace may abound? God forbid. How shall we, that are dead to sin, live any longer therein?"*

16. No. *1 John 1:8–9* says, *"If we say that we have no sin, we deceive ourselves, and the truth is not in us. If we confess our sins, He is faithful and just to forgive us our sins, and to cleanse us from all unrighteousness. If we say that we have not sinned, we make Him a liar, and His word is not in us."*

17. The prophetic word. *Matthew 16:21* says, *"From that time Jesus began to show to his disciples, that He must go to Jerusalem, and suffer many things from the elders and chief priests and scribes, and be killed, and be raised again the third day."*

18. Paul. *1 Timothy 1:12* says, *"And I thank Christ Jesus our Lord who has enabled me because He counted me faithful, putting me into the ministry. Although I was formerly a blasphemer, a persecutor and an insolent man; but I obtained mercy because I did it ignorantly in unbelief."*

19. "those who love God and are called according to His design and purpose"

20. The Lord that healeth thee.

21. "It is a strict adherence to the Law of Moses or a particular code of rules…"

22. Grace writes upon the heart of the "new man" within. The law commands the "old man" from without.

23. Yes.

24. Conviction is the state of being convicted or being found guilty.
25. Jesus. "I am the vine…" (John 15:5).
26. Tiredness and Frustration.
27. True.
28. Words. The main avenue for both blessings and curses is words—words which are spoken or written or spoken inwardly.
29. Jesus. *Matthew 11:30 says, "My yoke is easy and My burden is light."*
30. True.
31. False.
32. Kills. *2 Corinthians 3:6 says, "The letter (law) kills, but the Spirit gives life."*
33. Middle Wall of Petition. *Ephesians 2:13–15 says, "But now in Christ Jesus you who once were far away have been brought near through the blood of Christ, for He Himself is our peace who has made the two one and has destroyed the barrier [middle wall of petition]."*
34. Come boldly. *Hebrews 4:16 says, "come boldly to the throne of grace, that we may obtain mercy and find grace to help in time of need."*
35. Holy Spirit. *1 Corinthians 12:7, 11 says, "But the manifestation of the Spirit is given to each one for the profit of all… But one and the same Spirit works all these things, distributing to each one individually as He wills."*
36. True.
37. No. *Romans 4:4 says, "Now to him who works, the wages are not counted as grace but as debt."*
38. Paul. *1 Corinthians 15:10 says, "But by the grace of God I am what I am, and His grace toward me was not in vain, but I labored more abundantly than they all, yet not I, but the grace of God which was with me."*
39. One is by the works of the law and the other is by grace through faith (Romans 10:3–4).

40. The Holy Spirit. *Matthew 12:31* says, *"Therefore I say to you, every sin and blasphemy will be forgiven men, but the blasphemy against the Spirit will not be forgiven men."*

41. Sinners. The sinner is one of the most important reasons for the existence of God's grace. *Titus 2:11* says, *"For the grace of God that brings salvation has appeared to all men."*

42. Potiphar. *Genesis 39:5* says, *"the Lord blessed the Egyptian's house for Joseph's sake; and the blessing of the Lord was upon all that he [Potiphar's] had in the house, and in the field."*

43. To cure the temptation of spiritual pride. *2 Corinthians 12:7* says, *"And lest I should be exalted above measure by the abundance of the revelations, a thorn in the flesh was given to me, a messenger of Satan to buffet me, lest I be exalted above measure."*

44. Guilt.

45. Adoption.

46. Nineveh. *Jonah 4:11 (KJV)* says, *"And should not I spare Nineveh that great city, wherein are more than six score thousand persons that cannot discern between their right hand and their left hand; and also much cattle?"*

47. Death. *Hebrews 7:25 (KJV)* says, *"Wherefore He is able also to save them to the uttermost that come unto God by Him, seeing He ever liveth to make intercession for them."*

48. To form Christ in us. *Romans 8:29* says, *"For whom He [God] foreknew, He also predestined to be conformed to the image of His Son."*

49. God Forbid. *Romans 6:1–2 (KJV)* says, *"What shall we say then? Shall we continue in sin, that grace may abound? God forbid.*

50. Holy Spirit.

GLOSSARY

Adoption—the act of taking voluntarily a child of other parents as one's own child; in a theological sense; the act of God's grace by which sinful people are brought into His redeemed family. In the New Testament, the Greek word translated adoption literally means placing as a son. It is a legal term that expresses the process by which a man brings another person into his family, endowing him with the status and privileges of a biological son or daughter.

Atonement—the act by which God restores a relationship of harmony and unity between Himself and humanity. The word can be broken into three parts that expresses this great truth in simple but profound terms: "at-one-ment." Through God's atoning grace and forgiveness, we are reinstated to a relationship with God in spite of our past sin. The Hebrew term frequently translated "atone" has a basic meaning of "to wipe out, to erase, to cover" or perhaps more generally to remove. In short, atonement covers physical and spiritual healing.

Bondage—means repression, oppression, and burden; the condition of a slave; subjection to a power force or influence and the condition of being involuntarily under the power of another. Biblically, this describes the condition of people when they try to keep the law. Romans 8:15 says, "For you did not receive a spirit that makes you a slave again to fear but you received the Spirit of sonship. And by Him we cry, 'Abba, Father.'"

Calvary—from the Latin word *calvaria*, the skull, the name used in the KJV and NKJV for the place outside Jerusalem where the Lord Jesus was crucified (Luke 23:33 NIV; the skull). No one knows for sure why this place was called "the skull." The most likely reason is that the site was a place of execution; the skull is a widely recognized symbol for death. The site may have been associated with a cemetery, although its location near Jerusalem makes it improbable

that skulls could be viewed there. Perhaps the area was an out crop-
ping of rock that in some way resembled a skull.[17]

Charisma—is derived from the basic Greek abstract noun charis.
The word *charis* is normally translated as grace, the unmerited favor
of God toward the undeserving. If you join "ma" to the word *charis*
instead of it being an abstract noun, it becomes now a specific noun,
changing the word *charis* to *charisma*, which means grace made effective. Therefore, spiritual gifts or charisma is a manifestation of the
grace of God. It is grace acted out in a particular way.

Compassion—the quality of showing kindness or favor, of being
gracious, or of having pity and mercy: the aspect of Christ's love
that causes Him to help the miserable. The Lord shows compassion
by actively helping those who are miserable due to circumstances
beyond their control. Christ exemplified God's compassion in His
preaching, teaching, and healing (see Matthew 9:36, 14:14).

Condemnation—means to censure, blame, disapproval, denunciation and criticism, an expression of strong disapproval, pronounc-
ing as wrong or morally culpable. The condition of being strongly
disapproved like saying "he deserved nothing but condemnation."

Confession—an open, bold, and courageous proclamation of
one's faith. The word *confession* is derived from a word in the original
Greek of the New Testament that means "to say the same as." In its
scriptural context, it means we say the same as God says; that we
make the words of our mouths agree with God's Word. The word is
also related to the word *proclaim*. Proclaim is a strong word because
it comes from a Latin word that means to "shout forth." When we
look at the word *confess*, there is really not a lot of difference from the
word *proclaim* (see Hebrews 3:1).

Conviction—is an unshakable belief in something without need
for proof or evidence.

Covenant—an agreement between God and His people in
which God makes certain promises and requires certain behavior

---

[17] Definitions taken from Ronald F. Youngblood, Nelson New Illustrated Bible
Dictionary, copyright © 1995, 1986 by Thomas Nelson Publishers, Nashville,
Tennessee.

from them in return; a solemn agreement; covenant comes from the Hebrew word *B'rit*, which means to bind or binding. The Greek word is *Diatheke*, which means to set forth specific terms and conditions, an agreement, a mutual undertaking, between God and man.

Dispensation—a period of time under which mankind is answerable to God for how it has obeyed the revelation of God that it has received. The term *dispensation* is found twice in the NKJV. "The dispensation of the fullness of times" (Ephesians 1:10) and "the dispensation of the grace of God" (Ephesians 3:2 NIV; administration). The KJV uses the term four times (1 Corinthians 9:17; Ephesians 1:10, 3:2; Colossians 1:25).

Form of Godliness—it's basically a mannerism or outward appearance of righteousness. It would include but is not limited to things like going to the house of God, knowing Christian doctrines, and using all the right Christian clichés. Timothy said that "Some will have a form of godliness but denying its power" (see 2 Timothy 3:5).

Gentiles—a term used by Jewish people to refer to foreigners or any other people who were not a part of the Jewish race. The Apostle Paul became an effective missionary to the Gentiles (Acts 13:46–49, 15:14). At first, the early church was composed of converted Jews who accepted Jesus as the Messiah, God's Anointed One. But more and more, Gentiles came to accept the teaching of the Gospel. Some Jewish leaders warned that they could not enter the Church unless they also submitted to the Jewish ritual of Circumcision (Acts 15:1–31). But Paul fought against the requirement as a denial of the Gospel and ultimately convinced the churches. The only condition of salvation is repentance from sin and faith in Christ Jesus (Acts 20:21), "There is neither Jew nor Greek...for you are all one in Christ Jesus" (Galatians 3:28).[18]

Grace—the free and unmerited favor or beneficence of God. Favor or kindness shown without regard to the worth or merit of the

---

[18] Definitions taken from Ronald F. Youngblood, Nelson New Illustrated Bible Dictionary, copyright © 1995, 1986 by Thomas Nelson Publishers, Nashville, Tennessee.

one who receives it and in spite of what that person deserves. Grace is one of the key attributes of God. The Lord God is "merciful and gracious, longsuffering, and abounding in goodness and truth" (Exodus 34:6). The grace of God was supremely revealed and given in the person and work of Jesus Christ. Jesus was not only the beneficiary of God's grace (Luke 2:40) but was also its very embodiment (John 1:14), bringing it to humankind for salvation (Titus 2:11).[19]

Gracious—pleasantly kind, benevolent, and courteous; marked by kindness and warm courtesy and of a compassionate or merciful nature.

Healing—to make well; to restore to health of soundness; to cure; Jesus was firmly convinced that the Father's purpose for humankind was health, wholeness, and salvation.

Jehovah-Rapha—translated "I am the Lord, your Physician" or "I am the Lord that healeth thee." This name is given to reveal our redemptive privilege of being healed. Moreover, God's full name is found in Exodus 3:14 and means "I am who I am" or "I will be who I will be."

Justification—the process by which sinful human being are made acceptable to a holy God. Christianity is unique because of its teaching of justification by grace (Romans 3:24). Justification is God's declaration that the demands of His Law have been fulfilled in the righteousness of His Son. The basis of this justification is the death of Christ. Although the Lord Jesus has paid the price for our justification, it is through our faith that He is received, and His righteousness is experienced and enjoyed (Romans 3:25–30). Faith is considered righteousness (Romans 4:3, 9), not as the work of human beings (Romans 4:5) but as the gift and work of God (John 6:28–29; Ephesians 2:8; Philippians 1:29).[20]

Legalism—is a strict adherence to the Law of Moses or a particular code of rules. It's the attempt to achieve righteousness with God by keeping a set of rules. It is adding to what God has required for

---

[19] Definitions taken from Ronald F. Youngblood, Nelson New Illustrated Bible Dictionary.

[20] Definitions taken from Youngblood, Nelson New Illustrated Bible Dictionary.

righteousness. Scripture reference:2 Corinthians 3:6 says, "For the letter [Mosaic law] kills, but the Spirit gives life."

Mediator—one who goes between two groups or persons to help them work out their differences and come to agreement. A mediator usually is a neutral party, a go-between, intermediary, or arbitrator (Job 9:33 KJV; daysman) who brings about reconciliation in a hostile situation when divided persons are not able to work out their differences themselves. Jesus as Mediator in the New Testament, from the New Testament perspective, there is ultimately only "one Mediator between God and man" (1 Timothy 2:5)—Jesus the Messiah. He alone, being fully God, can represent God to man, and at the same time, being fully man, can represent man to God. He alone can bring about complete payment for our sin and sanctification of God's wrath. He alone can bring everlasting peace (Acts 15:11; 2 Corinthians 5:18; Ephesians 1:17).[21]

Mercy—the aspect of God's love that causes Him to help the miserable, just as grace is the aspect of His love that moves Him to forgive the guilty. Those who are miserable may be so either because of breaking God's law or because of circumstances beyond their control. God shows compassion toward those who have broken His law (Daniel 9:9; 1 Timothy 1:13, 16), although such mercy is selective, demonstrating that it is not deserved (Romans 9:14–18). God's mercy on the miserable extends beyond punishment that is withheld (Ephesians 2:4–6). Withholding punishment keeps us from hell, but it does not get us into heaven. God's mercy is greater than this.[22]

Middle Wall of Partition—a barrier or partition that divided the inner court of the Temple, open only to the Jews, from the Court of the Gentiles. The "middle wall of partition" between the Jews and Gentiles existed spiritually as well as physically. The Law of Moses, especially the practice of circumcision and the food laws, erected a barrier of hostility and contempt between the two people. The Jewish

---

[21] Definitions taken from Ronald F. Youngblood, Nelson New Illustrated Bible Dictionary, copyright © 1995, 1986 by Thomas Nelson Publishers, Nashville, Tennessee.

[22] Definitions taken from Ronald F. Youngblood, Nelson New Illustrated Bible Dictionary.

people scorn the Gentiles who were "without the law" and rejoiced in their superior religious traditions.

Mindset—the term *mindset* depicts a combination of both mind and set. In other words, the mind is already settled on a set of beliefs and therefore resistant to change. This means it is fixed and rigid. Most people who claim to be open-minded really are not. Their minds are closed and hardened to truth and revelation. Mindsets are the thought processes of people groups who have developed a way of thinking over centuries of time. It is a combination of their experiences and what they have been taught by their ancestors. Mindsets are not easy to change. It takes a strong anointing to break through the defensive barriers in their minds and overcome the pride associated with their way of thinking.[23]

Mosaic Law—the laws (beginning with the Ten Commandments) that God gave to the Israelites through Moses; it includes many rules of religious observance given in the first five books of the Old Testament (in Judaism these books are called the Torah).

Paraclete—a transliteration of the Greek word *parakletos*, which means "one who speaks in favor of" as an intercessor, advocate, or legal assistant. The word translated as "Comforter" or "Counselor," appears only in the Gospel of John. Jesus applied the term in the Holy Spirit who would be an advocate on behalf of Jesus's followers after His ascension; the Spirit would plead their case before God (John 14:16, 26, 15:26, 16:7).

Partition—KJV word for veil, curtain that separated the general worship area from the Holy of Holies in the tabernacle and Temple. Once a year, the priest passed through this partition or veil to make atonement first for his own sins and then the sins of the people (Exodus 26:31–35)

Pharisees—a member of an ancient Jewish sect noted for strict obedience to Jewish traditions; a self-righteous or sanctimonious person. They observed the Law carefully as far as appearances went, but their hearts were far from God. Their motives were wrong because

---

[23] Quotation taken from John Eckhardt, Moving in the Apostolic, copyright © 1991, by Chosen Books, Bloomington, Minnesota, pp. 45–46.

they wanted human praise. They also had evil desires that were hidden by their religious show. That is why they were often called hypocrites by Jesus because their hearts did not match their outward appearance (Matthew 23:5–7, 25–28).

Propitiation—the atoning death of Jesus on the cross, through which He paid the penalty demanded by God because of people's sin, thus setting them free from sin and death. The word means "appeasement." Thus, propitiation expresses the idea that Jesus died on the cross to pay the price for sin that a holy God demanded.

Reconciliation—the process by which God and people are brought together again. The Bible teaches that they are alienated from one another because of God's holiness and human sinfulness. Although God loves the sinner (Romans 8:5), it is impossible for Him not to judge sin (Hebrews 10:27). Therefore, in biblical reconciliation, both parties are affected. Through the sacrifice of Christ, people's sins are atoned for, and God's wrath is appeased. Thus, a relationship of hostility and alienation is changed into one of peace and fellowship.[24]

Redeemer—one who frees or delivers another from difficulty, danger, or bondage usually by the payment of a ransom price. In the New Testament, Christ is viewed as the ultimate Redeemer. Jesus gave His life as "a ransom for many" (Mark 10:45). Thus, the Apostle Paul speaks of believers as having "redemption through His blood" (Ephesians 1:7).

Redemption—deliverance by payment of price. In the New Testament, redemption refers to salvation from sin, death, and the wrath of God by Christ's sacrifice. In the Old Testament, the word *redemption* refers to redemption by a Kinsman (Leviticus 25:24, 51–52; Ruth 4:6; Jeremiah 32:7–8), rescue, or deliverance (Numbers 3:49), and ransom (Psalm 111:9, 130:7). The New Testament emphasizes the tremendous cost of redemption; "the precious blood of Christ" (1 Peter 1:19; Ephesians 1:7), which is also called an aton-

---

[24] Definitions taken from Ronald F. Youngblood, Nelson New Illustrated Bible Dictionary, copyright © 1995, 1986 by Thomas Nelson Publishers, Nashville, Tennessee.

ing sacrifice, "a propitiation by His blood" (Romans 3:25). Believers are exhorted to remember the "price" of their redemption as a motivation to personal holiness (1 Corinthians 6:19–20; 1 Peter 1:13–19). The Bible also emphasizes the result of redemption; freedom from sin and freedom to serve God through Jesus Christ our Lord.[25]

Regeneration—means spiritual revival, rebirth, resurrection, resurgence, and recovery. New Testament passage on regeneration is Titus 3:5, "Not by works of righteousness which we have done, but according to His mercy He saved us, through the washing of regeneration and renewing of the Holy Spirit."

Religion—belief in and reverence for God or some supernatural power that is recognized as the creator and ruler of the universe and organized system of doctrine with an approved pattern of behavior and a proper form of worship. The classic New Testament passage on religion is James 2:17, faith is divorced from deeds, says James, is as lifeless as a corpse.

Repentance—is a turning away from sin, disobedience, or rebellion and a turning back to God (Matthew 9:13; Luke 5:32). In a more general sense, repentance means a change of mind (Genesis 6:6–7) or a feeling of remorse or regret for past conduct (Matthew 27:3). True repentance is a "godly sorrow" for sin, an act turning around and going in the opposite direction (2 Corinthians 7:10).

Restoration—an act of restoring or the condition of being restored: such as a bringing back to a former position or condition; a restoring to an unimpaired or improved condition.

Righteousness—holy and upright living in accordance with God's standard. The word *righteousness* comes from a root word that means "straightness." It refers to a state that conforms to an authoritative standard. Righteousness is a moral concept. God's character is the definition and source of all righteousness (Genesis 18:25; Deuteronomy 32:4; Romans 9:14). Therefore, the righteousness of human beings is defined in terms of God's... The cross of Jesus is a public demonstration of God's righteousness. God accounts or trans-

---

[25] Definitions taken from Ronald F. Youngblood, Nelson New Illustrated Bible Dictionary.

fers the righteousness of Christ to those who trust in Him (Romans 4:3–22; Galatians 3:6; Philippians 3:9). We do not become righteous because of our inherent goodness; God sees us as righteous because of our identification by faith with His Son.[26]

Salvation—the Greek word for salvation is *soteria*. It implies all the deliverance, preservation, healing, and soundness that Christ promised with His death and resurrection. It is sometimes applied to the soul and at other times to the body only. The word *sozo*, translated "saved," also means healed, made sound, or made whole. Christ went to the cross in spirit, soul, and body to redeem man in spirit, soul, and body.

Sanctification—the process of God's grace by which the believer is separated from sin and becomes dedicated to God's righteousness. Accomplished by the Word of God (John 17:7) and the Holy Spirit (Romans 8:3–4), sanctification results in holiness or purification from the guilt and power of sin.

Self-Righteous—excessively or hypocritically pious; piously or smugly convinced of one's own righteousness. Synonyms associated with self-righteous are holier-than-thou, Pharisaic, pharisaical, and sanctimonious.

Supernatural—of or relating to existence outside the natural world; belief in Christ who is able to do exceedingly, abundantly above all we ask or even think (Ephesians 3:20).

Tradition—an inherited pattern of thought or action, a specific practice of long-standing customs and practices from the past that are passed on as accepted standards of behavior for the present. Jesus criticized the Pharisees for slavishly following their traditions and making them more authoritative than the Scriptures (Matthew 15:2; Mark 7:3).

Transform—means to change, alter, convert, make over, and renovate, change from one form or medium into another. To change the nature, function, or condition of. Scripture reference is Romans 12:2, "And do not be conformed to this world, but be transformed

---

[26] Definitions taken from Ronald F. Youngblood, Nelson New Illustrated Bible Dictionary.

by the renewing of your mind, that you may prove what is that good and acceptable and perfect will of God."

Transgression—is the violation of a law, command, or duty. The Hebrew word most often translated as "transgression" in the Old Testament means "revolt" or "rebellion." The psalmist wrote, "Blessed is he whose transgression is forgiven, whose sin is covered" (Psalm 32:1).

Yoke—it simply means repression, oppression, burden, and bondage; an oppressive power. Scripture reference is Galatians 5:1, "Stand fast therefore in the liberty by which Christ has made us free, and do not be entangled again with a yoke of bondage." Jesus bids all who want to be free from spiritual bondages to come to Him. Matthew 11:28–30 says, "Come to Me, all you who labor and are heavy laden, and I will give you rest. Take My yoke upon you and learn from Me, for I am gentle and lowly in heart, and you will find rest for your souls. For My yoke is easy and My burden is light."

OTHER BOOKS BY DONALD SPELLMAN

Christ Still Heals—Does Christ still heal? Author Donald Spellman emphatically says yes in his book *Christ Still Heals: The Atonement of Christ Made Provision for Spiritual and Physical Healing.* In this book, readers learn how the atonement of Christ provided not only for spiritual healing but physical healing as well. *Christ Still Heals* is filled with plenty of biblical case studies of God healing His people, including Apostle Spellman's personal testimonies.

<<Note to layout: IMAGE>>

In Words Have Great Power, you will learn what the Bible says about words and how they can affect you. Showing you how blessings and curses come from your words. Apostle Spellman explains the root problem of an uncontrollable tongue and the steps you can take to be healed. If you want to build up others as well as yourself, journey through this book to explore how your words can edify and strengthen those around you.

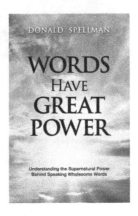

There are multitudes of well-meaning believers in Christ who have a distorted assessment of God the Father. Instead of knowing Him as loving, holy, righteous, and compassionate Father, they see Him as a tyrant who enforces man-made religious rules, their denominational agendas, and who is not concerned about their spiritual well-being. My friend, Jesus, came to set the captives free, and today, He's still setting those who are desiring to be liberated. *Freedom from Spiritual Bondage* does not simply expose religion/legalism for what it is; it offers the antithesis to spiritual bondage—the grace of the Lord Jesus in its place backed by Scriptural context.

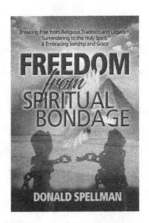

These books are available at www.lwogministries.org

FOR MORE INFORMATION AND ADDITIONAL MINISTRY MATERIALS

Email:
wordofgracerb@yahoo.com

Website:
www.lwogministries.org

Address:
Living Word of Grace Ministries, Inc.
Post Office Box 588
Baxley, Georgia 31515

ABOUT THE AUTHOR

Donald Spellman is an apostle and the cofounder of Living Word of Grace Ministries (LWOGM) Inc., a nondenominational ministry. He is an author, writer, Bible teacher, and has been in radio ministry since 1992. He was born in Elizabeth City, North Carolina, and graduated in 1982 from Northeastern High School. In 1983, he joined the US Armed Forces where he worked in Battalion S1 Headquarters as a Personnel Administrative Specialist in the army until he retired. After serving sometime in the military, he was diagnosed with cancer and was healed by Christ in 1988.

Subsequently, after giving his life to Christ in 1985 and serving as an ordained deacon in Germany, he was called to the ministry in 1989 and later ordained in 1991. After ministering and carrying out the work of an evangelist for a short period in 1992, he and his wife launched and founded LWOGM, Inc. In 1995, he joined the US Postal Service where he worked as a letter carrier until he retired in 2005 to begin full-time ministry.

As a result of serving in the pastorate for over twenty-one years, Apostle Spellman has a burden and compassionate heart for spiritual leaders and for those in the office of ministry. He and his wife operate as an apostolic ministry team. The primary objective of LWOG Ministries and the Healing Ministry Broadcast is to win souls for the kingdom of God.

Another aspect of their ministry is to bring healing and restoration (spiritually, physically, and emotionally) to the body of Christ and to equip the saints for ministry through expository teaching of the Word of God through the work of the Holy Spirit. He and his wife have been married for more than thirty-five years and reside in Baxley, Georgia. They have four grown sons.

CPSIA information can be obtained
at www.ICGtesting.com
Printed in the USA
BVHW080047061121
620873BV00001B/15